German Calvinism
in the Confessional Age

German Calvinism
in the Confessional Age

*The Covenant Theology
of Caspar Olevianus*

Lyle D. Bierma

Baker Books

A Division of Baker Book House Co
Grand Rapids, Michigan 49516

Published by
a division of Baker Book House Company
P.O. Box 6287, Grand Rapids, MI 49516-6287

Printed in the United States of America

Library of Congress Cataloging-in-Publication Data

Bierma, Lyle D.
    German Calvinism in the confessional age : the covenant theology of Caspar Olevianus / Lyle D. Bierma.
       p. cm.
    Includes bibliographical references and index.
    ISBN 0-8010-2111-1 (pbk.)
    1. Calvinism—Germany—History—16th century. 2. Covenant theology. 3. Olevian, Caspar, 1536–1587. I. Title.
BX9424.5.G3B54   1997
230′.42′092—dc21
                                      97-7373

For information about academic books, resources for Christian leaders, and all new releases available from Baker Book House, visit our web site:
http://www.bakerbooks.com

meiner Frau
gewidmet

Contents

Acknowledgments   *9*

1. Introduction   *11*
   Biographical Sketch of Olevianus   12
   Survey of Past Research   20

2. Continental Reformed Background   *31*
   Zwingli   31
   Bullinger   35
   Calvin   40
   Musculus   49
   Ursinus   55
   Conclusion   61

3. Olevianus and the Covenant of Grace   *63*
   Nature of the Covenant   63
   Foundation of the Covenant   76
   Signs of the Covenant   84
       Three Senses   84
   Unbelievers   96
   Infant Baptism   99
   Conclusion   104

4. Covenant or Covenants?   *107*
   Pretemporal Covenant   107
   Covenant of Creation   112
   Covenant with the Devil   120
   Legal Covenant   122
   Covenant with Creatures   126
   Old Covenant—New Covenant   130
   Conclusion   139

5. Olevianus's Covenant Theology in Historical-Theological Perspective   *141*
   Continental Reformed Context   141
       First Covenant Theologian?   141

Contents

   Synthesizer of Bullinger and Calvin?   148
      Antischolastic?   162
   Broader Context   168
      Medieval Background   168
      Late Sixteenth and Seventeenth Centuries   173

6. Conclusion   *183*

   Bibliography   *185*

   Index   *199*

Acknowledgments

As with most research projects of this size, there were a number of individuals without whose assistance this book could not have been completed. To the following I owe a special debt of gratitude: Dr. David C. Steinmetz, Professor of the History of Christianity at Duke University Divinity School, whose encouragement and critical suggestions while I was first preparing this work as a doctoral dissertation in 1979–80 were invaluable; the librarians of Duke University, the University of Tübingen, and Calvin College and Seminary—especially Mr. Donn Michael Farris, Professor of Theological Bibliography at Duke University Divinity School, who purchased for the library a number of materials essential to this study; the Fulbright-Kommission in der Bundesrepublik Deutschland, whose generous grant made it possible for me to do research for a year in Olevianus's homeland; Dr. Heiko A. Oberman, now Professor of History at the University of Arizona, who not only offered me working space in the Institut für Spätmittelalter und Reformation at the University of Tübingen but also went out of his way to make my wife and me feel welcome in a strange land; Drs. Fred H. Klooster, Emeritus Professor of Systematic Theology at Calvin Theological Seminary, and Richard A. Muller, P.J. Zondervan Professor of Historical Theology at Calvin Theological Seminary, both of whom read and evaluated the entire manuscript; the Rev. Dr. Norman Brooks Graebner, Episcopal priest in Hillsborough, North Carolina, who provided me with references to Olevianus in the works of seventeenth-century English theologians and read portions of the manuscript; Miss Connie Scheurwater, Registrar at Reformed Bible College, Grand Rapids, Michigan, who typed several drafts of the manuscript with commendable skill; and finally my wife, Dawn, whose careful typing of the first draft was only a small indication of her part-nership in this project. It is to her that this work is dedicated.

Portions of the second, third, and fourth chapters of this work have appeared in a somewhat different form in articles published in the *Westminster Theological Journal* 45 (Fall 1983) and the *Calvin Theological Journal* 22 (November 1987) and are reprinted here with the permission of the editors of those journals.

1

Introduction

The term "covenant" appears in the Bible nearly 300 times, most often to denote special relationships that God entered into with his people in the course of biblical history.[1] Christian theologians recognized the importance of this concept in Scripture already in patristic and medieval times,[2] but it was only in sixteenth- and seventeenth-century Reformed Protestantism that the covenant concept came to be viewed as a thread that wove together the entire message of Scripture. Continental Reformed as well as English and New England Puritan theologians developed what came to be called covenant or federal (from *foedus*, the Latin word for "covenant") theology, a systematic ordering of biblical teaching according to the various covenantal arrangements between God and humanity mentioned in Scripture. Covenant thinking became a fundamental part of the early Reformed and Puritan worldview[3] and has remained a distinctive feature of the Reformed interpretation of Scripture ever since.[4]

It is somewhat surprising to discover that there exists to date no full-length study of the thought of the man considered by

1. For a recent introduction to the various covenants in Scripture, see John M. Zinkand, *Covenants: God's Claims* (Sioux Center, IA: Dordt College Press, 1984).

2. See Chapter V, pp. 73–75.

3. Cf. J. Wayne Baker, *Heinrich Bullinger and the Covenant: The Other Reformed Tradition* (Athens, OH: Ohio University Press, 1980); Perry Miller, *The New England Mind: The Seventeenth Century* (New York: Macmillan, 1939); Leonard J. Trinterud, "The Origins of Puritanism," *Church History* 20 (March 1951):37–57.

4. I. John Hesselink, *On Being Reformed: Distinctive Characteristics and Common Misunderstandings* (Ann Arbor: Servant, 1983), 102. See also 57–62.

some to have been the founder of covenant theology—the German reformer Caspar Olevianus (1536–1587). Past studies of Olevianus have concentrated largely on his roles in the unsuccessful reformation of Trier, in the establishment of a Reformed church polity and liturgy in the Palatinate, and in the composition of the influential Heidelberg Catechism. Even though he wrote several major treatises on the concept of covenant in Scripture, the research on his covenant theology is scant, and what little there is has often arrived at contradictory conclusions. The importance of covenant thinking for continental, English, and American Calvinism and the inadequate research on Olevianus, allegedly a major covenant theologian, would seem warrant enough, therefore, for this monograph. My general purpose is to take a new and hard look at Olevianus's doctrine of covenant and to determine its place in the larger picture of sixteenth-century Reformed covenant thought. My more specific objectives will become clear once I have looked briefly at Olevianus's life and works and the current state of scholarship on his covenant theology.

Biographical Sketch of Olevianus

Caspar Olevianus was born on St. Laurentius's Day, August 10, 1536, in the ancient Roman imperial city of Trier.[5] His father

5. The oldest biography of Olevianus, Johannes Piscator's *Kurtzer Bericht vom Leben und Sterben Herrn D. Gasparis Oleviani,* was published as a separate work in 1587 and later appended to Olevianus's *Der Gnadenbund Gottes* (Herborn: C. Rab, 1590). Detailed biographical information can also be found in Melchior Adam, *Vitae germanorum theologorum* (Frankfurt, 1653), 596–603; G. Bouwmeester, *Caspar Olevianus en Zijn Reformatorisch Arbeid* (The Hague: Willem de Zwijgerstichting, 1954); *Allgemeine Encyklopädie der Wissenschaften und Künste,* 1832 ed., s.v. "Olevianus," by K. E. Förstemann; *Realencyklopädie für protestantische Theologie und Kirche,* 1904 ed., s.v. "Olevianus, Kaspar," by J. Ney; J. H. Steubing, "Lebensnachrichten von den Herborner Theologen," *Zeitschrift für die historische Theologie* 11 (1841):77–92; and Karl Sudhoff, *C. Olevianus und Z. Ursinus: Leben und ausgewählte Schriften,* vol. 8 of *Leben und ausgewählte Schriften der Väter und Begründer der reformirten Kirche* (Elberfeld: R. L. Friderichs, 1857).

Lists of Olevianus's works are given by Rotermund in *Jöchers Allgemeines Gelehrten-Lexikon,* s.v. "Olevianus" [incomplete and inaccurate] and by Steubing, "Lebensnachrichten," 95–8. For emendations of Rotermund's list see *Encyklopädie der Wissenschaften,* s.v. "Olevianus," by Förstemann.

Gerhard—baker, guild master, and later city councilman and tax collector in Trier—hailed from the nearby village of Olewig, from which the family had derived its surname. Until he was almost fourteen, Olevianus was educated in the home of his maternal grandfather and the schools of St. Laurentius, St. Simeon, the cathedral, and St. German—all in Trier. He would recall years later that it was the instruction of an aged priest at the St. German Collegium that awakened in him an early interest in the message of the Scriptures.[6]

In 1550 Olevianus's parents arranged for him to continue his education at the Sorbonne in Paris, and from there, like Calvin before him, he moved on to Orléans and Bourges to study civil law. Sometime during these years as a young law student he joined the underground Protestant movement in France,[7] but it was only after a frightening experience in Bourges that he decided to make a career of his newly found faith. While in Bourges he had developed a friendship with Pfalzgraf Hermann Ludwig, whose father would become Elector Frederick III of the Palatinate in 1559. As the two were strolling along the banks of a river one day in July 1556, they met a group of students, all wellborn and all rather drunk, who invited them along on a boat trip to the other shore. The prince joined the party; Olevianus refused. Halfway across the river, the rowdy bunch accidentally overturned the boat, and all occupants drowned. Olevianus, meanwhile, had dived into the water in an attempt to save his friend but soon found himself in danger of going under. In desperation he promised God that should his life be spared, he would devote himself to the service of the gospel in his homeland. Moments later a servant of one of the drowning students, mistaking Olevianus for his master, jumped in and brought him safely to shore.

Following his dramatic rescue Olevianus made good on his promise and began a course of intense personal study of the Bible and the writings of the reformers, especially the works

---

6. See the special preface to the youth in his *Expositio Symboli Apostolici* (Frankfurt: A. Wechel, 1584), xvi.

7. Piscator says only: "An welchen beyden orten [Orléans and Bourges] er sich zur heimlichen Gemeynde Gottes gehalten." *Leben und Sterben* (in the 1593 ed. of *Der Gnadenbund Gottes*), 11.b.

of Calvin. On June 6, 1557, he received his doctorate in jurisprudence from the Law Faculty in Bourges,[8] and in March
1558, after nine months as a lawyer in Trier, he pushed on to
Geneva to study theology with Calvin in person.[9] He also made
trips to Zurich, where he formed friendships with Peter Martyr Vermigli and Heinrich Bullinger, and to Lausanne, where
he first met Theodore Beza.[10] On the way back to Geneva he
encountered William Farel, who with Calvin and Viret in
Geneva strongly encouraged him to carry his Reformation
message back to Trier. In June 1559 Olevianus returned to his
birthplace.

Upon his arrival in Trier he applied to the city council for a
teaching position and was offered a post in the university's
Bursa (an old auditorium) as a lecturer in logic and philosophy. For a basic textbook he chose Melanchthon's *Dialectices*
(1547),[11] whose numerous biblical and doctrinal references
provided him with ample opportunity to do some Protestant
evangelizing. But the limited size of his audience frustrated
him, so on his twenty-third birthday (August 10, 1559), Olevianus used his lecture time at the Bursa to deliver a prepubli-
cized sermon (in German rather than the usual Latin) in which
he attacked a number of Catholic traditions and openly proclaimed the doctrine of justification by faith alone. His
preaching evoked an enthusiastic response from many of the
citizens present, but Catholic opposition on the city council
was strong enough to have the matter referred to the influen-

8. The diploma is quoted in Latin and translated into German by Piscator,
Leben und Sterben, 11b–12b.
9. Heppe, in his article "Der Charakter der deutschreformirten Kirche und
das Verhältniss derselben zum Lutherthum und zum Calvinismus" (*Theologischen Studien u. Kritiken* 23 [1850]:681), states that Olevianus contributed a confessional document to the Frankfurt Conference of 1558, but it seems highly unlikely that a 21-year-old lawyer, just back from seven years of study in France
and with theological training, would suddenly find himself in the thick of the
Lutheran doctrinal controversies in Germany.
10. Some of Olevianus's later correspondence with Martyr and Bullinger is
reprinted in Sudhoff, *C. Olevianus*, 479–85. Beza later edited three exegetical
works by Olevianus (see n. 22 below).
11. "Die Dialektik wird gefasst als 'ars seu via, recte, ordine, perspicue,
docendi, quod sit recte definiendo, dividendo, argumenta vera connectendo et
male cohaerentia seu falsa refutando.'" Sudhoff, *C. Olevianus*, 17, n*.

tial city guilds, which advised that Olevianus should not again use his lecture hall as a sanctuary. The city council did not forbid him to preach altogether, however, and the young reformer took his message elsewhere in the city to a rapidly growing following.

The struggle had only begun. Up to this point the only political body to take action against Olevianus had been the city council, which governed Trier's temporal affairs. The city also had an electoral council, however, which was responsible for religious affairs and was directly answerable to the Archbishop-Elector of Trier. The current Archbishop-Elector, Johann von der Leyen, was away at the time at the imperial diet in Augsburg, so it was up to the electoral council to take action against those sympathetic to the new movement. On August 25, 1559, the electoral council ordered Olevianus to refrain from any further preaching and, when he persisted, put pressure on the city council and the guilds to suppress the burgeoning heresy.

By early September a third of Trier's citizens and five of the thirteen guilds had declared for Protestantism, and the Archbishop-Elector in Augsburg ordered the city council to arrest Olevianus. The council, in the interests of peace in the city, thought it wiser to allow the Protestants freedom of worship, so on September 16, a week after their decision, Elector von der Leyen returned to Trier with 170 cavalrymen to deal with the matter himself. His attempts to rid Trier of Protestantism were no more successful, however, largely because the Catholic citizens of Trier feared that any additional authority granted the elector might place their own political liberties in jeopardy. Totally frustrated, Elector von der Leyen marched out of the city after just twelve days and proceeded to place it under siege.

Within two weeks (October 11) the situation in Trier had become so desperate that the Catholic members of the city council finally capitulated and had Olevianus and the Protestant representation on the council arrested. Finally, on October 26 the last of the elector's demands were met, and von der Leyen reentered the city in triumph. The Protestants were indicted in mid-November on criminal charges of sedition, rebellion, and breach of the religious peace. It was only through the intervention of six Protestant princes, led by Frederick III of the Palatinate, that Olevianus and the other ringleaders were released (December 19) and, upon payment of a fine of 3000 gulden, exiled from the city. Early the next year Elector von der Leyen summoned the Jesuits and other Catholic orders to Trier to help repair the religious damage, and Trier has remained largely a Catholic city ever since.[12]

By invitation of Elector Frederick III of the Palatinate, Olevianus moved on to Heidelberg and in January 1560 was engaged as an instructor in preaching at the *Collegium Sapientiae*, recently converted into a seminary. On March 4, 1561, he was promoted to Professor of Dogmatics at the University of Heidelberg and just four months later (July 8) received his doctorate in theology. Sometime in 1561 he also married a widow from Metz, Philippina, whom he had met during a trip to Strasbourg. Believing his real gifts to lie outside of the classroom, however, Olevianus soon exchanged his lectern for a pulpit[13]—first the pulpit of Heidelberg's St. Peter's Church and then, in 1562, that of the Church of the Holy Spirit—and devoted his energies to preaching and to the reorganization of the Rhenish-Palatinate Church along Calvinist lines. He was primarily responsible for the design of the Heidelberg Church Order of 1563[14] and for the establishment of a Genevan form of church discipline in the Pa-

---

12. James I. Good, *The Heidelberg Catechism in Its Newest Light* (Philadelphia: Publication and Sunday School Board of the Reformed Church in the United States, 1914), 201–41. Detailed accounts of the attempted reformation in Trier can also be found in Sudhoff, *C. Olevianus*, 15–59; J. Marx, *Caspar Olevian oder der Calvinismus im Trier im Jahre 1559* (Mainz: Kirchenheim, Schott, & Theilmann, 1846); Heinrich Heppe, "Urkundliche Beiträge zur Geschichte der Reformation in Trier im Jahre 1559," *Zeitschrift für die historische Theologie* 19 (1849):416–44; and J. Ney, *Die Reformation im Trier und ihre Unterdrückung*, nos. 88–9, 94 of *Schriften des Vereins für Reformationsgeschichte* (Halle and Leipzig: Verein für Reformationsgeschichte, 1906–1907).

13. Olevianus's *Lehrstuhl* on the theological faculty was filled by Zacharias Ursinus, the candidate recommended by Hubert Languet at the Naumburg Conference in January, 1561, after Peter Martyr refused the post because of his advanced age. Erdmann K. Sturm, *Der junge Zacharis Ursin: Sein Weg vom Philippismus zum Calvinismus (1534–1562)*, vol. 33 of *Beiträge zur Geschichte und Lehre der Reformierten Kirche* (Neukirchen-Vluyn: Neukirchener Verlag, 1972), 233, 237.

14. See Bouwmeester, *Olevianus*, 38–46.

latinate.[15] It is not clear what part he played in the composition
of the Heidelberg Catechism in late 1562,[16] but we do know that
by October 1563, he was hard at work on a homiletical exposition of Part II of the Catechism, *Vester Grundt, das ist, Die
Artickel des alten, waren, ungezweiffelten Christlichen
Glaubens*.[17] During these years in Heidelberg he also found
himself in the thick of the Protestant eucharistic controversies
in southern Germany, both as a participant in the Maulbronn
Colloquy with the Württemberg Lutherans in 1564[18] and as an

15. In his efforts to institute a Genevan church discipline in the Palatinate,
he encountered strong opposition from the court physician Thomas Erastus,
whose name is preserved in the familiar term "Erastianism." Erastus maintained
(with Zurich) that excommunication was the responsibility of the civil, not the
ecclesiastical, authorities. Olevianus and his sympathizers finally won the day,
and on July 15, 1570, Elector Frederick issued an edict that put all responsibility
for discipline, except the actual pronouncements of excommunication, under
the jurisdiction of the Palatine presbyteries. See Sudhoff, *C. Olevianus*, 339–370.

16. For a discussion of the controversy surrounding Olevianus's authorship
of the Catechism, see M. A. Gooszen, *De Heidelbergsche Catechismus. Textus Receptus met Toelichtende Teksten* (Leiden: E. J. Brill, 1890), 1ff. Gooszen himself
is of the opinion that "Olevianus . . . persoonlijk invloed op de redactie van den
H. C. naar vorm en inhoud beide, heeft geoefend" (p. 111), but even this more
modest estimate of Olevianus's contributions has been seriously challenged by
Walter Hollweg, *Neue Untersuchungen zur Geschichte des Heidelberger Katechismus*, vol. 13 of *Beiträge zur Geschichte und Lehre der Reformierten Kirche* (Neukirchen: Neukirchener Verlag, 1961), 124–152. For a response to Hollweg and
some new light on the question see Lyle D. Bierma, "Olevianus and the Authorship of the Heidelberg Catechism: Another Look," *Sixteenth Century Journal* 13,
no. 4 (Winter 1982):17–27.

17. Olevianus wrote to Bullinger in a letter dated October 25, 1563: "Ergo
praeter conciones diffusiorem Catechismum habeo prae manibus, eadem
methodo servata, quae est in minore." The entire letter is reprinted in Sudhoff,
C. Olevianus, 483–5. *Vester Grundt* was (first?) published in Heidelberg by
Michel Schirat in 1567, republished there by Harnisch in a corrected edition in
1573, and later included (in expanded form) in Christopher Rab's edition of
Olevianus, *Der Gnadenbund Gottes* (Herborn, 1590). Our citations are taken
from excerpts of the 1567 text reprinted in J. M. Reu, *Quellen zur Geschichte des
kirchlichen Unterrichts in der evangelischen Kirche Deutschlands zwischen 1530
und 1600*, pt. 1: *Quellen zur Geschichte des Katechismusunterrichts*, vol. 3: *Ost-,
Nord- und Westdeutsche Katechismen*, sec. 2: *Texte*, pt. 3 (Gütersloh: C. Bertelsmann, 1924), 1330–86; from the Schirat edition of 1567; and from a reprint of
the 1590 text in Sudhoff, *Fester Grund christlicher Lehre. Ein Hilfsbuch zum
Heidelberger Katechismus* (Frankfurt: K. T. Volcker, 1854).

18. For an account of the Maulbronn Colloquy see Sudhoff, *C. Olevianus*,
260–290, and Heinrich Heppe, *Geschichte des deutschen Protestantismus*, 4 vols.
(Marburg: R. G. Elwert, 1853), 2:73ff.

author of numerous polemical sermons and treatises on the sacraments.[19]

Frederick III died on October 26, 1576, around the time that Olevianus published his second major theological work, *Expositio Symboli Apostolici, sive Articulorum Fidei: in qua summa gratuiti foederis aeterni inter Deum et fideles breviter et perspicue tractatur.*[20] The new elector, Ludwig VI, was a Lutheran, and on November 17, after only six days in Heidelberg, he deposed the Calvinist Olevianus from his offices, placed him under house arrest, and finally expelled him from the city. In early 1577 Count Ludwig von Wittgenstein persuaded Olevianus to decline a call to Dort in the Netherlands and to come to Berleburg (50 miles northwest of Marburg), where over the next seven years he tutored the count's sons and directed a Calvinist reorganization of the church in Wittgenstein and the neighboring Wetterau districts.[21] During these years at Berleburg, he also published two

19. A collection of nine of Olevianus's "Predigten von dem heiligen Abendmahl des Herrn" is included in *Der Gnadenbund Gottes,* 1593 ed., 259–514, along with a "Kurtzer Unterricht von der predig des H. Evangelij und reychung der H. Sacramenten, nemlich des Tauffs und H. Abendmals unsers Herrn Jesu Christi," 515–21, and a more conciliatory treatise, "Fürschlag, wie Doctor Luthers Lehr von den heiligen Sacramenten (so in seinem kleinen Catechismo begriffen) auss Gottes Wort mit den reformirten Kirchen zu vereinigen seye," 523–44. Parts of the Lord's Supper sermons are reprinted in Sudhoff, *C. Olevianus,* 185–233 (on p. 233 Sudhoff mistakenly identifies the original Latin version of the second sermon, *Brevis admonitio de re eucharistica,* as a separate treatise). The "Kurtzer Unterricht" and "Fürschlag" are also found in *C. Olevianus,* 398–408, and in Reu, *Quellen,* 1318–20.

It is difficult to date most of these writings precisely, but four of the sermons (nos. 3, 4, 5, 6) appeared in 1563, the year before Flacius Illyricus published his *Widerlegung vier Predigten eines Sacramentierers, mit Zunamen Olevianus,* and at least one (no. 8) was printed as late as 1575. Sudhoff, *C. Olevianus,* 185, 226.

20. We are informed on the title page that this work was "desumta ex concionibus catecheticis Gasparis Oleviani." The first edition was published in Frankfurt in 1576 by Andreae Wechel. According to Steubing ("Lebensnachrichten," p. 95), the *Expositio* was republished in Herborn in 1580, 1584, and 1593, and in Frankfurt in 1618 (an English edition, translated by John Field, had appeared in London already in 1581). Förstemann (*Allgemeine Encyklopädie,* s.v. "Olevianus") suggests that the 1580 Herborn edition is probably confused with one published that year in Frankfurt. My own citations are from an edition published by Wechel in Frankfurt in 1584.

21. James I. Good, *Origin of the Reformed Church in Germany* (Reading, PA: Daniel Miller, 1887), 255.

handbooks on logic and three commentaries on the epistles of Paul.[22]

In 1584 Olevianus accepted a call from Count John the Elder of Nassau-Dillenburg to become the pastor in Herborn, and in July of that year Olevianus opened the Herborn Academy and became its first Professor of Dogmatics.[23] One year later he published his *magnum opus* on the covenant, *De substantia foederis inter Deum et electos, itemque de mediis, quibus ea ipsa substantia nobis communicatur. Libri duo e praelectionibus Gaspari Oleviani excerpti,*[24] presumably based on lectures delivered at the new academy. The last of his works published before his death was an instructional compendium of Calvin's *Institutes* in

22. *Fundamenta dialecticae breviter consignate e praelectionibus* (Frankfurt, 1581); *De inventione dialecticae liber, e praelectionibus Casp. Oleviani excerptus* (Geneva: Eustathius Vignon, 1583); *In epistolam D. Pauli Apostoli ad Galatas notae, ex concionibus Gasparis Oleviani excerptae, & a Theodoro Beza edita* (Geneva: E. Vignon, 1579); and *In epistolas D. Pauli Apostoli ad Philippenses & Colossenses notae, ex Gasparis Oleviani concionibus excerptae, & a Theodoro Beza editae* (Geneva: E. Vignon, 1580). My citations from the Romans commentary are from the second edition (1584), also published in Geneva by Vignon. Following his father's death in March 1587, Olevianus's son Paul put together an edition of *Notae Gasparis Oleviani in Evangelia, quae diebus dominicis ac festis populo christiano in plerique Germaniae ecclesiis proponi solent,* which was published in Herborn by Christopher Corvin (Rab) in late 1587. Sometime after October 1576 (according to the *Allegemeine Deutsche Biographie,* 1887 ed., s.v. "Olevian, Caspar," by F. W. Cuno), Olevianus composed a children's catechism, the *Bauern Katechismus,* which is included in *Der Gnadenbund Gottes* (1593 ed.), 235–58, and reprinted by Reu, *Quellen,* 1307–13.

23. For a description of the early growth and influence of the Academy under Olevianus and Piscator see Steubing, "Lebensnachrichten," 86–7, 103–13, and Gerhard Menk, *Die Hohe Schule Herborn in ihrer Frühzeit (1584–1660): Ein Beitrag zum Hochschulwesen des deutschen Kalvinismus im Zeitalter der Gegenreformation,* vol. 30 of *Veröffentlichungen der Historischen Kommission für Nassau* (Weisbaden: Selbstverlag der Historischen Kommission für Nassau, 1981).

24. (Geneva: Eustathius Vignon, 1585). Steubing ("Lebensnachrichten," p. 96), Ney (*Realencyklopädie,* s.v. "Olevianus"), Schaller (*Die Religion in Geschichte und Gegenwart,* 2nd ed., s.v. "Olevian"), and Ritschl (*Dogmengeschichte des Protestantismus,* 4 vols. [Göttingen: Vandenhoeck & Ruprecht, 1926], 3:417–8) all incorrectly identify Olevianus's *Der Gnadenbund Gottes* (Herborn: Christopher Rab, 1590) as a German translation of *De substantia. Der Gnadenbund Gottes* is actually a collection of some of Olevianus's earlier writings: *Vester Grundt,* the *Bauern Katechismus,* the nine "Abendmahlpredigten," "Kurtzer Unterricht," and "Fürschlag."

1586,[25] the year in which he also presided over the first general synod of Reformed churches from Nassau, Wied, Solms, and Wittgenstein.[26] Early in 1587, however, his health began deteriorating rapidly,[27] and on March 15, 1587, he died, five months short of his fifty-first birthday. He lies buried in the Evangelische Kirche in Herborn.[28]

Survey of Past Research

Over the last 150 years historians of the late Reformation period have recognized Caspar Olevianus as a major figure in the establishment of the Reformed church in Germany. He has been variously described as the most influential religious leader in the Palatinate,[29] the most significant German reformer from the Calvinist school,[30] next to Ursinus the most important father of German Reformed theology,[31] and even

---

25. *Institutionis Christianae Religionis Epitome: Ex Institutione Johanni Calvini excerpta, authoris methodo et verbis retentis. Cum praefatione Gaspari Oleviani, ad Theodorum Bezam, in qua editionis consilium exponitur* (Herborn: Christophorus Corvinus [Christopher Rab], 1586).

26. Good, *Reformed Church in Germany,* 264.

27. Sudhoff attributes this to "die jähen Wechselfälle seines Lebens, wie die harten Kämpfe, welche der eifrige Mann zu bestehen hatte" (*C. Olevianus,* 465), but in a letter of December 30, 1586, discovered by Knodt in the Wiesbaden archives, Olevianus himself explains to Count John the Elder that while on a pastoral call the day before he had twice slipped and fallen very hard and was now suffering from chest and head pains. Knodt is certain that these falls were "die Ursache seines zuletzt zum Tode führenden Leidens." D. Knodt, "Briefe von Caspar Olevianus," *Theologische Studien und Kritiken* 79 (1960): 628–30.

28. Piscator (*Leben und Sterben,* 20b–21a) records that at the time of his death Olevianus had several manuscripts ready for printing: 1) a book of sermons on I Corinthians; 2) *notae* on his sermons on the Sunday Gospel Lectionaries; 3) *notae* on his sermons on Ephesians; and 4) some additions to ". . . seinem buch de foedere [probably *De substantia*]. . . ." The Gospel sermons were published in 1587 as *Notae in Evangelia* (see n. 22 above) and the Ephesians sermons as *Notae in epistolam ad Ephesios ex Oleviani concionibus excerptae* (Herborn, 1588), but I have been unable to find any manuscripts or printed editions of the remaining materials.

29. Charles Miller, "The Spread of Calvinism in Switzerland, Germany, and France," in *The Rise and Development of Calvinism,* ed. John H. Bratt (Grand Rapids: Eerdmans, 1959), 48.

30. *Allgemeines Kirchen-Lexikon,* 1850 ed., s.v. "Olevian."

31. *Die Religion in Geschichte und Gegenwart,* 3rd ed., s.v. "Olevian," by J.F.G. Goeters.

one of the most prominent Reformed theologians of his time.[32] Until the late 1850s, however, Olevianus's importance was measured less by his reputation as a theologian or writer than by that as a promoter of Calvinist doctrine, polity, and discipline in Palatine Germany.[33] Ursinus (a colleague at Heidelberg) was supposedly the theologian, Olevianus the preacher; Ursinus was the more profound, Olevianus the more practical.[34] Even when historians of dogma in the 1840s and 1850s began acknowledging the sixteenth-century roots of Reformed covenant theology, Olevianus, who had written several lengthy treatises on the biblical notion of covenant, was left entirely unmentioned.[35] His image remained that of "the eloquent court preacher of Frederick the Pious."[36]

Between 1857 and 1879, however, two books and a long journal article appeared in Germany which for the first time assigned to Olevianus a place in the early development of Reformed covenant theology. In 1857 Karl Sudhoff published what is still the standard work on Olevianus's life and writings, *C. Olevianus und Z. Ursinus: Leben und ausgewählte Schriften.* Sudhoff devoted little space to actual analysis of Olevianus's thought, but he did at one point make the rather striking asser-

32. *Realencyklopädie,* s.v., "Olevianus," by J. Ney.
33. "His talents and his taste indicated that his vocation was rather in this sphere than in that of author, or even theological professor. . . . What writings he has left belong principally to preparations for the Heidelberg Catechism, and such as were published in its defence or explanation." *Cyclopedia of Biblical, Theological and Ecclesiastical Literature,* 1969 ed., s.v. "Olevianus," by Henry Harbaugh. Harbaugh's article on Olevianus is taken nearly verbatim from his earlier work, *The Fathers of the German Reformed Church in Europe and America,* 2 vols. (Lancaster, PA: Sprenger and Westhaeffer, 1857), 1:26ff.
34. This image can still be found in scholarly literature today. See, e.g., John P. Donnelly, *Calvinism and Scholasticism in Vermigli's Doctrine of Man and Grace,* vol. 18 of *Studies in Medieval and Reformation Thought* (Leiden: E.J. Brill, 1976), 186: "Olevianus was the more eloquent of the two but a less profound theologian; he made his mark mainly as a counsellor of the Elector rather than as a writer."
35. A. Schweizer (*Die Glaubenslehre der Evangelische-Reformirten Kirche,* 2 vols. [Zurich: Orell, Fussli and Comp, 1844], 1:103ff.) mentions only Zwingli, Calvin, and Hyperius, and W. Gass (*Geschichte der Protestantischen Dogmatik,* 4 vols. [Berlin: George Reimer, 1857], 2:265–6) only Zwingli, Jud, Bullinger, Hyperius, and Wendelin.
36. Harbaugh, *Fathers of the German Reformed Church,* 1:246.

tion that "by this work [*De substantia*] he became the actual founder of federal theology."[37] This conclusion was echoed in the next decade by Ludwig Diestel[38] and in the following decade by Heinrich Heppe, who in a major study of the history of Reformed pietism described Olevianus as the first person ever to employ the covenant motif as the organizing principle of an entire theological system.[39] This claim for Olevianus as the first real covenant theologian persisted into the twentieth century,[40] but other theses about his place in the history of covenant theology were also being proposed. Gottlob Schrenk, in an influential work in 1923 on the covenant theology of Johannes Cocceius (1603–1669), argued that Olevianus and his colleague Ursinus were important "middle links" in the transmission of federal theology to the seventeenth century but that it was Heinrich Bullinger of Zurich who was the first to use covenant as a constitutive theological principle.[41] According to Schrenk, Olevianus's originality lay largely in the practical, experiential dimension he added to the covenant theology of his predeces-

37. Sudhoff, *C. Olevianus*, 460.

38. Ludwig Diestel, "Studien zur Föderaltheologie," *Jahrbücher für deutsche Theologie* 10 (1865): 213.

39. Heinrich Heppe, *Geschichte des Pietismus und der Mystik in der Reformirten Kirche* (Leiden: E. J. Brill, 1879), 209–11. Already in 1857 Heppe had described the covenant idea as the "Grundbegriff" of early German Reformed dogmatics. *Dogmatik des deutschen Protestantismus im sechzehnten Jahrhundert,* 3 vols. (Gotha: F.A. Perthes, 1857), 1:143–44.

40. See, e.g., the *Encyclopedia of Religion and Ethics*, 1911 ed., s.v. "Covenant Theology," by W. A. Brown; Ritschl, *Dogmengeschichte,* 3:420; Karl Bauer, *Aus der grossen Zeit der theologischen fakultät zu Heidelberg* (Baden: M. Schauenburg, 1938), 27; Ernst Bizer, "Historische Einleitung des Herausgebers," in H. Heppe, *Die Dogmatik der Evangelisch-Reformirten Kirche* (Neukirchen: Kries Moers, 1958), xxxviii; Miller, "The Spread of Calvinism," 49; *Weltkirchen Lexikon,* 1960 ed., s.v. "Bundestheologie," by E.L. Evans; I. Breward, "The Life and Theology of William Perkins 1558–1602" (Ph.D. dissertation, University of Manchester, 1963), 62; Victor Priebe, "The Covenant Theology of William Perkins" (Ph.D. dissertation, Drew University, 1967), 30–1; W.K.B. Stoever, "The Covenant of Works in Puritan Theology: The Antinomian Crisis in New England" (Ph.D. dissertation, Yale University, 1970), 30–31, n. 15; and J.A.W. Verhoeven, "Caspar Olevianus: Een onderzoek naar plaats en funktie van het genadeverbond in zijn theologie" (Doctoraal Scriptie, Rijksuniversiteit Utrecht, 1982), 29.

41. Gottlob Schrenk, *Gottesreich und Bund im älteren Protestantismus, vornehmlich bei Johannes Coccejus* (Gütersloh: C. Bertelsmann, 1923), 44, 45.

sors.[42] Jacobs, too, argued that Olevianus gave pedagogical form and a pastoral touch to federal theology but that it was Zwingli who had discovered it and Bullinger who had first systematized it.[43] Goeters, Muller, and Verhoeven all credited him with combining Bullinger's covenant doctrine with some of the key themes in Calvin's thought,[44] while Baker insisted that "Olevianus's covenant of grace was the *Calvinistic* notion of unilateral testament."[45] Finally, in a ground-breaking article in 1951 entitled "The Origins of Puritanism," Leonard Trinterud labeled Olevianus and Ursinus "the architects of the *final* formulation of the covenant scheme" in "a wholly systematic reorganization of the covenant theology" around 1580.[46] Clearly, there has been little consensus in the secondary literature on the role Olevianus played in the development of sixteenth-century covenant thought.

There has also been considerable disagreement about his understanding of the covenant idea itself. This disagreement can be seen in four areas in particular. First of all, scholars as far back as Heppe[47] have seen in Olevianus's covenant theology an at-

42. "Ihnen [Ursinus and Olevianus] ist der Bundesgedanke nicht nur gut für einen dogmatischen Locus, vielmehr stellt tiefes persönliches Interesse diese Formulierung in den Vordergrund der religiösen Gesamtäusserung. Die gegenwärtige Heilserfahrung des Gläubigen ist der Ausgang "und Brennpunkt ihrer Föderaltheologie. . . ." Ibid., 57.

43. *Die Religion in Geschichte und Gegenwart*, 3rd ed., s.v. "Bund (Föderaltheologie, dogmengeschichtlich)," by P. Jacobs.

44. Goeters, *Religion in Geschichte*, 3rd ed., s.v. "Olevian"; Richard A. Muller, "Predestination and Christology in Sixteenth-Century Reformed Theology" (Ph.D. dissertation, Duke University, 1976), 314, 433: Verhoeven, "Olevianus," 114. Geerhardus Vos ("The Doctrine of the Covenant in Reformed Theology" [1891], trans. S. Voorwinde and W. Van Gemeren, in *Redemptive History and Biblical Interpretation: The Shorter Writings of Geerhardus Vos*, ed. Richard B. Gaffin [Phillipsburg, NJ: Presbyterian and Reformed Publishing Co., 1980], 236) and Charles S. McCoy ("The Covenant Theology of Johannes Cocceius" [Ph.D. dissertation, Yale University, 1957], 66) also held that Olevianus was heavily influenced by the Zurich theologians. Both Ritschl (*Dogmengeschichte*, 3:417) and Stoever ("Covenant of Works," 30–31, n.15) argued that he owed his greatest theological debt to Ursinus.

45. Baker, *Bullinger and the Covenant*, 205 (italics added).

46. Trinterud, "Origins of Puritanism," 48 (italics added). Cf. also Baker, *Bullinger and the Covenant*, 205: " Soon Olevianus's scheme would be standardized in the Reformed dichotomy between the covenant of works and the covenant of grace."

47. *Dogmatik des deutschen Protestantismus*, 1:139ff., 188ff.

tempt to mitigate the harshness of the Calvinist doctrine of predestination, which stressed that individual salvation or damnation depends not on human decision or behavior in history but
on God's inscrutable selection in eternity of some to be saved
(election) and others to be damned (reprobation). Covenant theology, it was claimed, shifted the focus back to history and to the
responsibility borne by the human partner in a covenant of salvation (or covenant of grace) established by God in history. W. A.
Brown, for example, described early German Reformed theology, including Olevianus's, as having "differed" with the "stricter
predestinarianism" of Switzerland and France.[48] Schrenk called
attention to a new emphasis in Heidelberg on the history of God's
self-revelation in Scripture, which "softened" the "rigid struc-
tures of post-Calvinian predestination doctrine"[49]; and Moltmann went so far as to portray Olevianus's covenant doctrine as
part of a widespread theological "counterattack" in the later
1500s against Theodore Beza's Aristotelian-based predestinarian
theology[50]—even though just a year before, he had stated that
election was the very "core" of Olevianus's covenant of grace![51]

Others, too, have maintained that Olevianus's doctrine of the
covenant in no way opposed Calvin's predestinarianism but, on
the contrary, rested on absolute election (Baker)[52] and encapsu-
lated the relationship between God and His elect (Lang).[53] As
Verhoeven put it, election for Olevianus determined both the
possibility and the boundaries of the covenant of grace.[54] Yet
even among some who saw in Olevianus a close relationship between election and covenant, there was still no consensus on

48. *Encyclopedia of Religion and Ethics,* s.v. "Covenant Theology," by W.A.
Brown. Evans (*Weltkirchen Lexikon,* s.v. "Bundestheologie") makes the same
point but appears to quote nearly verbatim from Brown's article. See also
Miller, "Spread of Calvinism," 49.
49. Schrenk, *Gottesreich und Bund,* 55–6; cf. also 60–61.
50. Jürgen Moltmann, "Zur Bedeutung des Petrus Ramus für Philosophie
und Theologie im Calvinismus," *Zeitschrift für Kirchengeschichte* 68 (1957): 317.
51. *Evangelisches Kirchenlexikon,* 1956 ed., s.v., "Bund (dogmengeschichtlich)," by Jürgen Moltmann.
52. Baker, *Bullinger and the Covenant,* 205.
53. August Lang, *Der Heidelberger Katechismus. Zum 350 jährigen Gedächtnis seiner Entstehung,* no. 113 of *Schriften des Vereins für Reformationsgeschichte*
(Leipzig: Rudolf Haupt, 1913), 21–22.
54. Verhoeven, "Olevianus," 113.

how he viewed the relation of the *non*elect to the covenant. Does the covenant of grace pertain only to the elect,[55] does it relate in some way also to the nonelect in the visible church,[56] or does Olevianus leave the question unanswered?[57]

These differences of opinion might be considered part of a larger disagreement about how closely tuned to Scripture Olevianus's covenant theology really was. As early as 1887, F. W. Cuno suggested a contrast between the thoroughly biblically grounded covenant doctrine of Olevianus and the more artificial dogmatic construction of Cocceius in the early seventeenth century.[58] Schrenk, too, felt that the Heidelberg theologians' emphasis on the biblical history of revelation provided an "opponent to the philosophically construed dogmatics" of the second half of the sixteenth century.[59] Klooster found in Olevianus "the beginnings of a redemptive-historical approach" that represented "a radical break with the old scholastic system of thought and paved the way for understanding the biblical message in the framework of the salvatory actions of God in history."[60] And Moltmann, as we have seen, described the Heidelberg-Herborn federal theology as part of a larger anti-Aristotelian movement that "liberated theology from the grasp of philosophy and gave biblical and humanistic thought a new lease on life."[61]

On the other hand, there are those who have felt that Olevianus's use of the covenant idea as a device for arranging theological material eclipsed the biblical picture of the covenant(s). According to Diestel, Olevianus borrowed the term *"covenant"* from the Bible but treated it in an "essentially dogmatic" fash-

---

55. Ludwig Diestel, *Geschichte des Alten Testaments in der christlichen Kirche* (Jena: Maukes Verlag, 1869), 288: Schrenck, *Gottesreich und Bund*, 61; Baker, *Bullinger and the Covenant*, 204.

56. Peter Y. De Jong, *The Covenant Idea in New England Theology* (Grand Rapids: Eerdmans, 1945), 25.

57. Louis Berkhof, *Systematic Theology* (Grand Rapids: Eerdmans, 1941), 285.

58. *Deutsche Biographie*, s.v. "Olevian."

59. Schrenk, *Gottesreich und Bund*, 55–56.

60. Fred H. Klooster, "The Heidelberg Catechism: Origin and History" (course syllabus printed at Calvin Theological Seminary, Grand Rapids, MI, 1981), 342.

61. Moltmann, "Bedeutung des Petrus Ramus," 317.

ion.[62] It was Cocceius, said Stoever, who developed the histori-cal (*heilsgeschichtlich*) element inherent in the covenant con-ception; in Herborn and Puritan federal theology "the *heilsgeschichtlich* progression is overshadowed by the theologi-cal architectonic."[63] Even Schrenk admitted that the historical dimension recedes in Olevianus's theology, though largely be-cause of Olevianus's interest in the ethical and experiential im-plications of the covenant of grace.[64]

A second area of disagreement regarding Olevianus's covenant doctrine has to do with the doctrinal direction of his view of the sacraments. Otto Ritschl argued in his *Dogmengeschichte* in 1926 that the consistent application of the covenant idea to every doc-trine in his system led Olevianus to adopt a more Lutheran con-ception of the objective character of the sacraments, namely, that divine grace is present in the sacramental elements themselves. It is not altogether clear from Ritschl's discussion why this was so, but he seemed to imply that, according to Olevianus, what is offered in the sacraments (signs of the covenant) to one has to be offered to all if the conditional nature of the covenant blessings is to be preserved. Thus the unbelieving participant in the sacra-ments receives more than a bare sign, but it leads ultimately to his or her greater damnation.[65] Sudhoff had asserted seventy years before, however, that Olevianus was completely in line with the general Reformed view of the Lord's Supper and had, in fact,

62. Diestel, "Studien zur Föderaltheologie," 213–4. Cf. Sudhoff's statement that even Olevianus's commentaries are "vorwiegend dogmatisch." *C. Olevi-anus*, 460.

63. Stoever, "Covenant of Works," 35, n.23.

64. Schrenk, *Gottesreich und Bund*, 60–61.

65. "Bei den Sakramenten endlich, die auch Olevian wieder als äussere Zeug-nisse und Siegel des Gnadenbundes auffasst, habt er im Unterschiede von der sonst den reformierten geläufigen Anschauung hervor, dass sie auf Grund der Einsetzung Christi auch für diejenigen Sakramente seien, die sie missbrauchen und daher gerechter Weise verdammt werden. So ist Olevian dadurch, dass er den Gedanken des Bundesverhältnisses und die Bedingungen eines solchen als den leitenden Gesichtspunkt seiner Darstellung der gesamten Dogmatik in folgerichter Durchführung zur Geltung brachte, in der Auffassung der Sakra-mente zu einem charakteristisch anderen Ergebnis gelangt, als Calvin, nach des-sen Lehre die ungläubigen Empfänger eines Sakraments nur ein seiner Wahrheit entblösstes Zeichen . . . behalten. Dadurch aber hat Olevian . . . in einem wichti-gen Punkt vielmehr mit der lutherischen Auffassung von dem objectiven Charac-ter der Sakramente übereingestimmt." Ritschl, *Dogmengeschichte*, 3:419–420.

been accused by some of his Reformed contemporaries of *Zwinglian* tendencies in his eucharistic doctrine.[66] Heppe, too, saw in Olevianus's *De substantia* the most complete discussion of the Reformed doctrine of the sacraments of his day.[67]

Ritschl's references to conditions in Olevianus's covenant of grace leads us to the third area in which there has been some difference of opinion. Whereas Ritschl understood the covenant of grace to be in some way conditional for Olevianus, Wayne Baker, in his recent volume on Bullinger's covenant theology, is convinced that Olevianus speaks of conditions only in reference to a so-called natural or legal covenant, not the covenant of grace. The latter is unilateral and unconditional, a testament of grace in no way dependent on human effort for ratification. It is a "purely gratuitous covenant."[68]

Baker's mention of more than one covenant in Olevianus's theology points, in turn, to the final disputed question in the scholarship to date: how many covenants does Olevianus actually find in the Bible? Diestel, writing in 1869, held that for Olevianus there was only one, a gracious covenant, established by God after the fall of Adam, although Olevianus's emphasis on the believer's union with Christ as the essence of the covenantal relationship soon led others to posit a pre-fall covenant with Adam as well.[69] Eleven years later Fisher had still found "no distinct mention of such a covenant with Adam either in the writers of the first age of the Reformation, or afterwards until near the time of Cocceius,"[70] some fifty years after Olevianus's death. Karl Barth did find a "double covenant" idea in Reformed theologians before Olevianus but was convinced that in Olevianus himself "the covenant is described uniformly, unequivocally and exclusively as the covenant of grace."[71]

66. Sudhoff, *C. Olevianus*, 237, 377–78.
67. Heppe, *Dogmatik des deutschen Protestantismus*, 2:221.
68. Baker, *Bullinger and the Covenant*, 204–5.
69. Diestel, *Geschichte des Alten Testaments*, 288.
70. George P. Fisher, *Discussions in History and Theology* (New York: Charles Scribner's Sons, 1880), 375.
71. Karl Barth, *Church Dogmatics*, vol. 4: *The Doctrine of Reconciliation*, trans. G.W. Bromiley (New York: Charles Scribner's Sons, 1956), 1:59. Cf. also Brian G. Armstrong, *Calvinism and the Amyraut Heresy* (Madison: University of Wisconsin Press, 1969), 48, n. 139: "Olevianus' *De substantia foederis* . . . presents but one covenant, the covenant of grace."

One also finds advocates, however, of precisely the opposite view. McCoy saw Olevianus "making clear and extensive use of the double covenant,"[72] and, in Heppe's judgment, Olevianus understood the pre-fall Adamic covenant (later called the "covenant of works") in "entirely the same way" as Cocceius did a half century later.[73] Trinterud, as we have already seen, pointed to Olevianus and Ursinus as the "architects of the final formulation of the covenant scheme," in which a pre-fall covenant of works played an important part.[74] Indeed, Baker believed that Olevianus "*introduced* the notion of a covenant of creation [works], which after the fall became the legal covenant or the natural covenant."[75]

In addition, Otto Ritschl discovered in Olevianus's writings the elements of a pretemporal covenant between the Father and the Son,[76] a concept that, in Schrenk's view, "is already clearly found in Olevianus"[77] and, according to Heppe, serves as the "center of gravity" of Olevianus's doctrine of redemption.[78] More recently, however, Verhoeven has argued that Olevianus does *not* speak expressly of such a covenant in eternity between the Father and the Son.[79] Finally, both Ritschl and John Murray noted references in Olevianus also to an "impious covenant" (*nefarium foedus*) contracted between the human race and the devil at the fall.[80]

---

72. McCoy, "Covenant Theology of Cocceius," 76.

73. Heppe, *Geschichte des Pietismus*, 211, n.1. According to Vos, however, when Olevianus discusses the covenant with Adam, he neither views Adam in a federal (i.e., representative) role nor clearly distinguishes Adam's covenant relationship to God from his relation as creature. "Covenant in Reformed Theology," 237–8.

74. Trinterud, "Origins of Puritanism," 48.

75. Baker, *Bullinger and the Covenant*, 204 (italics added).

76. Ritschl, *Dogmengeschichte*, 3:419.

77. Schrenk, *Gottesreich und Bund,* 61.

78. *Dogmatik des deutschen Protestantismus*, 2:218. Cf. also Heppe, *Geschichte des Pietismus*, 210: "so ist z.B. der auch von Coccejus vertretende Gedanke, dass der Gnadenbund auf der ewigen *sponsio* des Sohnes fur die Erwählten das Werk der Genugtuung vollbringen zu wollen und auf dem hierdurch begründeten ewigen Pact des Vaters mit dem Sohne beruhe, nach welchem dieser die Erwählten um der Verdienstes des Sohnes willen in seinen Gnadenbund aufnehmen will, schon von Olevian dargelegt."

79. "Olevianus," 114.

80. Ritschl, *Dogmengeschichte,* 3:418; *The Encyclopedia of Christianity*, 1972 ed., s.v. "Covenant Theology," by John Murray. It should be mentioned, however, that Ritschl found references to other covenants in Olevianus "nur an wenigen kurzen Stellen."

Past research on Olevianus, then, has left us with a highly confused, and at times contradictory, picture of his doctrine of the covenant and its place in the history of Reformed theology. Did Olevianus employ the covenant idea as the organizing principle of his theology? If so, was he the first to do so? If not the first, did he stand in the middle or near the end of the development of a systematic covenant theology? To whom did he owe his greatest theological debt? Exactly how did he relate the covenant to predestination and the sacraments? Did he understand the covenant to be conditional? Is his treatment of the covenant theme in Scripture dominated by a concern to systematize it? Are there other covenants in his theology besides the covenant of grace? In the past none of these questions has been answered with one voice. What follows, therefore, is a thorough reexamination of Olevianus's understanding of the covenant of grace, of other covenants in his writings, and of his place in the history of Reformed covenant thought. After an overview of the early history of Reformed covenant doctrine in Chapter II, these three topics will serve as the focus of Chapters III, IV, and V, respectively, followed by a concluding summary in Chapter VI.

2 Continental Reformed Background

Zwingli

Since the pioneer research of Von Korff early in this century,[1] historians of theology have almost without exception looked to the Swiss reformer Ulrich Zwingli (1484–1531) as the founder of Reformed covenant theology. It has, of course, been suggested that Zwingli's understanding of covenant was not original with him but was taken over from the French humanist tradition,[2] from Erasmus,[3] and from Bullinger.[4] Perhaps the most widely accepted thesis today is that first proposed by Schrenk in 1923, namely, that Zwingli hammered out his doctrine of the covenant in a defense of infant baptism against his Anabaptist opponents. It was the Anabaptists, said Schrenk, who actually introduced the idea of covenant into Reformation

---

1. *Die Anfänge der Föderaltheologie und ihre erste Ausgestaltung in Zürich und Holland* (Bonn: Emil Eisele, 1908).
2. "Den Bundesbegriff wird Zwingli (wie bald Calvin) Französisch-humanistischer Tradition (Budaeus) entnommen." Gottfried W. Locher, "Grundzüge der Theologie Huldrych Zwinglis im Vergleich mit derjenigen Martin Luthers und Johannes Calvins," *Zwingliana* 12 (1967):582.
3. "Die prägende Kraft der erasmischen Vorstellungen lässt sich vielfach erkennen. Hier sei nur auf Zwingli verwiesen, der in seinen ersten Schriften ebenfalls bei der ethischen Interpretation des Sakramentsbegriffs einsetzt." Martin Greschat, "Der Bundesgedanke in der Theologie des späten Mittelalters," *Zeitschrift für Kirchengeschichte* 81 (1970):61.
4. "Zwingli based his assimilation of New Covenantal baptism and Old Covenantal circumcision on Tertullian and Lactantius. It was Henry Bullinger who first pointed out to Zwingli these patristic texts demonstrating the unity of the Old and New Covenants and consequently the equivalence of circumcision and baptism." George H. Williams, *The Radical Reformation* (Philadelphia: Westminster, 1962), 131.

discussion, but it was Zwingli who first treated it from a Reformed perspective.[5]

Only recently has this thesis been challenged. In a dissertation in 1971 J. W. Cottrell convincingly argued that Zwingli was using covenant language well before his controversy with the Anabaptists—as early, in fact, as his first efforts at reform in 1522.[6] But Cottrell did agree that it was during the debates with the Anabaptists that the notion of the unity of the Old and New Covenants (Testaments) began to form an important part of Zwingli's argument for infant baptism and hence of his covenant doctrine in general.[7]

In his "Reply to Hubmaier" (November 1525) and particularly in his "Refutation of the Tricks of the Anabaptists" (July 1527) Zwingli defended the practice of paedobaptism on the grounds that there has been but one covenant of grace between God and his people from the time of Adam to the present. This "covenant that God had entered into with Adam" after the fall (Genesis 3:15) was renewed with Noah, with Abraham, with the nation of Israel, and finally, after its confirmation in Jesus Christ, with us in the New Testament church.[8] In both testaments we find a single people of God united in a common covenant by a common faith in the same Savior.[9] God's covenant

5. "Der erste Anfang der Bundeslehre wurde nicht in Wittenberg oder Genf, sondern in Zürich gemacht. Zwingli ist der eigentliche Erneuerer des biblischen Bundesgedankens für die reformierte Theologie, aber die Anregung dazu kam ihm wohl von täuferischer Seite. . . . Der Kampf gegen die Täufer und der Wille zur Volkskirche sind die treibenden Kräfte, die hinter diesen Gedanken stehen." *Gottesreich und Bund,* 36.

6. Jack W. Cottrell, "Covenant and Baptism in the Theology of Huldreich Zwingli" (Th.D. dissertation, Princeton Theological Seminary, 1971), 81. For a refutation of Williams's thesis that Bullinger's covenantal defense of infant baptism antedated Zwingli's "Reply to Hubmaier," see Cottrell, 339ff.

7. Ibid., 173, 243.

8. "In catabaptistarum strophas elenchus" (July 31, 1527), in *Huldreich Zwinglis Sämtliche Werke,* eds. Emil Egli et al., vol. 93/1 of *Corpus Reformatorum* [CR], (Zurich: Verlag Berichthaus, 1961): 156–57. "Idem ergo foedus, quod olim cum populo Israelitico, in novissimis temporibus nobiscum pepigit, ut unus essemus cum eis populus, una ecclesia, et unum foedus quoque haberemus." Ibid., 163.

9. "Idem enim testamentum et foedus, hoc est: eadem dei misericordia mundo per filium eius promissa salvum facit Adam, Noam, Abraham, Mosen, David, quod et Petrum, Paulum, Ananiam, Gamalielem et Stephanum salvos

promises to Abraham are promises to anyone who shares Abraham's faith, for God does not change.[10]

This does not mean that there are no differences between the Old and New Testaments. Zwingli lists six in particular: 1) In the Old Testament Christ is expected; in the New Testament He is already given. 2) In the Old Testament, believers at death descend into the bosom of Abraham; in the New Testament they pass directly from death into life. 3) The Old Testament is characterized by shadows, the New Testament by their removal. 4) The Old Testament is dominated by ceremonies, so open to priestly abuse; the New Testament is free of such ceremonies and thus clearer in its teaching. 5) In the Old Testament the covenant is limited to one nation; in the New Testament it is open to all. 6) Finally, in the New Testament we are for the first time given a perfect model for living—Jesus Christ.[11] These differences, however, are only minor when the heart (*principalia*) of the relationship between God and humanity in both testaments is considered. God as our God, Christ as our Savior, we as His people—these are themes that bind together, not separate, the two covenants: "so far as their substance is concerned, they are not a bit different."[12]

It is upon this foundation—the continuity of the history of salvation and the unity of the covenant of grace—that Zwingli goes on to make his case for infant baptism. If there is, indeed, one covenant and one people of God throughout redemptive history, children of New Testament believers are no less a part of that covenant than were the children of Old Testament believers, nor are they any less entitled to the sign of that covenant. New Testament baptism has replaced Old Testament circumcision, but like circumcision baptism signifies and seals covenan-

---

fecit. . . . Salvatorem igitur unum eundemque nobiscum habentes unus nobiscum atque nos cum illis populus sunt, una ecclesia." Ibid., 164–6.

10. "Dann was hie zu Abrahamen gsagt, wirt allen gsagt, die da gloubend wie Abraham Gal. 3. Gott wirt nit verwandlet." "Antwort über Balthasar Hubmaiers Taufbuchlein" (Nov. 5, 1525), in *Zwinglis Werke*, vol. 91 of *Corpus Reformatorum* (Leipzig: M. Heinsius Nachfolger, 1927): 630.

11. "Elenchus," 169–70.

12. Ibid., 169.

tal promises extended to God's people long before they them-selves are able to respond to them in faith.[13]

As far as the nature of this covenant is concerned, Zwingli recognizes both a divine and a human dimension to the cove-nant of grace. It includes both divine promise and human re-sponse and responsibility. More than once Zwingli makes it very clear that an upright walk before God is one of the "princi-pal parts" (*fürnemmen stück*) of the covenant[14] and even one of the several *conditiones* or provisions of the Abrahamic pact in Genesis 17.[15] God not only promised faithfulness to Abraham but expected faithfulness from him as well.[16] But Zwingli never described the covenant relationship in such a way that God's blessings of salvation *depend* upon human fulfillment of certain conditions, as Trinterud and others have argued.[17] For Zwingli the distribution of divine covenant favor is based solely on God's eternal decision, his free election. His covenant people are those whom He has selected long before they select Him.[18]

13. ". . . der Christen kinder glych im testament, kirchen, oder pundt sind wie der som Abrahams. Sind sy nun in der kirchen Christi, warumb wöllend ir inen das testamentzeichen abschlahen? . . . Die bschnydung ist den alten gewäsen, des zeychens halb, das uns der touf ist. Wie nun die den kinden gge-ben ist, also sol ouch der touf den kinden ggeben werden." "Antwort," 617, 629.

14. E.g., "Antwort," 630.

15. "Ut quum dominus cum Abraham ferit pactum sive foedus Gen. 17: 'Ego deus omnipotens', inquit, 'ambula coram me et sis integer'! . . . Hic nihil auditur quam foedus quod deus per gratiam suam dignatus est inire cum Abraham. Quid vero continet hoc foedus? Quibus conditionibus statuitur? Hae sunt ergo conditiones: 'Ego ero deus tuus. Tu ambulabis coram me integerrime. Ego patrem multarum gentium faciam te. Dabo tibi e Sara semen. Ero posteritatis quoque tuae illius, quam polliceor, deus. Dabor tibi et semini tuo terram, in qua nunc inquilinus es.'" "Subsidium sive coronis de eucharistia," in *Zwinglis Werke*, vol. 91 of *Corpus Reformatorum* (Leipzig: M. Heinsius Nachfolger, 927): 499.

16. "Promittit ergo ei [Abraham] primum bonitatem suam, quod sit deus eius futurus, atque ab eo vicissim requirit, ut *aristeuse*, hoc est: recte sese ger-endo coram eo ambulet." "Elenchus," 157.

17. Trinterud, "Origins of Puritanism," 45. For a fuller critique of Trinterud's thesis and its influence on recent scholarship see Lyle D. Bierma, "Federal Theology in the Sixteenth Century: Two Traditions?" *Westminster Theological Journal* 45 (Fall 1983):304–21.

18. "Certum est apud deum neminem esse de populo suo deque filiis eius, nisi quem elegirit; rursusque hoc certum est omnem eius esse, quem elegit. . . . Rur-sus electi eligebantur, antequam in utero conciperentur: mox igitur ut sunt, filii dei sunt, etiamsi moriantur, antequam credant aut id vocentur. . . . Eaque verum est: destinatus est, ergo salvus fit—electus est, ergo salvus fit." "Elenchus," 176.

The faith by which they finally do respond is a gift of God bestowed on His elect, and works of obedience are the natural outgrowth of that faith.[19] In short, God expects obedience as a covenantal *response* to His grace. Loving and fearing Him are the result, not the basis, of His favor. They are, in Zwingli's words, a visible *signum electionis*.[20]

Bullinger

When Zwingli died on the battlefield at Kappel in 1531, the mantle of his theological as well as political and ecclesiastical reform fell to his young protegé Heinrich Bullinger (1504–1575). With respect to the doctrine of the covenant, Bullinger indeed picked up the mantle and moved forward. Few today would challenge Von Korff's and Schrenk's conclusion early in this century that Bullinger's understanding of the covenant was essentially Zwinglian, though somewhat more carefuliy developed and complete than that of his mentor.[21]

19. "At ea vis non est ab ipso nomine (sic enim quisque vellet quam grandissimam habere fidem), quum non omnium sit fides; sed a solo deo est: ipsam enim Paulus spiritui sancto refert acceptam. . . . Dei ergo solius donum est." "De providentia dei," in *Huldrici Zuinglii Opera*, eds. M. Schuler and J. Schulthess, 8 vols. (Zurich: Ex Officina Schulthessiana, 1828–42), 4:121. "Trotzdem sind gute Werke heilsnotwendig, weil sie in einer Ketter göttlicher Taten stehen, die den Menschen nur dann zum Heil führen, wenn kein Glied in der Ketter fehlt: Gottes Vorsehung führt zur Erwählung, Gottes Erwählung führt zum Glauben, der gottgewirkte Glaube führt zu guten Werken." Christof Gestrich, *Zwingli als Theologe: Glaube und Geist beim Züricher Reformator*, vol. 20 of *Studien zur Dogmengeschichte und systematischen Theologie* (Zurich: Zwingli Verlag, 1967), 184.

20. "Signum enim electionis est, deum amare ac timere." "Zwingli an Urbanus Rhegius" (October 16, 1526), in *Zwinglis Werke*, vol. 95 of *Corpus Reformatorum* (Leipzig: M. Heinsius Nachfolger, 1914), 738.

21. "Wenn sich nun diese Gedanken [of Zwingli] bei Heinrich Bullinger wiederfinden, so liegt die Vermutung nicht fern, dass der noch jugendliche Amtgenosse und Freund Zwinglis diese Elemente von ihm übernommen hat. Bei seiner Selbstständigkeit aber hat er sie weiter entwickelt." Von Korff, *Anfänge der Föderaltheologie*, 15. "Diese Zwinglischen Gedanken hat Bullinger weitergeführt und noch sorgfältiger und umfassender begründet." Schrenk, *Gottesreich und Bund*, 40. Baker maintains that Bullinger had a more developed hermeneutical basis for his covenant idea, a clearer view of the conditionality of the covenant, and a broader understanding of the implications of covenant unity than Zwingli did, but he does conclude that "clearly Bullinger was greatly influenced by Zwingli." *Bullinger and the Covenant*, 15–18.

Bullinger's discussion of covenant, like Zwingli's, is found largely in two (related) contexts in his writings—in his treatments of the sacraments and of the development of salvation history. We turn first to the latter.

In establishing a covenant with humanity, says Bullinger, God was really accommodating Himself to human convention. Just as human beings bind themselves to a confederacy for, say, the common protection of its members against their enemies, so also God, in order that we might share in Himself and in His goodness, bound Himself to us in a covenant of goodwill.[22] He first made this covenant with Adam immediately after the fall when He received Adam back into favor. He promised him His Son, who would deliver to humanity an inheritance of heavenly blessings. This covenant was in turn renewed with Noah, Abraham and Moses on Mt. Sinai, and finally manifested in full clarity in Jesus Christ.[23]

It is not that there were no changes in the covenant along the way or that the covenant before Christ (Old Testament) and after Christ (New Testament) was identical. In the New Covenant: 1) the revelation of the way of salvation is much clearer; 2) the "very truth" of redemption through Christ prefigured in Old Testament types, shadows, and ceremonies has been realized; 3) the heavy yoke of the Old Testament cultus has been lifted; 4) the people of God are no longer confined to the land of promise but dispersed to the ends of the earth; and 5) the gifts of remission of sins and renewal of the mind (Jer. 31:31) are more liberally bestowed than before.[24] But, Bullinger continues, these changes in the covenant of grace have to do only with "the manner of administration, . . . a few accidents, and certain circumstances. . . . In the substantial and chiefest points, ye can find nothing altered or changed."[25] The differences lay largely in externals—organization, worship, manner of teaching—annexed in the Old Testament to the covenant promise. There were no substantial differences, however, in the covenant, the people, the church, the

22. *The Decades* (1557), 5 vols., ed. Thomas Harding (Cambridge: University Press, 1849–52), II.3.6:169.
23. Ibid.
24. *Decades*, II, 169–70; 3.8:294–99.
25. *Decades*, II, 3.8:294; 3.6:170.

doctrine, the faith, the Spirit, the hope, the inheritance, the expectation, the invocation, or the sacraments of the two testaments.[26] There has always been but one message of salvation through Christ and one means (faith) by which its blessings are appropriated.[27] The Old Testament fathers even passed directly into eternal life at their death, not (as Zwingli had believed) into an intermediary "prison" to await liberation by the Messiah.[28]

Like Zwingli, Bullinger places a good deal of emphasis on the unilateral divine promise of the covenant in which God commits Himself to the redemption of the human race. Like his predecessor also, however, Bullinger does not look upon the covenant as exclusively one-sided. It consists rather in two parts: God's promise to us, His confederates, and our obligation to respond to Him, our "confederate and sovereign prince."[29] Already in his covenanting with Adam God had promised us the bestowal through His Son of nothing less than Himself, both "by making us partakers of all his good and heavenly blessings, *and by binding us unto himself in faith and due obedience.*"[30] Human responsibility was set forth even more clearly in the Abrahamic covenant, where God explicitly enjoined us to walk before Him and be blameless.[31] Even the signs of the covenant of grace, be they circumcision, baptism, or the Lord's Supper, all testify to a resolve on the part of the participants "to do their endeavor by pureness of living to win the favor of God, their confederate."[32] Bullinger says about the Old Testament saints that "the blessing and partaking of all good things pertaineth to the circumcised, *if* they abide faithful to the Lord God entered into covenant with men."[33] It is our covenant obligation, too, to acknowledge and trust God alone, to call upon Him, worship Him, remain faithful to Him, and obey Him.[34]

26. *Decades*, II, 3.8:283.
27. Ibid., 236, 284, 285.
28. Ibid., 288–9.
29. *Decades*, II, 3.6:170.
30. Ibid., 169 (italics added).
31. Ibid., 171–72.
32. *Decades*, II, 178; 5.7:321, 339–40.
33. *Decades*, II, 5.7: 321.
34. *Common Places of Christian Religion*, trans. John Stockwood (London: Thomas East and H. Middleton, 1572), II.8:43a. This is a translation of Bullinger's *Summa Christlicher Religion* (1556).

It would almost seem that we have here a view of covenant in which the blessing of God is dependent on human obedience. But once again one must be careful. While circumcision (and later baptism) certainly testify to our responsibility in the covenant, they also testify to the fact, Bullinger says, that it is God who fulfills that responsibility in and through us. They are signs that God, solely by His grace and goodness, bound Himself in a

> covenant to justify and sanctify us through Christ who by his Spirit doth cut from us whatsoever things do hinder the mutual league and amity betwixt God and us; *He also doth give and increase in us both hope and charity in faith,* so that we may be knit and joined to God in life everlasting.[35]

Faith is entirely (*ganz und gar*) a gift of God bestowed on His elect.[36] It is "neither of our own nature, nor of our own merits, but it is by the grace of God poured into us through the Holy Spirit, which is given into our hearts."[37] And it is that same Spirit resident within us who inspires in us a love for God's law and a life of obedience patterned after the law.[38] For Bullinger, therefore, as for Zwingli, the benefits of God's covenant of grace do not ultimately depend on faith and obedience; they include faith and obedience.

The second context in which Bullinger devotes some attention to the covenant is in his discussion of the sacraments. Again, he says, just as human beings often resort to some form of written confirmation of a verbal commitment, God too, in place of a signed document, holds before us the sacraments as visible signs and seals of His everlasting covenant.[39] In the sacramental action He bears witness to our adoption into the covenant and to the work of salvation obtained for us and wrought

---

35. Decades, II, 3.6:174 (italics added).
36. "Dieser Glaube aber ist ganz und gar Gottes Gabe, die Gott allein um seiner Gnade willen und nach seinem Ermessen seinen Erwählten schenkt, wann, wem, und in welchem Masse er will." *Das Zweite Helvetische Bekenntnis. Confessio Helvetica Posterior,* trans. and ed. W. Hildebrandt and R. Zimmerman (Zurich: Zwingli Verlag, 1966), XVI:71–2.
37. *Decades,* II, 3.8:251.
38. Ibid.
39. *Common Places,* VIII.3:193–94.

in us by Jesus Christ.[40] As a matter of fact, the Lord's Supper is in a sense a covenant or testament itself, as Christ plainly said ("This cup is the new covenant in my blood"): Christ is the Testator, faithful Christians the heirs, the words of institution the will, the performance of the sacramental action the seal, and forgiveness and eternal life the legacy.[41] But the sacraments are more than a demonstration of God's pledge to us; by partaking in them we also bind ourselves to God and to all God's saints. They are, as it were, "an open confession made of the true religion, of free consent to the true religion, and of a binding by promise unto the same."[42] In receiving them, we "do profess and witness ourselves to be under Christ our captain's banner,"[43] and to wish to "bury the old Adam" and live in love and purity.[44]

The New Testament sacraments of baptism and the Lord's Supper have, of course, replaced Old Testament circumcision, sacrifices, and the Passover meal,[45] and for several reasons, Bullinger thinks, this was a change for the better: 1) the Old Testament sacraments were ordained for only a limited time; the New Testament sacraments will endure till time's end; 2) the Old Testament sacraments only prefigured blessings to come; the New Testament sacraments testify to their past and present reality; 3) the sacraments of the Old Testament were difficult, obscure, and a burden by their sheer number; the sacraments of the New Testament are simple, plain, and not of a burdensome quantity; 4) the former applied only to the Israelites, the latter to a much wider range of peoples.[46] But like the two testaments themselves, the sacraments of both testaments are substantially the same. If there is but one unchanging God, one way of salvation, one faith, one church, one (spiritual) baptism, and one spiritual meat and drink (I Cor. 10) in both testaments, the sacraments of both testaments must bear the same spiritual signif-

---

40. *Decades*, 5.6:244–45; *Common Places*, II.8:43.
41. *Decades*, 5.9:403.
42. *Decades*, II, 3.6:178.
43. *Decades*, II, 5.6:235–36.
44. *Decades*, II, 5.7:339–40.
45. *Decades*, II, 3.8:249, 269.
46. *Common Places*, VIII.4:195.

icance.[47] Only their signs differ. And if both the two testaments and their sacraments are substantially one, there is no good reason to withhold baptism from Christian infants. They do not at their age believe, but then neither did the infants of the Old Testament Jews, who were beneficiaries of both the sign of the covenant and its full blessings.[48]

Calvin

In Calvin, according to such scholars as Trinterud, Moller, Greaves, and Baker, we encounter a view of covenant quite different from that of Zwingli and Bullinger.[49] The covenant for Calvin is a divine promise (not a mutual agreement) fulfilled by God (not by us) in the life and death of His Son (not in human faith and obedience).

This, however, is only half of Calvin's doctrine. It is certainly true that for Calvin the covenant established with Abraham includes a divine promise, the promise of a redeemer to come. So far as this promise is concerned, the covenant is "perfectly gratuitous";[50] it does not "spring from either the worthiness or the merits of men" but rather "has its cause and stability, and effect, and completion solely in the grace of God."[51] In this sense the covenant is unconditional.

47. "I say further that the Scripture witnesseth that the sacraments of the Old Testament and ours are of the same force, inasmuch that Paul calleth them circumcised which are baptized, and them baptized which are circumcised. And he also teacheth that our fathers did eat that spiritual meat which we eat and drank of that spiritual drink, i.e., the rock." *Decades,* 5.7:298.

48. *Decades,* II, 322; 5.8:372, 374, 383, 390; *Common Places,* VIII.5:199a.

49. Trinterud, "Origins of Puritanism," 50; Jens Moller, "The Beginnings of Puritan Covenant Theology," *The Journal of Ecclesiastical History* 14 (April 1963):66–7; Richard Greaves, "The Origins and Early Development of English Covenant Thought," *The Historian* 31 (November 1968):23–26; Baker, *Bullinger and the Covenant,* xxi–xxiii. It should be noted that Baker does concede that Calvin speaks of a condition of obedience or piety that concerns the life of the faithful *after* God gives them faith. He concludes nevertheless that faith is really only a "hypothetical condition" for Calvin since this condition is fulfilled by God in the elect and is unable to be fulfilled by the reprobate (195). For an elaboration and critique of the above views, see n. 59 below.

50. *Calvin's Commentaries,* 45 vols. (Edinburgh: Calvin Translation Society, 1844–1856), comm. on Psalm 132:12. Cf. *Institutes,* IV.ii.11.

51. *Commentaries,* comm. on Daniel 9:4.

But Calvin considers the covenant to be much more than a unilateral divine promise. If Zwingli and Bullinger no less than he emphasize divine initiative in the covenant, he no less than they leaves room for human response and responsibility, including the response of faith. For whereas "the covenant *begins* with a solemn article concerning the promise of grace, faith and prayer are required above all things to the proper *keeping* of it."[52] The covenant with Abraham, he explains, had not one but two parts: God's declaration of love and promise of happiness, on the one hand, and "an exhortation to the sincere endeavor to cultivate uprightness," on the other.[53] This was a "mutual covenant," containing a "mutual obligation" and requiring "mutual faith."[54] As "mutual consent is required in all compacts, so when God invites His people to receive grace, He stipulates that they should give Him the obedience of faith . . . ."[55] To the promise of redemption in Christ, therefore, "a *condition* was appended, to the effect that God would bless them *if* they obeyed his commandments."[56] In fact, Ishmael, Esau, and others were cut off from their covenantal inheritance precisely because they had not kept this condition. They had not been faithful.[57] Is there any reason, then,

> why He should keep His promise, when we have broken His covenant? Yet when we reject His covenant, and set light by it through our wicked life, we may not look that He should be any longer bound to us. Why? For He has become our God upon this condition, that we also should be His people. And how shall we be His people? It is not by saying simply with our mouth, We are the people of God, . . . but we must show by our deeds that we are the people of God, in that we obey Him.[58]

52. Ibid., comm. on Psalm 103:18 (italics added).
53. Ibid., comm. on Genesis 17:2.
54. *Ioannis Calvini opera quae supersunt omnia,* 59 vols. (Brunswick: C. A. Schwetschke et Filium, 1863–1900), 26/2:236 (serm. on Deut. 4:44–9); *Commentaries,* comms. on Romans 9:4, Exodus 24:5.
55. *Commentaries,* comm. on Exodus 24:5.
56. Ibid., comm. on Psalm 132:12 (italics added); Cf. also *Calvini opera* 28:286 (serm. on Deut. 26:16–9).
57. *Institutes,* III.xxi.6.
58. *Sermons of Master John Calvin upon the Fifthe Book of Moses called Deuteronomie,* trans. Arthur Golding (London, 1583), 915b (serm. on Deut. 26:16–19). For this and the following quotations from Golding's translation and for parts of this argument concerning Calvin I am indebted to Anthony A. Hoekema,

There is a sense, then, in which the covenant for Calvin is also bilateral and conditional: "For as God binds himself to keep the promise given to us, so the consent of faith and of obedience is demanded from us."[59]

One should not conclude from this, as Trinterud did about the Zurich theologians, that the burden of fulfillment rests on the human partner, that divine grace awaits human response. "As soon as the ignorant sort hear of the word 'condition,'" Calvin states, "it appears to them that God makes some payment and that when he shows us any favor, he does it in recompense

---

"The Covenant of Grace in Calvin's Teaching," *Calvin Theological Journal* 2 (November 1967):133–61. A cogent defense of this same thesis was written ten years earlier by Elton M. Eenigenburg, "The Place of the Covenant in Calvin's Thinking," *Reformed Review* 10 (June 1957):1–22. See also James F. Veninga, "Covenant Theology and Ethics in the Thought of John Calvin and John Preston" (Ph.D. dissertation, Rice University, 1974), 16ff.

59. *Commentaries*, comm. on Genesis 17:9. It is puzzling why Baker especially sees a fundamental difference between Bullinger's and Calvin's doctrines of covenant. Baker is correct in pointing to a tension in Bullinger's theology between salvation *sola gratia* and a conditional covenant that takes human responsibility for faith and piety very seriously. But precisely the same tension is present in Calvin and in all of early Reformed theology for that matter. To suggest, as Baker does, that Calvin resolves this tension by making faith a gift rather than a condition does justice neither to Calvin's many references to the conditional nature of the covenant nor to Bullinger's own insistence that faith is a gift of God bestowed on those whom He has elected from eternity.

It is also curious that Baker ascribes the differences in Calvin's and Bullinger's views of the covenant to their doctrines of double and single predestination, respectively. Faith as a condition of the covenant of grace is only apparent in Calvin, he argues, because for Calvin this condition is always fulfilled for the elect, and the reprobate, by God's will, can never fulfill it. Baker implies that Bullinger's single predestination, on the other hand, helps to preserve the conditional nature of the covenant because the reprobate, not God, bear final responsibility for their rejection (27–54, 195). It is difficult to see, however, how these two views of reprobation affect the conditionality of the covenant. By locating the ultimate cause of reprobation in human *unbelief* Bullinger does not mean to suggest the possibility that nonelect persons after the fall are capable of fulfilling the condition of *belief.* The unregenerate continue to sin willingly, without coercion from the outside, but their wills are not free to the extent that they are able to love God or do any good (*Second Helvetic Confession*, IV.2, 3; VIII.2). That ability is a gift reserved for the elect, and the ultimate cause of one's election is found, of course, solely in God (ibid., XVI.2). The possibility of fulfilling the condition of the covenant, therefore, is really no greater in Bullinger's view of predestination than in Calvin's.

for our merits."[60] Not at all. Both faith and works of obedience are the fruit not of our own efforts but of the renewing power of the Spirit within us.[61] That is to say, we can fulfill our obligations in the covenant only because the Holy Spirit stimulates us to do so. For Calvin, as for Zwingli and Bullinger, "whatever acceptable obedience man yields to God is itself inspired in him by God, and is therefore not properly his own, with respect to origin."[62] That is why our pledges of obedience are really implicit pleas for divine help.[63]

Of course, even when we are reformed within by the Holy Spirit to the point where we show some inclination toward the good, we still fall short of the mark. There is no one who of himself serves God with complete heart and soul.[64] The godly are still sinners, "and their good works are as yet incomplete and redolent of the vices of the flesh." Therefore it is only as God "embraces [the godly and their works] in Christ rather than in themselves" that they both become acceptable in His sight.[65] It is not because our works after justification are intrinsically good but because God accepts them as good that we receive His covenantal favor. Indeed, His acceptance is part of

60. *Sermons upon Deuteronomie*, 322 (serm. on Deut. 7:11–15).

61. "But again, let us keep in mind that the fulfillment of the Lord's mercy does not depend upon believers' works but that he fulfills the promise of salvation for those who respond to his call with an upright life, because in those who are directed to the good by his Spirit he recognizes the only genuine insignia of his children. . . . Therefore if one seeks the first cause that opens for the saints the door to God's Kingdom . . . at once we answer: Because the Lord by his own mercy has adopted them once and for all, and keeps them continually. But if the question is of the manner, we must proceed to regeneration and its fruits." *Institutes*, III.xvii.6. "God also binds himself to his people, on condition that he will govern them by his Holy Spirit, and write his word in their hearts; moreover, when he has so touched them, he will also be favorable to them in bearing with their infirmities and in forgiving their sins." *Sermons upon Deuteronomie*, 1175 (serm. on Deut. 32:44–47).

62. Eenigenburg, "Covenant in Calvin's Thinking," 10.

63. *Institutes*, IV.xiii.6.

64. "If we take the promises of God so crudely as to make them mean that God will bless none but those that serve Him, we shall all of us be shut out from hope. . . . Nay, even when God has reformed us by His Holy Spirit, so that He has given us some good disposition through which we are inclined to serve Him . . . yet we still come far short of the mark." *Sermons upon Deuteronomie*, 322 (serm. on Deut. 7:11–15).

65. *Institutes*, III.xvii.5.

that favor.[66] For Calvin, then, the covenant is in the fullest sense of the term a covenant of grace. God graciously enters into covenant with us, graciously regenerates us to respond in faith and obedience, and by the righteousness of Christ graciously supplies whatever is lacking in our response.

Not only does Calvin understand the covenant of grace in essentially the same way as Zwingli and Bullinger, he also uses the concept in the same limited theological contexts. In the first place, the covenant provides the key to the unity of salvation history. God entered into a covenant with Abraham,[67] confirmed it with Moses, ratified it with David, and ratified it again with us in the coming of Christ.[68] This covenant was made once and for all,[69] and was "firm, sure, . . . eternal, and not changeable or temporary."[70] Like us of the New Testament, the fathers of the Old Testament were adopted as heirs of a spiritual inheritance. Their covenant status no less than ours depended not on their merits but on the righteousness of faith imparted to them by God's grace. And they too were joined to God and His promises through Christ the Mediator, the sole foundation of this one covenant.[71]

66. "For whereupon is his covenant grounded? Even upon his mercy. Now, then, let us see what his mercy is, and whereto it ought to be referred. First of all, it is his choosing of us. Though we are utterly perverse, and deserve to be rejected by him, yet he takes us into his favor. . . . And secondly, . . . he continues his favor towards us for love of his only Son, though he might find just cause in us to shake us off and to hate us. And thirdly, . . . he accepts our works and takes them for good, so that, though they be (as you would say) but half done, and always have some fault mingled with them, nevertheless he does not cease to receive them as if they were righteous and sound—and all this, as I said before, by virtue of this covenant." *Sermons upon Deuteronomie,* 321–2 (serm. on Deut. 7:11–15).

67. Calvin never explicitly identifies the Protoevangelium as a covenant, but he does imply that the promise to Adam was the first step in "this orderly plan in administering the covenant of his mercy." *Institutes,* II.x.20. He also mentions that God's heirs "*since the beginning of the world* were covenanted to him by the same law and by the bond of the same doctrine as obtains among us." Ibid., II.x.1 (italics added).

68. *Commentaries,* comms. on Isaiah 55:3, Jeremiah 31:31, 32.

69. *Institutes,* IV.ii.11.

70. *Commentaries,* comm. on Isaiah 55:3.

71. *Institutes,* II.x.2; II.x.3; II.vi.2; *Commentaries,* comm. on Isaiah 42:6; *The Second Epistle of Paul the Apostle to the Corinthians and the Epistles to Timothy, Titus, and Philemon,* ed. D. W. and T. F. Torrance, trans. T. A. Smail (Edinburgh: Oliver and Boyd, 1964), 22 (comm. on II Cor. 1:20); Ibid., 42, 44 (comm. on II Cor. 3:6, 7).

But even if, as Schrenk suggested, Calvin can hardly keep from giving the impression that there are no differences between the testaments,[72] he does not ignore the differences altogether. Like Bullinger before him he employs the distinction between "substance" and "administration": "The covenant made with all the patriarchs is so much like ours in substance and reality that the two are actually one and the same. Yet they differ in the mode of dispensation."[73] He lists five differences in particular:[74] 1) In the Old Testament/Covenant the heavenly heritage was apprehended under earthly benefits; in the New Testament/Covenant it is apprehended directly. 2) In the Old Covenant the eternal priesthood of Christ, the blotting out of our sins, and "true sanctification" are only foreshadowed; in the New Covenant they are really present. The contrast between the two dispensations appears rather sharp here, but earlier Calvin had described the revelation of God's covenant promises as a slowly progressing manifestation. The initial promise to Adam "glowed like a feeble spark" which became increasingly brighter as the day of full revelation approached. "At last— when all the clouds were dispersed—Christ, the Sun of Righteousness, fully illumined the whole earth."[75] 3) In the Old Testament we find a ministry of law, condemnation, and death; in the New Testament we find a ministry of gospel, righteousness, and life. 4) The Old Testament was a covenant of bondage and fear, the New Testament a covenant of freedom and assurance. 5) In the Old Testament the covenant of grace was confined to one nation; in the New Testament the gospel call goes forth to all peoples.

As Calvin himself goes on to point out, the middle three comparisons of the Old and New Testaments have to do with the differences between law and gospel. For him Old Testament/New Testament, Old Covenant/New Covenant, *foedus legale/foedus evangelicum,* and law/gospel were in many respects synony-

---

72. "Ja, so stark hat Calvin die innere Einheit der Testamente hervorgehoben, dass er wie Zwingli nachher den Schein abwehren muss, als ob er keine Unterschiede statuiere." *Gottesreich und Bund,* 47.

73. *Institutes,* II.x.2.

74. Ibid., II.xi.1–12.

75. Ibid., II.x.20.

mous terms.[76] But how then can he say, on the one hand, that the two covenants are "in substance and reality . . . one and the same"[77] and, on the other, that there is a "great difference"[78] and even "antithesis"[79] between the law and the gospel? The answer lies in a distinction he makes between law and gospel in their "broad" and "narrow" senses. In its narrower sense the law is only precept, only "the bare commandments,"[80] only that proclamation of condemnation and death which "belongs peculiarly to the ministration of Moses."[81] In its broader sense, however, the law is "the *whole* doctrine contained in the Law and the prophets," "the teaching of Moses as a whole." As such it contains not just God's commandments but His promises of grace as well, including the promise of Christ.[82] So too with the gospel. Taken in its broad sense, the gospel "includes those testimonies of his mercy and fatherly favor which God gave to the patriarchs of old"; in its narrow sense it is restricted to the proclamation of grace displayed in the incarnate Christ.[83] The law or Old Testament, therefore, is antithetical to the gospel or New Testament only in its narrow sense, that is, only insofar as it "is distinguished from the word of grace and mercy. . . . Where the *whole* law is concerned, the gospel differs from it only in clarity of manifestation."[84]

It is by a fusion of this double distinction between substance and administration and the broad and narrow senses of the law and gospel that Calvin resolves the tension suggested by the eternity of the Abrahamic covenant, on the one hand, and the establishment of the New Covenant mentioned in Jeremiah 31, on the other. He confronts the problem directly: Jeremiah's

76. Andrew J. Bandstra, "Law and Gospel in Calvin and Paul," in *Exploring the Heritage of John Calvin,* ed. David E. Holwerda (Grand Rapids: Baker, 1976), 12.

77. *Institutes,* II.x.2.

78. *Calvin: Commentaries,* trans. and ed. Joseph Haroutunian, vol. 23 of *The Library of Christian Classics* (Philadelphia: Westminster, 1963):60 (comm. on II Cor. 3:6–10).

79. *Commentaries,* comm. on John 1:17.

80. *Calvin: Commentaries,* 103–4 (comm. on Acts 7:38).

81. *Second Corinthians,* 44 (comm. on II Cor. 3:7).

82. Ibid.; *Calvin: Commentaries,* 103–4 (comm. on Acts 7:38).

83. *Institutes,* II.ix.2; *Commentary on John,* 21.

84. *Institutes,* II.xi.10; II.ix.4.

statement cannot be gotten around "by any cavils."[85] By their unfaithfulness the people of the Old Testament "had made God's covenant void."[86] But neither do we have a God who is undependable, inconsistent with Himself, or mutable in His purpose. A new covenant could never be one "contrary" to the first (or Abrahamic) covenant, for that covenant was inviolable.[87] The "newness" that Jeremiah was talking about pertained to the new form or administration of the covenant of grace, that is, to the fulfillment in Christ of the types of the old administration; to the inscribing of hearts, not tablets of stone, by the Holy Spirit; and to the unveiled proclamation of the gospel. The substance, namely, the doctrine or teaching of the two covenants, remained the same, for the New Testament gospel added nothing substantially new to the promises of salvation included in the Old Testament law.[88] What Jeremiah had in view, then, was the abolition of the Old Covenant or law only in its narrow sense, only "insofar as it was opposed to the gospel,"[89] only with respect to "what properly belongs to it."[90] In their broad sense or in substance, law and gospel are identical.

Calvin discusses the covenant at greatest length in the context of the relationship between the testaments and of the development of redemptive history. The covenant also appears in his doctrine of the sacraments, however, though with far less frequency and detail. From the first, he says, the sacraments have been tokens or signs of God's covenant promises.[91] In baptism and circumcision these promises were first made; in the Lord's Supper they are renewed.[92] The sacraments have, of course, changed with the transition in the testaments. But this was a change only in "outward ceremony . . . , a very slight factor." What is essential to these sacraments (in this case, circumcision and baptism)—the promises (God's favor, forgiveness, eternal life), the thing signified (regeneration), and the foundation

---

85. Ibid., II.v.9.
86. *Commentaries,* comm. on Jeremiah 31:31, 32.
87. Ibid.
88. Ibid.; *Institutes,* II.xi.4.
89. *Calvin: Commentaries,* 106 (comm. on II Cor. 3:6–10).
90. *Institutes,* II.xi.7.
91. Ibid., IV.xiv.6.
92. Ibid., IV.xvi.3, 4; IV.xvii.1.

(Christ)—is the same: "There is no difference in the inner mystery by which the whole force and character of the sacraments are to be weighed."[93] Hence, if the covenant with Abraham is one and eternal, and if the infants of the Jews participated in both the promise and the sign of this covenant, it stands to reason that Christian infants are no different. They quite properly receive the New Covenant sign of baptism.[94]

It should be noted, finally, that while in many respects Calvin's doctrine of the covenant resembles that of Zwingli and Bullinger and very likely reflects their influence,[95] Calvin does move beyond his colleagues in Zurich in the way he treats the relationship between covenant and election. The connection is there in Zwingli and Bullinger, but it is not always obvious or direct. Calvin spells it out much more clearly. He distinguishes a twofold election of God: one general, the other particular; one public, the other "secret." By His general election God selected from the nations of the earth one especially to be His own—"the whole offspring of Abraham." These He marked out to be the recipients of His special revelation and His special care. He made a covenant with them and sealed it with the sign of circumcision. But this decree of general election was not always "firm and effectual." Those within the covenant who failed to keep its condition lost their status as adopted children of God. They were cut off from their inheritance. Those who did and do remain faithful, however, were the focus of a more limited decree of election. They have been graciously chosen to receive the Spirit of regeneration, whereby they are enabled to persevere in meeting their covenant responsibilities.[96]

---

93. Ibid., IV.xvi.4.

94. Ibid., IV.xvi.5, 6.

95. "Bemerkenswert ist, dass er nach Bullingers Schrift gerade die Bundesgedanken in seiner Institutio in der gleichen Richtung wie jener ausgestaltet hat. Dass er sich dabei durch Zwingli und Bullinger befruchten liess, scheint mir zweifellos. Darum sei er nach den Zürichern behandelt." Schrenk, *Gottesreich und Bund*, 44.

96. "God has attested this [predestination] not only in individual persons but has given us an example of it in the whole offspring of Abraham, to make clear that in his choice rests the future condition of each nation. . . . We must now add a second, more limited decree of election, or one in which God's more special grace was evident, that is, when from the same race of Abraham God rejected some but showed that he kept others. . . . Ishmael had at first obtained

Calvin, therefore, does not identify covenant membership with particular election. The covenant of grace serves rather as the "middle ground" (*medium quiddam*) between the reprobate and the special elect. As Hoekema has put it, "Covenant membership is here pictured as a circle wider than particular election, but narrower than mankind as a whole."[97]

Musculus

Wolfgang Musculus (1497–1563), reformer of Augsburg and later professor of theology at Bern (1549–63), introduced three new features into the Reformed doctrine of the covenant: 1) he assigned the covenant a separate locus in his system of theology (*Loci Communes*, 1560); 2) he no longer identified the biblical

---

equal rank with his brother Isaac, for in him the spiritual covenant had been equally sealed by the sign of circumcision. . . . By their own defect and guilt, [however,] Ishmael, Esau, and the like were cut off from adoption. For the condition had been laid down that they should faithfully keep God's covenant, which they faithlessly violated. . . . It is easy to explain why the general election of a people is not always firm and effectual: to those to whom God makes a covenant, he does not at once [*protinus*] give the spirit of regeneration that would enable them to persevere in the covenant to the very end. Rather the outward change, without the working of inner grace, which might have availed to keep them, is intermediate [*medium quiddam*] between the rejection of mankind and the election of a meager number of the godly." *Institutes*, III.xxvii.5–7. Hoekema's translation of *protinus* as "invariable" instead of "at once" ("Covenant in Calvin," 150) seems more appropriate to the context and is, in fact, supported by Calvin's French translation of the text: ". . . la raison est claire, c'est que Dieu ne donne point l'esprit de regeneration à tous ceux ausquels il offre sa parolle pour s'allier avec ceux." *Calvini opera*, 32:466. Cf. also Calvin, *Commentaries on the First Twenty Chapters of the Book of the Prophet Ezekiel*, trans. Thomas Myers, 2 vols. (Grand Rapids: Eerdmans, 1948), 2:121–2 (comm. on Ez. 16:21): "We may remark that there was a twofold election of God: since speaking generally, he chose the whole family of Abraham. For circumcision was common to all, being the symbol and seal of adoption: since when God wished all the sons of Abraham to be circumcised . . . he at the same time chose them as his sons: this was the one kind of adoption or election. But the other was secret, because God took to himself out of that multitude those whom he wished."

97. "Covenant in Calvin," 150. Joseph McLelland seriously misunderstands Calvin when he argues that in *Institutes* III.xxi.5 Calvin "understands the Divine activity of covenant-making as derivative from the Divine activity of decree-making" and relates the covenant of grace "to a supralapsarian scheme of double predestination." "Covenant Theology—A Re-evaluation," *Canadian Journal of Theology* 3 (July 1957):184.

terms "covenant" and "testament"; and 3) he distiguished between a *foedus generale* and a *foedus speciale* in Scripture.

Musculus begins his discussion of the covenant by emphasizing that God's decision to bind Himself to the conditions of a covenant or bargain with humanity was totally free. He was in no way driven by necessity or lured by the prospect of benefitting Himself. Had He chosen not to enter into a covenant with us, He would have been at liberty to declare His goodness and to withdraw it again at His pleasure.[98] But since "the purpose of his will is appointed from ever to the health of mankind,"[99] He decided to covenant with us for our sake, not His. He could have given us just His promises. But He wished to underscore the steadfastness and reliability of those promises by taking the oath of a covenant, for a covenant to which God has committed Himself is as immutable and everlasting as God Himself. He is free to make covenants but not to break them. And therein lies our assurance, our "most strong comfort . . . and . . . fast anchorhold to rest upon until the end."[100]

This covenant of God is of two sorts: the one general and temporary, the other special and everlasting. First, God made a general covenant "with his whole frame of the earth and all that dwelleth therein."[101] From the biblical texts that Musculus quotes (Genesis 8:21–22; 9:9–11; Jeremiah 33:20ff.) it is clear that he has in mind here God's postdiluvian promise to preserve the regular cycles of day and night, summer and winter, and seedtime and harvest and never again to destroy every living creature. This covenant, however, is only temporal, touching only "the steadfastness of earthly matters," and temporary, of no longer duration than the world itself.[102]

The special covenant is so called because it embraces only the "elect and believing, that is to say, Abraham, the father of all believers, and his seed."[103] Musculus has no quarrel with those who prefer to call this covenant general or universal also, if by

---

98. *Common Places of Christian Religion,* trans. John Man (London: Henry Bynneman, 1578), 284.

99. Ibid., 289.

100. Ibid., 284, 289.

101. Ibid., 285.

102. Ibid.

103. Ibid., 285–86.

that they mean that it includes believers from all nations of the world. Elect Gentiles are as much a part of Abraham's seed as elect Israelites. To designate it a "special" covenant is only to distinguish it from the former or "general" covenant, which applies to beasts as well as people, wicked as well as elect, unbelievers as well as believers.[104]

This special covenant is also everlasting. When God promised Abraham that He would establish His covenant also "with thy seed after thee in their generations for an everlasting covenant" (Gen. 17:7), He had in view not only the continuity in the life and death of each individual member. God is our gracious God not just in life but in the afterlife as well.[105]

Finally, this special covenant is bilateral. The "principal part" of the covenant is God's promise to be our God, our Savior as well as Creator. But His "partners" or "confederates" in this covenant have certain responsibilities. They are to walk before God and be upright, which includes "all kind of welldoing and faith towards God."[106] Musculus does not mention the term "condition" here or suggest in any way that the fulfillment of the covenant hinges on human endeavor. Elsewhere in the *Loci* he insists that faith is a gift of God distributed only to those whom God of His free choice has elected.[107] And good works are stimulated in the heart by the Holy Spirit.[108] But from the human point of view, at least, we are called "to live in the conscience of God as it were under his eyes, after the manner of servants, continually depending at their master's beck . . . and to be of a simple, faithful, clear and right heart."[109]

Like Zwingli, Bullinger, and Calvin, Musculus finds no "substantial" differences in the order of salvation before and after Christ:

104. Ibid.
105. Ibid., 287–88. Musculus, in fact, makes a case for immortality on the basis of God's covenant promise: "If he be not God of the dead but of the living, and is my God by an everlasting covenant, it must needs follow that when I am dead in body, I shall not be exempt out of this covenant, and therefore it is necessary that I must live forever." Ibid., 288.
106. Ibid., 288.
107. Ibid., 483.
108. Ibid., 561.
109. Ibid., 288.

There is one God and father of all. . . . There is one Lord Savior and redeemer of all, Christ Jesus; there is one holy spirit, there is one kingdom prepared from the beginning of the world for the elect and blessed, there is one grace of heavenly calling, there is one faith, one hope of everlasting life, there is one body, one people, and one Catholic Church of the elect, which comprehendeth all the elect and faithful from the beginning of the world until the end; and there is one only and perpetual covenant of God, made and confirmed with all his elect.[110]

But although there is but one covenant for all time, redemptive history has been divided into three periods (*ante legem, sub lege, post legem*), each with its appointed leader (Abraham, Moses, Christ) and each with its "peculiar order of Religion."[111] The period before the law stretched from Adam to Moses. Musculus recognizes that there was no "manifest making of covenant before Abraham's time" but argues that through the Protoevangelium and the special revelations of God, the older fathers became beneficiaries of the same grace of salvation that in the Abrahamic covenant "was made . . . more express and confirmed."[112] The sign of circumcision and the promise of the land of Canaan added in the Abrahamic covenant were but "accessories" to the one covenant of salvation. Unlike the substance of the covenant ("I am the Lord your God. . . . Walk before me and be upright") these accessories were neither universal nor everlasting. They served a limited people (Israel) for a limited time (until Christ).[113]

During the period under the law, from Moses to Christ, a "new" covenant was introduced. This covenant with Moses was new, however, only because of the new accessories joined to the older covenant with Abraham. To accommodate a rapidly multiplying population and to prepare the Israelites for entry into pagan Canaan, the law, the Aaronic priesthood, and a variety of other ceremonies were added to the circumcision and sacrifices of the past.[114] Yet all of this "policy of the Church of Israel"

110. Ibid., 291.
111. Ibid.
112. Ibid., 289.
113. Ibid., 290.
114. Ibid., 292.

served an even more profound purpose: "to be a certain lesson-ing [i.e., tutor] to the nation towards Christ."[115]

In the period after the law, inaugurated with the coming of Christ, yet another "new" covenant (and testament)[116] was insti-tuted. The economy of grace under this New Testament is "much better" than that under the Old (or Mosaic) Testament[117] for a number of reasons:

Old Testament

1. The mediator Moses was faithful in a house not his own.
2. God's people were delivered from an earthly bondage (to Pharaoh).
3. The Israelites inherited the land of Canaan.
4. The law was given at Mt. Sinai, by the ministry of angels, by fearful means, "in letter," and engraved on tablets of stone.
5. The Old Testament was characterized by a ministry of bondage, fear, and death; many difficult and bloody cere-monies; a continuous sacrificing of beasts; outward bodily cleansings; and figures, shadows, and promises.
6. The dispensation gave way to another.
7. The Old Covenant was restricted to a single nation.

---

115. Ibid., 290.

116. As we noted earlier, Musculus distinguishes rather than identifies the biblical terms "covenant" and "testament." Covenants, for example, are broken up by death; testaments are ratified by death. Covenants are confirmed by an oath; testaments do not require an oath. Musculus believes, therefore, that it is appropriate to describe the redemptive work of Christ first and foremost as a testament: Christ, as the Testator, has the legal right to draw up this testament, for the Father has conferred upon Him the lordship of all things; His inherit-ance is bequeathed to His heirs, not owed them; He owns the goods He is be-queathing; He has appointed executors of this testament (the Apostles); and the testament is confirmed or put into effect by His, the Testator's, death. At the same time, however, Musculus regards this new testament instituted by Christ as the new dispensation of the one, eternal covenant with Abraham. Ibid., 283–84, 742–43, 292–94.

117. Musculus calls the second or Mosaic covenant old "not because it is the first and most ancient, . . . but in respect of the New." In relation to the Abra-hamic covenant both the Old and the New Covenants are "new" in a chronolog-ical sense. The labels "old" and "new" are attached to the latter two covenants, however, by virtue of their relation to each other. Ibid., 293–94.

New Testament

1. The Mediator Christ was faithful in the house which He built (Hebrews 3).
2. God's people are delivered from a spiritual bondage (to Satan).
3. We inherit the "country of Heaven."
4. The law is given at Mt. Zion, by the presence of the Lord, by "a wonderful mildness," "in spirit," and wrought in the hearts of the elect.
5. The New Testament was characterized by a ministry of liberty, cheerfulness, and life; fewer, easier, and non-bloody ceremonies; Christ as the sacrifice once and for all; inward, spiritual cleansings; and fulfillment of all figures and promises.
6. The dispensation gives way only to the "fruition of Heaven."
7. The New Covenant is universally applied.[118]

Yet once again what is old and new in these two covenants has to do only with their "accessory points," not their substance. Christ's institution of the New Testament by no means nullified the eternal covenant established with Abraham; it rather confirmed and fulfilled it. For example, from year to year the representatives and laws of a city's senate often change, so that while the structure of the senate itself remains unaltered, one often speaks of the "old senate" and the "new senate." So too with the testaments. The new testament "is not called New considered of itself, but in respect of that covenant which was before," the former dispensation of the same covenant in substance.[119]

The sacraments are signs of, among other things, the covenant.[120] Circumcision and baptism signify incorporation into the covenant; Passover and Lord's Supper, the redemption offered in the covenant.[121] This does not mean that the sacraments of the two testaments are without any differences. The

118. Ibid., 294–95.
119. Ibid., 293–94.
120. Musculus states, for example, that baptism is "the Sacrament of regeneration, purgation, profession, sanctification, consignment, and incorporation into Christ our Savior," though "principally . . . of the covenant of God and of his heavenly grace." Ibid., 674, 691.
121. Ibid., 650, 663–67, 674.

New Testament sacraments make use of signs that are not only different but fewer in number, void of bloodshed, and less difficult to perform.[122] The Lord's Supper, moreover, signifies not merely the redemption available in the covenant but also the institution of the most recent dispensation of that covenant, the New Testament.[123] But the sacraments of both orders do have the same author, the same purpose (to testify to God's grace, to strengthen faith, and to bind the Christian community together), the same distinction between sign and signified, the same meaning, and the same requirement for spiritual profit (faith). Finally, both sacraments of admission into the covenant are intended also for children. If infants of the faithful in the Old Testament partook of both the grace and the sign of the covenant, and there is no indication in Scripture that their participation has since been prohibited, it is not necessary that the command to admit children into the covenant be repeated in the New Testament. By insisting on such an express command, the Anabaptists "reprove and condemn the counsel and purpose of God."[124]

Ursinus

Zacharias Ursinus (1534–1583), professor of dogmatics at the University of Heidelberg (1561–76) and a principal author of the Heidelberg Catechism (1563), was the last Reformed theologian before Olevianus to make a significant contribution to the continental doctrine of the covenant. That his covenant doctrine was to some extent influenced by Bullinger, Calvin, and even Melanchthon has been widely accepted.[125] And in his

122. Ibid., 662ff.

123. "So that when he had . . . taken his leave of the figure of the old Testament, meaning to initiate the new Testament, he took bread, and gave thanks. . . . Likewise the cup. . . . Thus he doth initiate the new Testament to succeed the Old." Ibid., 722. Cf. also ibid., 742–43.

124. Ibid., 693, 691.

125. See, for example, Gooszen, *Heidelbergsche Catechismus*, 65; August Lang, *Der Heidelberger Katechismus und vier verwandte Katechismen* (Leipzig, 1907), LXIV–LXVII; and Schrenk, *Gottesreich und Bund*, 58–9. Schrenk (ibid., 48–9) argued for Melanchthon's general influence on Reformed covenant theology both through his widely used *Examen ordinandorum* (1554), where he describes infant baptism as a *mutuum foedus* and a *mutua obligatio* (*CR* 23:42),

treatment of the covenant of grace, many of the themes from the older covenant doctrine recur: the identification of covenant and testament,[126] the familiar similarities and differences between the testaments and their sacraments,[127] the distinction between the substance and mode of administration of the covenant of grace,[128] the view of the sacraments as covenant signs,[129] and the covenantal rationale for infant baptism.[130] He also speaks of the mutuality of the covenant of grace and of the conditions of faith and obedience,[131] though like his theological forebears he insists that faith and good works are unmerited

and through his 1558 edition of the *Loci communes,* in which he takes a striking *heilsgeschichtlich* approach to Old Testament history and its fulfillment in Christ (*CR* 22:308f.). Even more significant is his treatment in the *Loci* (*CR* 21:711ff.) of the *lex naturae* in relation to both the Decalogue and the Gospel, which, according to Schrenk, strongly influenced Ursinus in his development of the concept of the *foedus naturale*. To keep Schrenk's claims in perspective, however, three things should be remembered (see Sturm, *Der junge Zacharias Ursin,* 253–8): First, Melanchthon rarely uses the term "covenant" in his writings. Second, when he does refer to *foedus,* it is only with respect to divine promises in general, the hypostatic union, and baptism; "der Begriff wird . . . nicht föderaltheologisch verwendet" (Ibid., 257–8). Finally, whatever influence Melanchthon might have exerted on Ursinus, he did not serve as the *source* of Ursinus's covenant doctrine. The most that can be said is that Ursinus combined Melanchthon's doctrine of law and gospel with a covenantal theology inherited from Calvin, Vermigli, and Bullinger (ibid.), and even here Melanchthon's special influence on Ursinus is open to serious question (see Peter Alan Lillback, "Ursinus' Development of the Covenant of Creation: A Debt to Melanchthon or Calvin?" *Westminster Theological Journal* 43 [Spring 1981]:247–88).

126. *The Commentary of Dr. Zacharias Ursinus on the Heidelberg Catechism,* trans. G. W. Williard (Grand Rapids: Eerdmans, 1954), 97; *Catechesis, summa theologiae per questiones et responsiones exposita in D. Zachariae Ursini . . . opera theologica,* ed. Quirinus Reuter (Heidelberg: John Lancellot, 1612), 14 (Q. 32).

127. *Summa theologiae,* 14 (Q. 33); *Commentary,* 99–100, 346–47.

128. *Commentary,* 98–99; *Summa theologiae,* 14 (Q. 33).

129. *Summa theologiae,* 29 (Qs. 274, 276, 277, 279, 284), 31 (Q. 295); *Commentary,* 342, 354, 373–75. Like Zwingli and Bullinger, Ursinus regards the sacraments as signs of our commitment to God as well as of His commitment to us—a "mutua foederis contestatio." *Summa theologiae,* 29 (Q. 279); *Commentary,* 342, 354.

130. *Summa theologiae,* 31 (Qs. 293, 294); Commentary, 366–67.

131. "Quod est illud foedus? Est reconciliatio cum Deo . . . in qua Deus promittit, se credentibus, propter Christum perpetuo fore Patrem propictum, ac daturum vitam aeternam & ipsi vicissim spondent, se haec beneficia vera fide accepturos, & sicut gratos & obedientes filios decet, perpetuo celebraturos: & utique hanc promissionem mutuum signis visibilibus . . . publice contestantur." *Summa theologiae,* 11 (Q. 31). ". . . foedus Dei nullis ratum est, nisi illud servantibus. Obligavimus autem nos non tantum ad credendum in Christum, sed

blessings dispensed by God to those whom he had chosen from eternity as their beneficiaries.[132]

Nevertheless, Ursinus did break new ground in his doctrine of the covenant of grace. In the first place, in late 1561 or early 1562 he composed a 323-question *Summa theologiae* (often called the *Catechesis maior,* or Larger Catechism) with the covenant as the central motif. Covenant appears in the first question and answer, "What firm consolation do you have in life and in death? That . . . God, out of His infinite and free mercy, has received me into His covenant of grace";[133] in the last, "Why is this [ecclesiastical] discipline necessary? . . . In order that the desecration of the sacraments and of the divine covenant might be avoided";[134] and at nearly every important juncture in between: incorporation into Christ (Questions 2, 3), the law (Qs. 10, 148), the testaments (Q. 33), the gospel (Q. 35), the difference between law and gospel (Q. 36), the Mediator (Qs. 72, 73), the sacrifice of Christ (Q. 224), preaching (Q. 272), the sacraments (Qs. 274ff.), and infant baptism (Qs. 293, 294). The range of theological topics under which Ursinus's predecessors had discussed the covenant had widened considerably.

Second, he defined the covenant for the first time not just as a promise, or even a mutual promise, but as the actual reconciliation between God and humanity achieved through these promises.[135] What is of particular importance here is the direct link he draws between this reconciliation in the covenant and the mediating work of Christ. For Ursinus, Christ is still the focus and foundation of the covenant but primarily in His role

---

etiam ad sancte coram Deo vivendum." Ibid., 21 (Q. 141). See also *Commentary,* 99–100.

132. "Omnibus ne hominibus illa gratia contingit vel exposita est? Minime vero: sed illis tantum, quos ab aeterno Deus in Christo ad vitam aeternam eligit." *Summa theologiae,* 25 (Q. 216). "The first and chief efficient cause" of justifying faith is the Holy Spirit, who instills it in the elect "by his special working." *Commentary,* 112. "Good works are possible only by the grace and assistance of the Holy Spirit, and that by the regenerate alone, whose hearts have been truly regenerated by the Spirit of God." Ibid., 479–80.

133. "Quam habes firmam in vita et morte consolationem? Quod . . . Deus ex immensa et gratuita misericordia me recipit in foedus gratiae suae." *Summa theologiae,* 10.

134. "Quaere haec disciplina est necessaria? . . . Ut sacramentorum et foederis divini profanatio vitetur," Ibid., 33 (Q. 323).

135. See n. 131 above.

as Mediator, "inasmuch as every mediator is the mediator of some covenant and the reconciler of two opposing parties."[136] Because of human sin the original covenant relationship between God and us had been destroyed. The justice of God did not permit Him to keep company with any who had willfully deserted Him. But in His capacity as Mediator, Christ appeased God's wrath against our sin, satisfied His justice, and opened the way toward reconciliation. It was, indeed, the *office* of the Mediator to restore the covenant between the parties at variance.[137]

Third, Ursinus was the first to explain the *foedus gratiae* (in the *C. maior*, at least) in relation to a second covenant, a *foedus naturale*. This natural covenant was initiated by God with humanity in creation and is known by nature, that is, it is engraved on the heart of every rational creature. Natural knowledge of God is that perception of His divine will, that ability to distinguish right from wrong, which constitutes in part His image in us.[138] This covenant was repeated in the Decalogue given at Sinai.[139] But whether expressed in the written or the unwritten law, the *foedus naturale* requires of us perfect obedience and of-

136. *Commentary*, 96.

137. "Quod ergo est Mediatoris officium? Foedus inter Deum et homines, qui a Deo defecerant, restituere. Cur foedus hoc sine Mediatore sanciri non poterat? Quia iustitia Dei postulabat, ut Deus hominibus propter peccatum esset in aeternum iratus. Cum igitur esset impossibile, ut contra suam iustitiam Deus ullam cum genere humano societatem iniret, necesse fuit aliquem intervenire, qui Deum nobis exorans iustitiae Dei satisfaciens & omnem in posterum offensionem tollens, homines a Deo avulsos, rursus cum eo coniungeret." *Summa theologiae*, 16 (Qs. 72, 73). It is interesting to note that Ursinus's excursus on the covenant in the *Commentary* appears in the Heidelberg Catechism under his exposition of the question on the Mediator (Q. 18).

138. "Quid docet Lex divina? Quale in creatione foedus cum homine Deus iniverit; quo pacto se homo in eo servando gesserit . . . hoc est, qualis & ad quid conditus sit homo a Deo, in quem statum sit redactus. . . . Qualis est homo conditus? Ad imaginem Dei. Quae haec est imago? Vera Dei et divinae voluntaris agnitio, et secundum hanc solam vivendi, totius hominis inclinatio et studium." *Summa theologiae*, 10 (Qs. 10, 11, 12). Cf. also *Commentary*, 490–91: "The *moral law* is a doctrine [Ursinus no longer uses covenant terminology here] harmonizing with the eternal and unchangeable wisdom and justice of God, distinguishing right from wrong, known by nature, engraven upon the hearts of creatures endowed with reason in their creation."

139. " . . . quia Deus non tunc primum tulit legem, in Decalogo comprehensam, sed in populo Israelitico repetivit et declaravit, non tantum quid ab ipsis requirat, sed ad quid omnes creaturae rationales sint conditae." *Summa theologiae*, 22 (Q. 158).

fers us our just reward: eternal life to those who obey, eternal punishment to those who do not.[140]

Because God is immutably righteous and true, He accepts fallen humanity into the covenant of grace only in such a way that the integrity of the covenant of nature is preserved. He does not deem us just or award us eternal life unless we conform perfectly to the standards of righteousness required in the *foedus naturale* or, failing that, unless someone else satisfies the stipulations of the law in our stead.[141] The covenant of grace thus complements the covenant of nature. The gospel (which contains the *foedus gratiae)* reveals to us the fulfillment in Christ of the righteousness demanded by the law (which contains the *foedus naturale)* and promises to us through Christ the eternal life no longer within our reach under the covenant of nature.[142]

Fourth, in Ursinus's covenant doctrine the Holy Spirit plays a much more vital role than before. If the Father is the initiator of the covenant and the Son its mediator, the Holy Spirit is both Himself a benefit of the covenant[143] and the one who seals in our hearts the other benefits of forgiveness, righteousness, and eternal life.[144] He is the "first and chief efficient cause" of justi-

140. "Lex continet foedus naturale, in creatione a Deo cum hominibus initum, hoc est, natura hominibus notus est; et requirit a nobis perfectam obedientiam erga Deum, et praestantibus eam, promittit vitam aeternam, non praestantibus minatur aeternas poenas." *Summa theologiae,* 14 (Q. 36).
141. "Cur nobis satisfactionem & iustitiam Christi imputari necesse est, ut iusti simus coram Deo? Quia Deus, qui immutabiliter iustus & verax est, ita nos in foedus gratiae vult recipere ut nihilominus contra foedus in creatione initum non faciat, id est, nec pro iustis nos habeat, nec vitam aeternam nobis det, nisi integre ipsius legi vel per nos ipsos, vel, cum hoc fieri non possit, per alium pro nobis satisfactum sit." *Summa theologiae,* 20 (Q. 135).
142. "Lex continet foedus naturale, in creatione a Deo cum hominibus initum, hoc est, natura hominibus notus est; et requirit a nobis perfectam obedientiam erga Deum. . . . Evangelium continet foedus gratiae. . . : ostendit nobis eius iustitiae, quam lex requirit, impletionem in Christo, et restitutionem in nobis per Christi Spiritum, et promittit vitam aeternam gratis propter Christum, his qui in eum credunt." Ibid., 14 (Q. 36).
143. "Quis fructus ad nos redit ex passione et morte Christi? Sacrificium est unicum, quo nobis receptionem in foedus gratiae divinae, hoc est, remissionem peccatorum, donationem Spiritus sancti, iustitiam et vitam aeternam meruit." Ibid., 17 (Q. 87).
144. ". . . Deus ex immensa et gratuita misericordia me recepit in foedus gratiae suae, ut . . . donet mihi credenti iustitiam et vitam aeternam; atque hoc foedus suum in corde meo per spiritum suum . . . obsignavit." Ibid., 10 (Q. 1).

fying faith in the elect[145] and the agent of their sanctification—
including the sanctification of children of covenant parents.[146]
He regenerates God's covenant people, teaches them what is required of them in the covenant, and fashions them into temples
of God and members of Christ.[147] He is also a constant source
of the grace they need to keep their side of the covenant.[148]
Zwingli, Bullinger, Musculus, and especially Calvin also perceived these as operations of the Holy Spirit but not as explicitly
covenantal functions.

Finally, one is struck by the new emphasis in Ursinus's covenant doctrine on the believer's personal union with Christ. For
him reconciliation in the covenant involves not merely a new
legal status before God but also an intimate spiritual relationship with Him in the person of His Son. We are members not
just of the covenant but of Christ Himself.[149] We participate not
just in the benefits of the covenant but in Christ Himself.[150] In
short, to be in league with God is first and foremost to be in

145. *Commentary*, 112–13. Cf. also *Summa theologiae*, 29 (Q. 266): "Quare
per ministerium in foedus Dei nos recepi et in eo retineri dicis? Quia instrumen-
tum Spiritus sancti est, quo fidem et conversionem, quam in foedere suo Deus
a nobis requirit, in electorum cordibus operatur et confirmat."

146. "At cum infantes nondum fide sint praediti, recte ne baptizantur?
Recte. Fides enim et eius confessio ante baptismum in adultis requiritur, ut qui
aliter in foedere Dei comprehendi nequeant. Infantibus vero, Christi spiritu pro
aetatis modo sanctificari, satis est." *Summa theologiae*, 31 (Q. 294).

147. "Quid efficit Spiritus sanctus per praedictionem verbi Dei? Primum
docet nos, quid Deus in foedere suo nobis polliceatur, et quid vicissim a nobis
requirat." Ibid., 29 (Q. 272). "Quod est [Spiritus sancti] officium? Sanctificatio
electorum. . . . Quid est sanctificatio electorum? Est a Spiritu sancto per ministerium Evangelii doceri electos de voluntate Dei erga ipsos, et regenerari, et per
fidem effici templa Dei et membra Christi, ut actiones carnis mortificent." Ibid.,
19 (Qs. 109, 110).

148. "Quaere necessaria est Christianis invocatio Dei? . . . Secundo, quia hic
modus est, quo vult Deus electos impetrare et retinere tam Spiritus sancti gratiam ad servandum foedus suum necessariam quam omnia reliqua sua beneficia." Ibid., 26 (Q. 224).

149. Ibid., 14 (Q. 38), 17–8 (Q. 92), 19 (Q. 110), 27 (Qs. 239, 240), 33 (Qs.
315, 316).

150. "Nunquid Evangelium docet, foedus gratia Dei ad omnes homines per-
tinere? Omnes quidem ad illud vocet, sed nulli eius sint participes, nisi qui illud
amplectuntur & servant, hoc est, qui vera fide oblatum sibi Christum & beneficia eius accipiunt." Ibid., 14 (Q. 37). "Quod est [Spiritus Sancti] officium? Sanctificatio electorum, qua Christi et beneficiorum eius fiunt participes." Ibid., 19
(Q. 109).

union with Christ. Our incorporation into Christ testifies to our status as Christians and our status as Christians to our inclusion in the covenant.[151] Calvin, of course, had also stressed this mystical union between Christ and the believer but never in a covenantal context. Once again, Ursinus had cast an older doctrine in a new mold.

Conclusion

It is our judgment, then, that there were no fundamental differences in the conception of the covenant in the major first-generation (Zwingli) and second-generation (Musculus, Bullinger, Calvin) Reformed theologians who dealt with the doctrine. All these figures were contending with a common opponent—the rival covenant theology of the Anabaptists. All discussed the covenant in the same two theological contexts—the sacraments and the relationship between the testaments—which intersected in the doctrine of infant baptism. All considered the boundaries of the covenant (blessings) to extend to peoples of every nation but no further than the numbers of the elect. All stressed both the conditions of human faith and obedience in the covenant and the divine sovereignty and initiative by which the elect are led to fulfill them. What has not always been recognized is, first, that in each of these thinkers there was both a monopleuric and a dipleuric dimension to the covenant of grace and, second, that the dipleuric dimension was never treated in such a way as to threaten the monergistic soteriology that underlay all early Reformed doctrine. That Calvin and the northern Swiss Reformed were not in agreement on all points of doctrine and practice cannot be denied, but their disagreements were not rooted in fundamentally different views of the covenant.

The most far-reaching changes in Reformed covenant thought took place in the third-generation theologians, led by Ursinus in his first catechism, the *Summa theologiae*. Ursinus became the first Reformed thinker to free the covenant of grace

---

151. "Qui scis, tale foedus a Deo tecum esse initum? Quia vere Christianus sum. Quem dicis vere Christianum? Qui vera fide Christo insitus, et in eum baptizatus est." Ibid., 10 (Qs. 2, 3).

from the limits of a single locus (cf. Musculus) and from the two contexts mentioned above and to apply it to a whole range of topics within a unified system of theology. He also introduced into Reformed theology the idea of a covenant of nature initiated at creation—the forerunner of the covenant of works. Musculus, to be sure, had also employed a double covenant scheme a few years before. But what Musculus called God's "general covenant," His promises to Noah never to suspend the laws of nature and never again to eradicate the human race, bears no resemblance to Ursinus's "natural covenant." The *foedus naturale* was contracted with Adam, not Noah, and concerned humanity's innate obligation to obey God, not God's revealed obligation to preserve the physical universe.[152] Indeed, the swiftness with which both the natural covenant disappeared and the covenant of grace returned to its traditional stations in Ursinus's later works may indicate how innovative his covenant ideas actually were.

---

152. Stoever's failure to recognize these important differences led him to the erroneous conclusion that "the notion of a covenant in creation was not necessarily original with Ursinus. Wolfgang Musculus . . . distinguished a temporal *foedus generale* in which God established the orders of the universe." "Covenant of Works," 28, n. 12. The same mistake can be found in R. T. Kendall, *Calvin and English Calvinism to 1649* (Oxford: University Press, 1979), 39, n. 2, and Holmes Rolston III, *John Calvin versus the Westminster Confession* (Richmond: John Knox, 1972), 12.

3   Olevianus and the Covenant of Grace

Nature of the Covenant

Q. In what does human happiness consist?
A. In being united and in fellowship with God, the only source.[1]

This is not only the first question and answer in Olevianus's first theological work but also the first clue to his understanding of the covenant of grace. One's happiness, he says, consists in union and communion with God.[2] The problem is that through the sin of Adam the human race had broken this union. God and humanity had suddenly become separated. In place of communion, there was now enmity and estrangement; in place of *Seligkeit* (happiness), only utter *Unseligkeit*.[3] But, he continues, God did not wait for humanity to repair the relationship. Out of His great mercy He took the initiative and devised a plan of reunion in the form of a covenant (*Bund*). Just as human enemies will bind themselves to each other in an oath or covenant of peace, God too bound Himself to us with a promise (*Verheissung*) and oath (*Eid*) that He would send His Son in the flesh and through His sacrifice establish an eternal peace with humanity. Since only those who are holy and pure can be united with Him, He would remove our guilt and purge us of our impurities. The warring parties would be reconciled in an inseparable union.[4]

---

1. Sudhoff, *Fester Grund*, 1590 ed., 1.
2. Cf. also Reu, *Vester Grundt*, 1567 ed., 1355–56; "Abendmahlpredigten," no. 5, *Gnadenbund*, 1593 ed., 387.
3. Reu, *Vester Grundt*, 1567 ed., 1355–56.
4. ". . . vergleicher Gott den handel von unser seligkeit einem Bund. . . . Dann gleich wie die menschen nach schwerer feindschaft dann aller erst gerüwige

Olevianus understands the covenant of grace, then, first of all as a statement of God's saving intention, a unilateral promise of reconciliation through Jesus Christ. When Scripture speaks of the "covenant of God," he maintains, it means the "oath of God," an oath with which God promises us His grace and thus binds Himself to us.[5] It is nothing other than the "word of the Gospel," what Scripture calls the "covenant of peace" (Is. 54:8,10), the "word of the eternal covenant" (Is. 59:21), and the "word of reconciliation" (2 Cor. 5:19)—God's *promissio* of grace in which the whole substance of the covenant or content of the gospel promise is offered.[6] It is even appropriate to call this covenant a "testament," as do the New Testament apostles when they refer to this Old Testament *berith* (Latin: *foedus*) as a *diatheke* (Latin: *testamentum*). For like a last will and testament, this covenant promise is ratified only by death—the death of Christ the Testator.[7]

When did God make such a pledge? We will be looking at this question in some detail in Chapter IV, but it should be mentioned here that for Olevianus this covenant of grace or gospel

<hr/>

gemüter haben, wenn sie sich beides theils mit versprechung und geschwornem eidt verpflicht und verbunden haben, das sie mit gewissem geding frieden haben wollen: Also thut im Gott auch auff das wir in unserm gewissen ruhe und fried hetten, hatt er sich auss seiner lautern güte und gnaden unss, die wir doch seine feindt waren, mit seiner verheissung, ja auch mit seinem eidt wollen verpflichten, das er seinen eingeborenen Sohn wolte lassen mensch werden, für unss in den todt geben, und das er durch sein opffer eine bestendige versönung und ewigen frieden machen und auffrichten wolt, Isa. 54. Und das er also unser Gott sein wolte und unss benedien, das ist, die Sünde vergeben und den H. Geist und das ewig leben mittheilen." Ibid., 1333.

5. "Nu aber ist gewiss, dass wo die heilig Schrifft von dem bund Gottes . . . meldung thut, so verstehet sie den eyd Gottes, damit er uns seine gnad verheisset, und sich also uns verbindet." "Abendmahlpredigten," no. 1, *Gnadenbund*, 313–14. Cf. also Sudhoff, *Fester Grund*, 1590 ed., 163: "Die Verheissung und der Eid Gottes. . . . Der Gnadenbund und der Eid Gottes."

6. *De substantia*, 272. Cf. also 17: ". . . foedus gratuitum seu promissionem Evangelij . . . ," and 249: ". . . igitur Deus substantiam illam foederis a testimonio [Evangelii] . . . non vult esse separatum."

7. "Apostolos interpretationem Bibliorum, ut tum versabatur in manibus Gentium retinuisse. Ii *berith*, id est, foedus, verterunt plerunque *diatheke*, dispositio, sive Testamentum. Neque sine causa versionem illam retinuerunt. Quia foedus hoc habet aliquid diversum ab allis foederibus, & commune cum Testamentis, quia morte confirmatur, ut docetur ad Heb. 9." Comm. on Romans 11:27, pp. 590–1. "Etsi enim alia foedera morte dissiliunt, hoc tamen aeternum foedus in eo testamentis est simile, quod morte interveniente confirmatur." *De substantia*, 56. Cf. also "Bund oder Testament," Sudhoff, *Fester Grund*, 1590 ed., 163, and "promissionem hanc foederis seu testamenti," *De substantia*, 55.

of forgiveness and life was proclaimed to the Old Testament fathers from the beginning:[8] to Adam after the fall ("The seed of the woman shall crush [Satan's] head");[9] to Abraham and his descendants ("In your seed shall all the nations of the earth be blessed");[10] to the remnant of Israel in Jeremiah 31 ("I will put my laws in their minds . . . and will remember their sins no more");[11] and still to hearers of the Word today.[12] To be sure, this oath or testament was not confirmed until the suffering and death of Christ. Christ was still the only way to *Seligkeit,* since it was only through His sacrifices that the blessing promised to Abraham could be applied to us and the forgiveness and renewal promised through Jeremiah made possible.[13] Neverthe-

8. "Et sane unum erat foedus aeternum gratuitum seu Evangelium promissum Patribus ab initio." *De substantia,* 295. ". . . Jesus Christus, . . . welcher der einige weg zum ewigen leben ist, den Gott selbst von anfang dem armem verlorenen menschlichen geschlect auss dem Himmel gezeigt hatt." Reu, *Vester Grundt,* 1567 ed., 1332. Cf. also 1356; Comm. on Rom. 1:2, pp. 2–4; *De substantia,* 97.

9. "Primum enim Deus ipse . . . primus Evangelium in Paradiso protulit: Semen mulieris conculcabit caput serpentis." Comm. on Gal. 1:9, p. 9. "Una est promissio remissionis & vitae aeternae omnium temporum edito initio his verbis: Semen mulieris conculbat caput serpentis." Comm. on Rom. 1:2, pp. 3–4. See also Reu, *Vester Grundt,* 1567 ed., 1332; "Abendmahlpredigten," no. 3, *Gnadenbund,* 349.

10. Reu, *Vester Grundt,* 1567 ed., 1322; Comm. on Galatians 3:15–7, p. 66; Sudhoff, "Abendmahlpredigten," no. 1, 187–88.

11. *Expositio,* 182–83.

12. ". . . denn das neue Testament ist die Verheissung und Eid Gottes von der Vergebung der Sunden und Erneuerung des hl. Geistes um des Verdienstes Christi willen, . . . welche Ding, anders nicht denn durch der wahren Glauben und Vertrauen mögen empfangen werden." Sudhoff, "Abendmahlpredigten," no. 1, 193. "Christus accipiendus est qualem se in Evangelio offert (offert autem se cum integro foedere, hoc est, salvatorem merito & efficacia, sive in iustitiam & sanctificationem)." *De substantia,* 256–7. "Das Evangelium ist ein offenbarung des vetterlichen und unwandelbaren willen Gottes, darin er verheist allen glaubigen, das jhre sunden von ewigkeit jhnen verzeigen seindt und in ewigkeit verzeigen bleiben." Reu, *Vester Grundt,* 1567 ed., 1336. See also *De substantia,* 267, and Sudhoff, *Fester Grund,* 1590 ed., 12.

13. "Itaque Paulus admonet Christum maledictionem Legis a nobis sustulisse dum pro nobis in cruce factur est maledictio, ut Abrahae promissa benedictio ad nos pervenirit." *De substantia,* 51. "Quae autem potest maior esse confirmatio huius foederis sive Testamenti [in Je. 31] quam dum *logos* . . . morte sua, qua carne subit, idipsum quod promisit, confirmare dignatur?" *Expositio,* 183. Cf. also "Abendmahlpredigten," no. 1, *Gnadenbund,* 270, and *De substantia,* 55–56, 296–97.

less, even before ratification it was still a covenant—a declaration of God's will awaiting its final fulfillment.

In some contexts, however, Olevianus understands the covenant of grace in a broader sense than as God's unilateral promise of reconciliation ratified in Jesus Christ. He employs some of the same terms as before—*Bund, Gnadenbund, foedus, foedus gratiae,* and *foedus gratuitum*—but this time to mean a *bilateral* commitment between God and believers. The covenant so understood is more than a promise of reconciliation; it is the realization of that promise—reconciliation itself—through a mutual coming to terms. Not only does God bind Himself to us in a pledge that He will be our Father; we also bind ourselves to Him in a pledge of acceptance of His paternal beneficence. Not only does God promise that He will blot out all memory of our sins; we in turn promise that we will walk uprightly before Him. The covenant in this sense includes both God's *promissio* and our *repromissio*.[14]

This semantical shift from a unilateral to a bilateral promise is most clearly seen in two passages in Olevianus's writings where he compares the covenant of grace to a human *Bund.* In *Vester Grundt,* as we have seen, he portrays the covenant strictly as a divine pledge. While we were yet sinners, God bound Himself to us with an oath and a promise that through His Son He would repair the broken relationship. It was expected, of course, that we accept the Son (whether promised or already sent) in faith, but Olevianus here does not treat this response as part of the covenant. The emphasis is on what God would do because of what we could not do.[15]

In a similar passage in the *Expositio,* however, Olevianus not only identifies the covenant with reconciliation itself but describes it as a mutual agreement (*mutuus assensus*) between the

14. "Imprimis vero foedus gratiae, quo se iuramento obstrinxit, se fore nobis in Patrem, & nos vicissim ipsi nos obstrinximus, velle nos in ipsius paterno affectu acquiescere." Comm. on Matthew 4:1–12, *Notae in Evangelia,* 87. "Quid foedus? Promissio ac iuramentum Dei, quod propter mortem Filii non meminisse velit peccatorum nostrorum: & repromissio, quod per gratiam Christi ei fidere velimus, & integre ambulare." Comm. on Luke 2:21, *Notae in Evangelia,* 42. ". . . foederis mutui inter Deum & nos." *De substantia,* 411. See also Comm. on Rom. 2:17, pp. 108–10.

15. See n. 4 above.

estranged parties.[16] Here God binds Himself not to us "who were yet sinners"[17] but to us "who repent and believe," to us who in turn are bound to Him in faith and worship. This "covenant of grace or union between God and us"[18] is not established at just one point in history; it is ratified personally with each believer. Christ the Bridegroom enters into "covenant or fellowship" with the Church His Bride by the ministry of the Word and sacraments and through the Holy Spirit seals the promises of reconciliation in the hearts of the faithful.[19] But this is also a covenant into which *we* enter, a "covenant of faith."[20] As full partners in the arrangement we become not merely God's children but His *Bundgesnossen,* His *confoederati.*[21]

When he discusses the covenant of grace in this broader sense, i.e., as a bilateral commitment between God and us, Olevianus does not hesitate to use the term *conditio.* We see already in the establishment of the covenant with Abraham that the covenant of grace has not one but two parts: not merely God's *prom-*

16. "Reconciliatio autem hominis cum Deo, sive hoc salutis negotium, . . . ideo foedus vocatur, & forma etiam foederis a Deo nobis proponitur, quia nulla forma sive ratio agendi aptior est, ad constituendum mutuum inter pares assensum, stabiliendumque fidem. Quemadmodum enim homines post graves inimicias, tum demum pecatis sunt animis cum promissionibus ac iureiurando sese mutuo ad [componendum?] pacem obstrinxerunt: Sic etiam Deus ut tranquillae essent nostrae conscientiae, non dubitavit ex mera bonitate vel iureiurando ac foedere se nobis resipiscentibus & credentibus, obstringere . . . ut vicissim in huius veri Dei Patris, Filii, & Spiritus sancti fidem cultumque obstricti, hanc tantem ipsius bonitatem celebremus." *Expositio,* 9–10.

17. Reu, *Vester Grundt,* 1567 ed., 1333.

18. Ibid., 1360–61; Cf. also *Expositio,* 96: ". . . foederis gratiae sive coniunctionis inter Deum & nos."

19. "[Christus] init foedus sive *koinonian* cum Ecclesia per ministerium Verbi & Sacramentorum." *Expositio,* 36. ". . . der Sohn Gottes aus dem ganzen menchlichen Geschlect . . . sich ein Volk . . . sammelt. . . . Er macht auch einen ewigen Bund, und verlobt sich mit diesem Volk als mit seiner Braut." Sudhoff, *Fester Grund,* 1590 ed., 157–58. ". . . is foedus proprie nobiscum percutit cum promissionem reconciliationis gratuitae in Evangelio oblatam per Spiritum Sanctum cordibus obsignat." *De substantia,* 15–16.

20. ". . . Deum, quocum foedus fidei iniimus." *Expositio,* 46.

21. "So haben alle Christgläubigten nicht einen geringen, sondern vortrefflichen Bund mit Gott, diewil er seine gläubigen Bundesgenossen für seinen Kinderhalten will." Sudhoff, *Fester Grund,* 1590 ed., 67–68. See also Reu, *Vester Grundt,* 1567 ed., 1351. For *confoederati* see *Expositio,* 46, 57, 81. Cf. *De substantia,* 408: ". . . mutuae confoederationis inter Deum & nos."

issio to be the God of Abraham and his seed, but that promise on the condition (*qua conditione*) of Abraham's (and our) *repromissio* to walk before Him and be perfect.[22] Simply put, God's covenantal blessings are contingent upon our faith and obedience. It is to those who repent, believe, and are baptized that He reconciles Himself and binds Himself in covenant.[23]

Olevianus is quick to point out, however, that this is not a conditional covenant in the ordinary sense of the term. It is not a *contractus mutuus*, based on full reciprocation.[24] That would imply that we come to the covenant with something to offer, that we are able to fulfill the conditions of the covenant *ex propriis viribus*. The fact is, we are wholly incapable of meeting these conditions. The fall of Adam dealt such a blow to the human race that no one has the personal resources to produce even a "drop" of righteousness or eternal life.[25] The grace of reconciliation is not ours for the taking. Were the work of faith left to us, we would never believe. Were the enjoyment of the benefits of the covenant dependent on our works, we would remain forever unfulfilled.[26]

God's covenant initiative, then, is in no sense founded on our ability to meet the conditions of the covenant on our own merits, capabilities, or worthiness; it is founded rather on His good-

22. "Itaque non est quod allegetis tantum unam partem foederis: quam Deus promiserit & confirmarit; sed addite etiam alteram qua conditione promiserit, sive quid vos repromiseritis, nempe vos fore integros & ambulataros coram ipsium facie. . . . Gen. 17. Ero Deus tuus & seminis tui: sub conditione repromissa, Ambula coram me & esto integer, id est, fidas mihi & serves mandata mea." Comm. on Rom. 2:17, pp. 108–10. Cf. also Comm. on Rom. 2:25–8, pp. 110–1.

23. ". . . dass allein, allein sage ich, in dem Leiden Jesu Christi und sonst nirgends die Vergebung der Sünden zu suchen sei und denselbigen (laut der Verheissung Gottes) gewisslich zugeeignet wird, die ihres Herzens Vertrauen darauf setzen." Sudhoff, "Abendmahlpredigten," no. 1, 185–86. "Sic etiam Deus . . . non dubitavit ex mera bonitate vel iureiurando ac foedere se nobis resipiscentibus & credentibus, obstringere." *Expositio,* 9–10.

24. ". . . non est hic contractus mutuus, exempli causa, facio ut tu facias vicissim, vendo, solvas. Nihil horum." Comm. on Gal. 3:18, p. 68.

25. "Quomodo, inquis, faciam, ut non abiiciam gratiam Christi? Cogitare & sentire debes te ne guttam iustitiae & vitae aeternae ex propriis viribus habere." Comm. on Gal. 2:21, p. 37.

26. ". . . nequaquam . . . (ut quidam imaginantur sparsam esse illam oblationis gratiam in aerem ut eam ad se rapiat qui volet)." Ibid., 211–12.

ness and grace. The fountain of salvation flows only in one direction—from God to us.[27] Since we in our own strength, therefore, are unable to fulfill the conditions of the covenant, He fulfills them for us, or better yet, in and through us. The covenant is ratified not by our coming first to God in faith and obedience but by Christ's instilling first in us an "eagerness for reconciliation" (*studium reconciliationis*) and *creating* in us faith and obedience.[28] This is entirely God's work, not ours. Fulfillment of the conditions of the covenant, like the benefits of the covenant, is a gift, a free gift, of God.[29] That is what Olevianus implies is so distinctive about this covenant of grace. In ordinary covenants both parties have something to give; in the covenant of grace it is God alone who gives. We only receive, and the ability to receive is itself a gift of God.[30]

Olevianus does not mean, however, to minimize the ethical responsibility of the human partner in the covenant. It is true that our inchoate righteousness does not become the cause of our eternal life or that our good works after conversion in any way add to the obedience and righteousness of Jesus Christ.

27. ". . . quod nulla pars dilectionis Dei erga nos fundata est in nostra dignitate, viribus vel meritis, sed in sola bonitate Dei . . . Ezech. 16: Aeternum foedus nominat, non quod nos ipsum diligamus, sed quod ipse diligat nos." Comm. on Rom 8:35–6, p. 404. "Der brun laufft nicht den berg hinauf sonder herab zu uns." Comm. on Rom. 8:29, 30, p. 382.

28. "Efficacia vero, qua ut Rex Ecclesiae primum corda ad agnitionem sui mali & divinae iustitiae considerationem adducit, studiumque se reconciliandi Deo, & convertendi se ad ipsius voluntatem in iis creat. Deinde vero ita dispositis verbum reconciliationis offert, fidemque in iis generat." *Expositio*, 4–5. ". . . acceptatio ex parte nostra etiam est gratuita, quia est Dei actio in nobis, qua promissionem suam obsignat cordibus, ut acti agamus, hoc est, effecti ab ipso credentes credamus & vivificati sive conditi a Christo ad bona opera in iis porto ambulemus, Ephes. 2. v.1 usque ad v.10." *De substantia*, 16. "Itaque interna mentis renovatio, sive internae qualitates & quae ex iis proficiscuntur cogitationes & actiones bonae, id est bona opera etiam non a nobis oriuntur, sed gratis a Deo dantur." Comm. on Rom. 9:11, p. 434. Cf. also Reu, *Vester Grundt*, 1567 ed., 1373, 1383; *Expositio*, 11–12; and Sudhoff, *Fester Grund*, 1590 ed., 166.

29. At one point Olevianus even includes faith as *part* of one of the benefits of the covenant: "Ad vivificationem hanc & renovationem ad Dei imaginem quod attinet, (quae in se continet donum fidei & resipiscentiae . . .)" *De substantia*, 93.

30. "Deus est qui donat gratis; homo accipit solummodo; imo hoc ipsum acceptare sive credere etiam gratuitum Dei donum est." Comm. on Gal. 3:18, p. 68.

Whatever good we possess is still of the Holy Spirit.[31] But that is not to say that works play no role whatsoever in the Christian life. They serve, first of all, to prove whether ours is a genuine or a counterfeit faith. It should be easy to tell from our actions whether the Holy Spirit has truly granted us new powers of belief and obedience. It is rather difficult to convince someone that a statue is alive when it remains absolutely motionless or that a drunk is sober when he is staggering from wall to wall.[32] Works are the fruit and thus the measure of faith. Second, they are a means by which we demonstrate our gratitude to God for our share in the inheritance of His covenant and for a place in His Kingdom.[33] Finally, it is through the example of our good deeds that others are attracted to Christ and built up in their faith.[34] It is our responsibility, then, both to "strive that [we] may have those same marks by which [Christ] through his Spirit identified his sheep," and at the same time to recognize that it is not we ourselves but the Holy Spirit who brings forth these "fruits worthy of repentance."[35]

This broader understanding of the covenant as a bilateral commitment must be kept in view in any analysis of two important themes in Olevianus's covenant theology, the Kingdom of Christ and the mystical union with Christ. As Heppe and Schrenk pointed out, Olevianus, especially in his *Expositio,* welds the biblical–theological concept of "kingdom" to the cov-

31. "Etsi igitur Pater cum Christo nos excitando e morte spirituali, simul cum dono fidei inchoat in nobis iustitiam seu conformitatem cum Deo, tamen iustitia illa inchoata seu resipiscentia causa vitae aeternae non est." *De substantia,* 286. ". . . muss man gar und gantz kein stücklein, wie gross oder klein es auch sey, von unsern [guten] wercken hinzuflicken zu dem gehorsam oder gerechtigkeit Jesu Christi." Reu, *Vester Grund,* 1567 ed., 1378. "Quidquid boni, vel minima gutta, nobis est, a Spiritu sancto est." Comm. on Gal. 5:22, p. 121.

32. ". . . ex actionibus vitae nostrae facile erit iudicare, quis spiritus nos regat. Quemadmodum si quis mihi persuadere velit statuem vivere, quae tamen neque ambulare neque quicquam movere possit. Aut, quemadmodum si ebrius, qui ab uno pariete cadat in alterum, mihi persuadere velit, se esse sobrium." Comm. on Gal. 5:25, p. 127.

33. Sudhoff, *Fester Grund,* 1590 ed., 141; *De substantia,* 184.

34. ". . . das wir durch gute exampel der guten werck andere Christo gewinnen und die so schon gewonnen seindt, nicht abfellich machen, sondern bey Christo erhalten und jhe länger, je mehr erbawen." Reu, *Vester Grundt,* 1567 ed., 1379–80.

35. *Expositio,* 170–1; Comm. on Gal. 2:21, p. 33; *De substantia,* 181.

enant idea.[36] The *regni Christi administratio* is, in point of fact,
the administration of the new covenant promised in Jeremiah
and ratified by Christ on Calvary. The citizens of the Kingdom
of God are one and the same with God's *confoederati*.[37] But
when Olevianus places kingdom alongside covenant, he always
has in mind the broader sense of covenant. The Kingdom of
God is not merely a promise of reconciliation but the realization
or fulfillment of that promise in the lives of its citizens. It is the
administration of salvation whereby Christ the King calls and
gathers to Himself His subjects through the Gospel and sacraments and whereby He applies the *double benefit* of the covenant, forgiveness and inner renewal, to their hearts.[38] This is a
gradual process, never complete in this life. Day in and day out
the fire of the Holy Spirit burns away the rubbish of our old al-
legiances and advances the Kingdom of God in us a little further.[39] But here, as elsewhere in his discussion of covenant in
the broader sense, Olevianus emphasizes that the reconciliation
between King and subject involves a mutual commitment. The
Kingdom of Light is peopled by those who, for their part, have
responded to God's initiative. Only those who repent and be-

36. Heppe, *Dogmatik*, I:149; Schrenk, *Gottesreich und Bund*, 60–61.
Schrenk goes on to suggest that "hier begegnet uns zum ersten Male die system-
atische Verbindung von Bund und Reich."
37. "Universa haec regni Christi administratio foedus illud novum est, quod
Deus promiserat per Ieremiam Prophetem. . . . Hoc foedus Christus sacerdos &
Rex Ecclesiae inter Deum et nos merito suo in aeternum sancivit, & efficacia
sua quotidie in nobis administrat." *Expositio*, 4. ". . . confoederatis sive fidelibus
regni Dei civibus." Ibid., 48.
38. "Das Reich Christi ist eine ordentliche, kräftige Wirkung und Mit-
theilung des Heils." Sudhoff, *Fester Grund*, 1590 ed., 128. "Regnum Christi in
hoc mundo, est administratio salutis, qua Rex ipse Christus externe per Evangelium & Baptismum, populum sive Ecclesiam visibilem . . . sibi colligit & vocat
ad salutem, eam ipsam salutem ad quam vocat . . . ipsemer administrat & largitur." *Expositio*, 3. ". . . credimus eum . . . cum potentia regnum suum administrare, ita ut Spiritu suo quam efficacissime promissionem gratiae de abolita
peccatorum memoria cordibus nostris obsignet, indiesque ad sui imaginem
sibi insitos longe efficacius renovet atque gubernet." *De substantia*, 123.
39. "Derhalben regieret Christus uns . . . dass er uns . . . von Tag zu Tag sein
geistliches Reich in uns fordere . . . bis dass er uns vollkommen erneuert und
von Sünden und aller Verderbniss gereiniget." Sudhoff, *Fester Grund*, 1590 ed.,
133–4. ". . . wird [der Heilige Geist] auch genannt ein Feuer, darum, dass er die
Herzen mit wahrer Liebe Gottes anzundet, und was dem Reich Gottes zuwider
ist, ausbrennet und lautert." Ibid., 151.

lieve in Christ and are baptized in His name can truly be said to be in the Kingdom of Christ.[40]

Past research on Olevianus's covenant theology has also noted the importance of the mystical union with Christ for his doctrine of the covenant of grace. Heppe described it as "die Realität, die Substanz, und das Mittel" of the covenant for the early German Reformed dogmaticians, including Olevianus;[41] Diestel, as part of the "content of the covenant";[42] and Schrenk, as a new relationship to Christ given in the covenant.[43] It is interesting that all three identified this ingrafting and incorporation into Christ with the content or benefits of the covenant. In a certain sense they read Olevianus correctly here, for when he uses covenant in the narrower sense, he does indeed include the mystical union among the benefits of the covenant promise. The new covenant referred to by Christ in the Last Supper, for example, is God's offer not only of forgiveness of sins and eternal life but also of incorporation into Christ.[44]

But the mystical union plays a far more significant role when Olevianus speaks of covenant in the broader sense, i.e., as actual reconciliation between God and believers. Here union with Christ is the vital link in the covenant between our faith, on the one hand, and God's promises, on the other. Only through faith

---

40. "Regnum Christi, in quo revera sunt quicunque resipiscunt, & credunt, & in eius nomen baptizati sunt." *Expositio,* 1–2. "Die an Christum glauben, ihm vertrauen auf seinen Namen getauft sind, wissen, dass sie in diesem Leben im Reiche Christi sind." Sudhoff, *Fester Grund,* 1590 ed., 54–55.

41. Heppe, *Dogmatik des deutschen Protestantismus,* 1:144. Brown (*Encyclopedia of Religion and Ethics,* s.v. "Covenant Theology") makes a similar point but appears to rely on Heppe.

42. Diestel, *Geschichte des Alten Testaments,* 288.

43. "[Olevianus's] Besonderheit besteht endlich noch darin, dass er . . . das im Bund gegebene neue Verhältnis zu Christo als Eingliederung und Einverleibung beschreibt. Hier liegt ein mystiches Moment vor, das einem überall bei Olevianus entgegentritt, und das auf eine besondre Innigheit des Gemeinschaftserlebnis mit Christus schliessen lässt." Schrenk, *Gottesreich und Bund,* 61–62.

44. ". . . denn das neue Testament ist die Verheissung und Eid Gottes . . . von der Vergebung der Sünden, eine Einleibung in Christum durch den hl. Giest und ewiges Leben." Sudhoff, "Abendmahlpredigten," no. 1, 193. "Unionem quoque per Spiritum Sanctum & fidem fieri, abunde constat ex natura novi testamenti, quod Christus promittit. . . . Quod non aliam quam talem communionem nostri cum capite in se continet." *De substantia,* 368–69. Cf. also *Expositio,* 81–82.

are we incorporated into Christ and only through that incorporation are we accepted as children of God and coheirs with Christ.[45] Furthermore, it is only as we are truly engrafted into Christ through faith that we experience the forgiveness of sins and the restoration of the *imago Dei* (true knowledge, righteousness, and holiness) within us.[46] As Mediator of the reconciliation or covenant between God and us, then, Christ is the channel through which God's favor flows, and we possess that favor only insofar as we possess Christ Himself.[47] It is in union with Him that the terms of the covenant set down in the Creed are put into effect.

Olevianus claims that, aside from the trinitarian union of Persons and the hypostatic union of Christ's natures, there is no greater (*maior*) or tighter (*firmior*) bond than this *mystica unio* between Christ and His Church.[48] But he is always careful to point out that this union is not a mixture of essences.[49] One cannot, he suggests, describe the union between the person of Christ and Peter or Paul in the same way that one describes the union between the person of Christ and His own natures.[50] The mystical union is rather a *spiritual* union, spiritual in the highest sense of the term, for the "bond" between Christ and us is none other than the Holy Spirit. It is He who

45. " . . . dass er verheissen hat und mit der that bewisen, dass er . . . unss durch den glauben als ware glieder seinem Sohn eingeleibet und also unss zu seinen kindern angenommen hatt." Reu, *Vester Grundt*, 1567 ed., 1345. ". . . Spiritus sanctus, qui nos in possessionem Christi inducit, eidem nos inserit atque ita Filios Dei & cohaeredes facit." *De substantia*, 37.

46. "Quotquot enim vere Christo per fidem sumus insiti, praeter illud beneficium remissionis, . . . alterum simil incipimus possidere, nempe instaurationem imaginis Dei." *Expositio*, 184. "Vult ut crescamus in coniunctione cum Christo, & in illa coniunctione apprehendamus . . . potentiam ipsius resurrectionis sive conformitatem in gloria." Comm. on Philippians 3:11–4, p. 58. For Olevianus's definition of the image of God see his Comm. on Colossians 3:10, pp. 160–61.

47. "Ita enim immutabiliter constituit divina sapientia, ut semen Abrahae sit organum intermedium in cuius manu Deus nobiscum paciscitur, ut nullus promissae benefictionis seu foederis gratuiti sit particeps nisi per Spiritum huic carni seu semini Abrahae inseratur." *De substantia*, 208–9.

48. Ibid., 43, 227.

49. "Cuius unionis, non commixtionis respectu fideles dicuntur caro de carne eius, os de ossibus eius, ad Eph. 5." Ibid., 44. Cf. also ibid., 232–4.

50. Reu, *Vester Grundt*, 1567 ed., 1360.

through our faith engrafts us into Christ like branches into a tree. Living both in Christ in heaven and in the heart of the believer, He is, as it were, the "living nerve" (*lebendige Senader*) by which the believer is bound to Christ and made a partaker of the covenantal riches.[51] Our reconciliation or *mutua confoederatio* with the Father is thus secured by two intermediate bonds: Christ is the link between the Father and us, and the Holy Spirit the link between us and Christ. Or as Olevianus himself puts it, "God unites Himself to us with an indissoluble bond in Christ our Head through the fetter of the Holy Spirit."[52] What we really have in this covenant is communion with the entire Trinity.[53]

For Olevianus, then, the covenant of grace is much more than an "unconditional . . . unilateral testament";[54] it has a carefully qualified conditional, bilateral dimension as well. It is true that he never explicitly mentions these two dimensions of the covenant. The closest he comes to acknowledging them is in a distinction he introduces in *De substantia* between the substance (*substantia* or *essentia*) and the administration (*administratio*) of the new covenant referred to in Jeremiah 31. Here God promised His people that there would come a time when He would inscribe His laws on their hearts and remember their sins no more. When Olevianus discusses the substance of this covenant, he seems to think of the covenant in the narrower sense. The substance of the covenant, he asserts, is the essence, content, or fulfillment of the *promise*, the very "gift promised and sworn to by God"—namely, remission of sins and renewal.[55] When he discusses the administration of these covenant blessings through the Word and sacraments, however, he seems to think of covenant in the broader sense. The visible

---

51. *Expositio*, 173–4; Sudhoff, "Abendmahlpredigten," no. 5, 213. Cf. also ibid., 216–17, and *De substantia*, 227–29.

52. ". . . atque [Deus] in capite Christo per . . . vinculum Spiritus Sancti cum iis indissolubili nexu se uniat." Ibid., 226–27.

53. Ibid., 216.

54. Baker, *Bullinger and the Covenant*, 204, 205.

55. "Deus promiserat per Ieremiam Prophetam se percussurum nobiscum foedus novum. . . . Dupliciter autem accipitur foedus: primum pro ipsa foederis substantia, sive pro rebus ipsis a Deo promissis. . . . Foedus itaque gratuitum, si essentiam eiis spectes, est promissa & iurata a Deo donatio." *De substantia*, 1–2.

signs bear witness to a *mutual* agreement (*mutuus consensus*) or a mutual covenant of grace (*mutuum foedus gratuitum*) between God and us.[56] God offers us His grace; we assent thereto in faith.[57]

But even though Olevianus never explicitly mentions this distinction between unilateral and bilateral covenant, it is difficult to make sense of his doctrine of the *foedus gratiae* without it. It explains why, for example, he can speak of the covenant with Abraham as both a promise confirmed in the sacrifice of Christ and a two-sided *Bund und Freundschaft*;[58] why he can state that the new covenant promised in Jeremiah 31 is established both by Christ through His atoning death and by God with us through faith;[59] why in the same sentence he can refer both to God's testimony "by an everlasting covenant" that He will be our God and also to a "covenant of faith" into which we have entered with God;[60] and, why, finally, the sacraments can demand

56. ". . . testimonium mutui consensus inter Deum et nos." Ibid., 3. ". . . sigilla . . . mutui foederis gratuiti," Ibid., 408. Cf. also ibid., 410–12, 414–16.

57. "Signi seu visibilis testimonii administratio continet . . . stipulationem solemnem assensus seu fidei in oblatam in promulgatione doctrinae gratiam." Ibid., 343–44.

58. "That same everlasting covenant that God had stricken with Abraham ['in your seed shall all nations of the earth be blessed'], the son of God in man's nature, taken of the seed of Abraham, hath confirmed by satisfying the righteousness of God perfectly. Now it resteth that the Holy Ghost engraft us into Christ through faith, the true seed of Abraham, and so pour out that blessing promised to Abraham and his seed upon us." *Expositio*, 233 (this page is missing in my Latin text). "Gott hat . . . diesen Bund und Freundschaft mit [Abraham] gemacht, dass er wolle sein Gott sein und seines Samens nach ihm und Abraham solle aufrichtig vor ihm wandeln." Sudhoff, "Abendmahlpredigten," no. 1, 187–88.

59. "Ipsum autem Iehovam esse, qui testamentum seu foedus illud promittit, constat ex Ierem 31. cap. Eundem Iehovam esse qui idem testamentum morte sua confirmat, docetur ad Hebr. 8. cap. ac deinde 9. Ubi testamentum, inquit, mors testoris intercedat necesse est. Quo in loco eundem Christum, qui moritur, testament, in Ieremia promissi conditorem dicit." *Expositio*, 183. Cf. also Sudhoff, *Fester Grund*, 1590 ed., 163. "Promiserat autem Deus per Ieremiam Prophetam se percussurum nobiscum novum. . . . Hoc foedus in Christum per fidem nobiscum pactus est Dominus." *Expositio*, 10. "Haec de forma, qua Deus nobiscum foedus percutit per oblationem gratiae in Evangelio cum mandato, ne obduremus corda nostra, seu fidel: & simul per usum Sacramentorum, per quem & fidei sit contestatio & gratiae obsignatio." *De substantia*, 319.

60. ". . . Deum, quocum foedus fidei iniimus, quique se nobis in Deum testatus est foedere sempiterno." *Expositio*, 46.

our assent to the covenant of grace offered in them and at the same time signify the mutual covenant of grace between God and us.[61] In every case Olevianus has in mind, first, the promise of reconciliation and, second, reconciliation per se; first, a monopleuric divine oath and, second, a dipleuric divine-human pledge.

Foundation of the Covenant

A search for the ground or basis of the covenant of grace in Olevianus will uncover not one but three such foundations, better understood, perhaps, as a single foundation with three levels. The first and uppermost level is Christ Himself in His role as eternal High Priest. It is as Priest that He offered up Himself as a sacrifice for our sin and obtained our righteousness before God. And it is as eternal Priest, ascended and seated at God's right hand, that He preserves forever the covenant blessings obtained below.[62] The death of Christ is the foundation of the covenant promised to Abraham, therefore, in the sense that it was on the cross that the covenant promise was "founded," or established or confirmed.[63] Indeed, it was both a necessary and sufficient foundation. The establishment of the eternal covenant of grace depended on the death of Christ, but His death would

61. ". . . [Deus] testimonia visibilia instituit, quibus assensum nostrum in gratuitum foedus in verbo oblatum . . . stipuletur." *De substantia,* 311. ". . . sigilla . . . mutui foederis gratuiti." Ibid., 408.

62. "Sequitur ut explicemus, cur non in Regem modo, sed etiam Sacerdotem unctus sit. Ratio est, quia regnum Christi ita stabiliendum erat, ut in aeternum satisfieret Dei iustitae atque ita firmo solidoque fundamento niteretur pax inita promissa gratia. Fundamentum autem est, Sacerdotium Christi aeternum." *Expositio,* 72–73. "Quoniam autem Sacerdotium, sive aeterna reconciliatio regni fundamentum est . . . priore loco dicamus, foedus gratuitum semel in terra in humilitate sancitum, in aeternum conservari intercessione huius Mediatoris." Comm. on Rom. 8:34, p. 396. Cf. also *De substantia,* 128–30.

63. "Fundamentum itaque foederis gratiae & aeterna confirmatio est mors testatoris sanguinolenta. . . . Etenim in iuramento illo foederi gratuiti, PER MEIPSUM IURAVI IN SEMINE TUO BENEDICENTUR OMNES FAMILIAE TERRAE Gen. 22. mortem testatoris (ceu fundamentum benedictionis) per quam iurata bendictio rata futura esset velut ob oculos nobis proponi docet Paulus Gal 3. ve. 13–14." *De substantia,* 296–97. "Quae etiam maior huius testamenti confirmatio esse potuisset de certa remissione peccatorum quam mors ipsius Dei, nempe Filii incarnati in quo per quem testamentum promissum atque conditum erat." Ibid., 55–56.

have been in vain if it were not also the *only* way our reconciliation with God could have been procured.[64]

The very possibility of the work of Christ, however, rested on an even deeper foundation, the person of Christ.[65] Time and again Olevianus stresses that the *fundament und grundt* of the priesthood of Christ—and thus of the eternal covenant between God and us—is comprehended in the person of Christ, more particularly in the union of natures in that person. The covenant of grace or union between God and us is grounded first and foremost in Immanuel, the highest expression of the divine and human in union. Without this union there is no true Christ, and without this Christ there is no true covenant or reconciliation with God.[66] This hypostatic union, moreover, must be preserved into all eternity if our covenant of reconciliation with God is to remain intact.[67] The Logos's habitation of His assumed human

64. ". . . enim aeternum foedus sine morte Christi constare non potest." Ibid., 297. "Nam finis atque scopus victimae propitiatoriae seu mortis Christi est satisfacere pro peccatis atque ita comparare iustitiam soluto precio. Qui scopus si aliunde haberi potuisset aut etiamnum posset, Christus frustra fuisset mortuus." Ibid., 64–65.

65. ""Ut fundamentum foederis gratuitae adoptionis coniunctionisque inter Deum & nos esset firmissimum, voluit coelestis Pater Filium suum aeternum assumere nostram naturam." Ibid., 26–27.

66. "Das fundament und grundt des Königlichen priesterthumbs Christi und derwegen des ewigen Bundts zwischen Gott und den menschen wirdt begriffen in diesem Artickel von der person Christi, zu welcher person Substanz und wesen diese zwo naturen gehören . . . , welche also zusammen verhafftet sein, das sie ein wesentlicher, wahrhaftiger Christus sein." Reu, *Vester Grundt*, 1567 ed., 1355–56. "Fr. Nuhn zeig an, warumb diese beide naturen in Christo müssen persönlich vereiniget sein. A. Auff das der grundt des gnadenbundts oder der vereinigung zwischen Gott und unss fest und unbeweglich were, so hatt Gott gewolt, das diese zwo naturen in Christo auff eine besondere weiss verbunden und vereiniget weren, nemlich durch eine persönliche vereinigung . . . damit sie seligkeit durch solche mittel erworben und auch in ewigkeit erhalten würde." Ibid., 1360–1. "In Christo Immanuele ceu fundamento est summa Dei & hominis unitio. Quamobrem Immanuel, id est, nobiscum Deus vocatur Ies. septime." *De substantia*, 227–28. Cf. also ibid., 36–37, 232–34, and *Expositio*, 96–100.

67. "Dann gleich wie es vonnöten war, den bundt und die versöhnung des Menschen mit Gott [anzufangen], das beide naturen am mitler wahrhafftig und gantz weren sampt jhren eigenschafften. Also auch, dieweil der bundt und vereinigung mit Gott in ewigkeyt were solt. . . , so ist es vonnöten, das auch im fundament, nemlich im Mitler des bundts, . . . unss in ewigkeyt selig zumachen, die menschliche natur wahrhafftig gantz und volkommen an leib und seel, fleisch und gebein bleibe und behalten werde in ewigkeyt." Reu, *Vester Grundt*, 1567 ed., 1361–62.

nature into all eternity assures us of the constancy and eternity of God's covenant promises. If there were no personal union of natures for eternity, the covenant would be torn from its foundations and destroyed.[68] That is why the Devil has always been hard at work trying to deny, or at least undermine, Jesus Christ as very God and very man. He knows that just as damage to the root of a tree saps the branches of their ability to bear fruit, so also damage to the person of Christ will rob Him of His fruit of redemption and us of our enjoyment of it.[69]

If the covenant is founded upon the priestly work of Christ and that work upon His person, the person of Christ as the cornerstone of our salvation is grounded in the deepest level of the foundation, the eternal decree of God.[70] To use another of Olevianus's metaphors, the covenant of grace "flows out of the fountain" of God's gracious election in Christ.[71] Or, covenant and election are different "links" in the same "golden chain" of salvation described in Romans 8. At the head of the chain stands God's decision to save, then his *electio* of a specific portion of the corrupted human race. To this decree of *electio* is joined the effectual *vocatio*, the gift of faith by which the elect are incorporated into Christ. And to faith in turn is linked the

---

68. "Postremo ut sciremus dilectionem, qua nos Pater in Filio gratis adoptavit sepulta peccatorum nostrorum memoria, esse constantem, & instaurationem ad Dei imaginem esse aeternum, ita ut porro vita aeterna excidere non possimus, ipsum *logon* aeternum Dei Filium, consubstantialem ipsum nimirum fontem, in quo vita est ab initio (Ioan. 1) in natura humana assumpta in omnem aeternitatem personaliter habitare, nosque per eundem *logon* ei institos cum ea uniti oportet, ut semper in illo capite censeamur, & de plenitudine eius continenter hauriamus gratiam pro gratia, Ioan. 1, Iesai. 12, Col. 1:3, 9, 10; denique ut habitatio in nobis per regenerationis gratiam, firma sit tanto fundamento subnixa, Col. 1:15 usque ad 20, Rom. 8:37, 38, 39." *De substantia*, 37–38. "Cum igitur foedus salutis inter Deum & homines aeternum sit, statuendum est in persona Christi tanquam in fundamento ita in aeternum esse unitas duas hasce naturas, ut veritatem utriusque naturae cum suis proprietatibus in aeternum constare, neutramque ab altera absorberi oporteat, nisi velimus foedus ab ipsis fundamentis convelii atque everti, Luc. 24:38, 39; Ioan. 20:27, 28." Ibid., 38.

69. Reu, *Vester Grundt*, 1567 ed., 1355–56, 1362; *Expositio*, 89–90.

70. "Das fundament und grundt des Königlichen priesterthumbs Christi und derwegen des ewigen Bundts zwischen Gott und den menschen wirdt begriffen in diesem Artickel von der person Christi, zu welcher person, Substanz und wesen diese zwo naturen gehoren. . . . Diss ist im Rath Gottes der anfang und Eckstein unserer seligkeyt." Reu, *Vester Grundt* 1567 ed., 1355.

71. ". . . ex electione gratuita, fonte scilicet foederis . . . ex fonte electionis gratuitae, unde foedus fluit." Comm. on Rom. 9:24–5, pp. 460, 462.

double benefit of the covenant, *iustificatio* or forgiveness of sins and *glorificatio* or renewal of mind and (ultimately) body.[72] These benefits are secured in history, of course, by the suffering and sacrifice of Jesus Christ on behalf of the elect.[73] But conformity *to* Christ, through which covenant or reconciliation with God is attained, is grounded ultimately in election *in* Christ, decided by God from all eternity.[74]

If we probe behind the decree of election for an even deeper cause of the covenant, says Olevianus, we get no further than the fathomless goodness and grace of God. Those whom God chose to be His covenant partners, He chose out of His boundless love.[75] The question remains, of course, why He selected only

72. "Ordinem itaque pulcerrimum proponit causarum nostrae salutis, & veluti catenam auream, ab una parte coeli, usque ad alteram, in qua qui unum annulum habet, reliquos etiam connexos habet. Catena autem haec est:

1. Ponite vobis ob oculos totum genus humanum in peccato originali conceptum & morte aeterna, & non idoneum ad cogitandum quicquam boni, captivum Satanae. Ex hac damnatorum turba Deus proposuit sibi salvare quos voluit. Propositum igitur servandi est primum, inde electio. . . .
2. Vocatio efficax & externa & internum alterum est. . . . Haec est donatio fidei per quam inserimur Christo. . . .
3. Iustiticatio, id est, pronuntiatio nos esse solutos a peccatis in corpore Christi. . . .
4. Glorificatio, renovatio mentis & corporis fit & fiet. . . ."
Comm. on Rom. 8:28, pp. 375–77, 379–80. Cf. also Comm. on Rom. 8:29, 30, pp. 381–82.

73. "In aeterno Dei consilio et ipsius Christi oratione non aliis destinatum esse hoc *lutron* quam quos filius Dei fecit aut facturus est credentes. . . . Intercedere et sacrificare sunt coniuncta. Pro quibus ergo Filius Dei non orat, pro iis etiam non sacrificat, Ioan. 17:9. Item Luc. 22:31, 32. . . . Ergo etsi sufficienter sit passus pro omnibus hominibus, tamen efficaciter pro solis electis (ut etiam Scholastici loquuntur) quos ipse facit credentes." *De substantia*, 67. "Fons enim applicationis consistit in decreto aeterno Patris pro quibus eum offerre velit, quod arcanum Dei decretum est notum, sicut apud Ioan. 17, ait, Pro iis oro, quos dedisti mihi. Deinde in voluntate Mediatoris obediente huic decreto Patris, ut cum intercessione pro iis se offert. . . . Atque ita dum non tantum se offert, sed pro certis hominibus offert oratione sua expressis." Ibid., 69.

74. ". . . die gleichformigkeyt der glieder Christi mit jrem haupt, erstlich im leiden, darnach in der herligkeyt, ist gegründet in dem ewigen Raht Gottes, darin auch das leiden und herligkeyt Christi selbs gegründet ist, wie unss lehret das 8. Cap. an die Römer, Vers. 28 und 29." Reu, *Vester Grundt*, 1567 ed., 1353. Cf. also ibid., 1331, and *Expositio*, 63.

75. ". . . credo Deum non aliam habuisse causam cur nos fide donaret, & per fidem universam foederis substantiam unam donaret, quam gratuitam suam bonitatem, qua nos quantumvis indignos & perditos in Christo elegit." *De substantia*, 216. ". . . dass Gott aus dem ganzen menschlichen Geschlect sich ein neues Volk, welches er zuvor aus Gnaden erwählt, schaffen will." Sudhoff, *Fester Grund*, 1590 ed., 157. "Ja, dieser Bund ist in einer solchen überaus grossen Liebe Gottes gegen uns gegründet." Ibid., 68. Cf. also *Expositio*, 82.

some and not all hearers of the Word, but this decision had nothing to do with the worth or worthiness of those chosen. If election is not purely of grace, the entire substance of the covenant is destroyed.[76] The explanation lies rather in the nature of God Himself. God is wholly free, truthful, just, and wise.[77] As a free agent, He is at liberty to choose what and whom He wishes. The only restriction on His freedom is that He is bound to His own decisions; He never reneges on a promise. To ask why God made certain choices is both irrelevant and irreverent, moreover, because God is also wholly good, the *summum bonum*, and that in which He finds pleasure must perforce also be good.[78]

Do the nonelect, then, have no status at all with respect to the covenant of grace? If the covenant for Olevianus is founded on the eternal decree of election, we would expect that those in

76. ". . . sed totam substantiam foederis esse merum & gratuitum donum Dei, cui omnes debitores sumus, ipse autem nulli est debitor. Ergo aut oportet omnem supra positam substantiam perire sine fructu (quod fieret si ullam bonam cogitationem a nobis stipularetus) aut oportet eum sibimet causam esse, & e gratuito bonitatis suae fonte eligere, quibus substantiam illam foederis . . . donare gratuito velit." *De substantia*, 211–12.

77. "Ut electio Dei ita defendatur, ut consentiat cum vocatione atque adeo cum natura Dei libera, veraci, iusta, sapiente." *De substantia*, 327. ". . . vero non addita erga reprobos incomprehensibili quidem, sed iusto tamen & adorando Dei iudicio." Ibid., 3.

78. ". . . causae omnes cur Deus non nisi poenitentibus & credentibus in Filium peccatorum remissionem annunciet atque promittat, & annunciando poenitentiam & fidem simul generet, & quidem non in omnibus audientibus verbum, sed in quibus & quando ipse vult, cum sit agens liberum, in natura Dei inclusae sunt." *De substantia*, 291. (The Dutch rendering of this passage in *Geschriften van Caspar Olevianus* [Den Haag: Het Reformatorische Boek, 1963], 321, mistranslates the Latin to mean that the elect, not the causes of election, are included in the nature of God: "Hij verwekt tevens het berouw door de verkondiging, weliswaar niet in allen, die het Woord horen, maar alleen in diegenen, die naar Zijn wil in de natuur van God besloten zijn.") "Etsi enim Deus sit agens liberum (unde etiam electio & secundem eam efficax vocatio libera ei est & manebit in aeternum), tamen promittendo singulis & promissionem signando obligat se, & sic infirmitati nostrae se accomodans adimit sibi ultro libertatem mutandi sententiam." *De substantia*, 324. "Validissimam firmissimamque causam passionis Domini adducit, aeternum inquam Dei consilium & beneplacitum. Ita, inquit, placuit Deo. Quod autem Deo placet de eo nefas est, inquirere cur placeat. Quia credimus, Deum esse summe bonum, summeque sapientiam. Unde sequitur, ea, in quibus ipse beneplacitum (ut ita dicam) habet, optime esse." Comm. on Isaiah 53:10, *Notae in Evangelia*, 114. Does Olevianus mean here that they are "optima" because of or independent of God's good pleasure?

whom God fulfills the condition of the covenant should coincide exactly with those whom He had chosen from eternity as
His covenant partners. In other words, the covenant should
have to do only with the elect. This is, in fact, the way Olevianus
argues in his earlier writings. Predestination and the *duplex
beneficium* of the covenant are links in the same chain of salvation: God justifies and purges those whom He has chosen for
union with Him.[79] It is the elect whom He awakens from eternal
death and gathers to Himself through the power of His Word
and Spirit; *in electis* that He fulfills the mandate of the covenant;
to the elect that Christ betroths Himself in an eternal covenant
and communicates His benefits.[80] Indeed, the justice of God demanded that He not enter into covenant with the godless, for
that would have created the soteriological absurdity of the Just
(i.e., Christ) dying for the unjust (i.e., the nonelect). Christ is the
Savior only *corporis sui*.[81] The boundaries of the covenant of
grace do not extend beyond the boundaries of election.

In his *magnum opus* on the covenant in 1585, however, Olevianus refines this position somewhat. As we noticed earlier, he
works in this treatise with a distinction between the *substantia*
of the covenant, the blessings themselves that God has promised, and the *administratio* of the covenant, the application of
these blessings in the context of the visible Church. He implies
a further distinction, however, between a general administration of the covenant promise to all within the visible Church—

79. Comm. on Rom. 8:28, pp. 375–77, 379–80 (see n. 72 above for quotation). ". . . ideo certo confido Deum quos ad hanc *koinonian* elegit, iustificare,
atque etiam purgare ad sanctitatem vitae innocentiam." *Expositio,* 178.

80. "Ich glaube, dass der Sohn Gottes aus dem ganzen menschlichen Geschlect . . . sich ein Volk, dass er zum ewigen Leben aus Gnaden, ohne alles Ver-
dienst, auserwählt hat, sammelt, welches er durch die Predigt seines Wortes
und die Kraft seines Geistes jetzt in diesem Leben auferwecket von dem ewigen
Tod. . . . Er macht auch einen ewigen Bund, und verlobt sich mit diesem Volk
als mit seiner Braut." Sudhoff, *Fester Grund,* 1590 ed., 157–58. ". . . Deus mandat
& mandando efficit in electis hoc ipsum quod mandat." Comm. on Rom. 2:25–
28, pp. 113–14. Cf. also Comm. on Rom 9:11, pp. 431, 434, and *Expositio,* 177.

81. "Zu dem erfordert auch die gerechtigkeit Gottes, der gesagt hatt, Exod.
13 vs. 7: Ich will den gottlosen nicht gerecht sprechen, das er nit mit gottlosen
und ungerechten einen bund und freundtschafft machte, es were dan, das der
gerechte (nemlich Christus) stürb für die ungerechten, I Petr. 3, vs. 18." Reu,
Vester Grundt, 1567 ed., 1334; *De substantia,* 71.

elect and nonelect alike—and a special administration of the *substance* of this promise to the elect alone. When, for example, the Lord stated in Genesis 7:10ff, "This is my covenant which you shall keep between me and you: . . . every male child among you shall be circumcised . . . and so shall my covenant be in your flesh," He had in view, according to Olevianus, the outward administration of the covenant promise to all of Israel. Every (male) Israelite was to receive this physical circumcision. But not all of those circumcised physically were also circumcised spiritually. Moses's promise in Deuteronomy 30:6 that "the Lord your God shall circumcise your hearts and the hearts of your seed" referred to the administration of the substance of the covenant promise only to the elect. Only they received this spiritual circumcision.[82]

The same is true in the Church today, Olevianus argues later on. It is not within the Church's power to exclude from the sacramental administration of the covenant (promise) any who outwardly profess their faith and testify to their conversion. Nevertheless, while the reprobate in the visible Church partake of the visible signs of the covenant, they do not partake of its substance.[83] By their refusal to believe the promises of remission and renewal, they become, in fact, covenant profaners.[84]

82. *De substantia,* 1–3. "Also da Gott sagt im ersten buch Mosis am 17.cap. Das ist mein bund den jn halten solt zwischen mir und euch, unnd deinem samen nach dir, Ein jegliches knablein, wann es act tag alt ist, solt jhr beschneiden, usw. wil er nicht, dass die beschneidung das wesen des bunds selbst sey, welches war die innerliche beschneidung oder reinigung des hertzen durch Christum, . . . sonder dass die Beschneidung diss ampt unnd gebrauch haben solte, dass so fern sie dem Glauben Abrahae folgeten, Gott jhnen damit zusagte an eyds statt, . . . dass er jhr und jhrer kinder gnediger gott seyn wolte durch Christum." "Abendmahlpredigten," no. 8, *Gnadenbund,* 468.

83. "Cum enim in arbitrio Ecclesiae non sit eos a testimoniis foederis arcere, qui fidem & resipiscentiam profitentur, ad communem eorum usurpationem eos admittere cogitur; sed ita ut iis non sanctificentur, verum ipsi contactu suo ea polluant . . . ; non autem per externam testimoniorum usurpationem, sine fide unius illius sanctae Ecclesiae membra fiant. . . . Sic accipiendae parabolae de sagena, de agro, de decem virginibus, nempe de externa usurpatione testimoniorum absque communione, absque substantia foederis eiusque effectis." Ibid., 220–21.

84. "Sic non vult Dominus ut impius assumat foedus ipsius in os suum: Quia cum foederis finis sit fides & poenitentia, impius autem reipsa finem hunc a foedere avellat, foedus ipsum corrumpit atque profanat, Psalm 50." Ibid., 197.

As we saw in Chapter I, there has been considerable disagreement in the secondary literature on Olevianus about how he understood the relationship of the covenant to both election and nonelection. We are now in a position to draw some conclusions of our own. First of all, we have found no evidence for the common argument that Olevianus's covenant of grace serves to temper the doctrine of double predestination. On the contrary, there is at the center of his theology an integral relationship between covenant and predestination, a relationship in which the covenant, by its very definition as reconciliation with God through justification and sanctification, is seen as part of the *unfolding* of God's decree to elect, to call the elect, to justify the called, and to sanctify the just (Rom. 8:29–30). Sometimes, in fact, Olevianus goes so far as to place the covenant of grace within what later Reformed theologians would call a "supralapsarian" predestinarian framework. In deciding to choose some and reject others, God also decided that to reach this two-fold goal He would create a perfect human race, that this race would fall of its own volition, and that through His incarnate Son He would reconcile to Himself the part of fallen humanity He had selected from eternity. It certainly lay within God's power to create a humanity not only pure but incapable of falling, but that would have eliminated any possibility of demonstrating His holiness and righteousness to those whom He had decreed to reprobate or His boundless mercy to those whom He had decreed to save.[85]

---

85. ". . . fons salutis nostrae erat, aeternum illud & immutabile Dei decretum, ut in Filio suo unigenito nos adoptaret, eos nimirum quos fide donare decreverat: alios quos non decreverat donare fide, iusto iudicio puniret. . . . Ad utrunque scopum perveniret, hunc simul decrevit exequendi modum: 1. Ut hominem purum conderet. 2. Is autem sponte, nulla coactione peccaret. 3. Ut Deus ex tota multitudine aeque damnatorum eligerit quos ab aeterno in Christo adoptare decreverat. . . . Omnipotentiam quidem suam testari potuisset primum condendo hominem non modo purum, sed etiam ita labi non posset; verum eo pacto non fuisset strata via tum ipsius iustitae in declaranda iusta sua ira in puniendis iis ob peccata sponte commissa, quos non eligere, sed reprobare decreverat; nec etiam via perveniendi ad manifestationem summae suae misericordiae in eligendis iis & gratis servandis, qui non minus sponte sua in exitium corruerunt, quam alij." *De substantia*, 28–30. To Verhoeven ("Olevianus", 78, n. 7) it appears from this passage "dat Olevianus het zgn. infralapsaristische standpunt benadert," but I think he has misread Olevianus here. The decree of predestination is shaped and controlled by God's desire to manifest his mercy through election and his justice through reprobation. This most closely resembles what would later be termed a "supralapsarian" position.

Divine omnipotence cannot be divorced from the divine will, and God had willed to judge and to reconcile.[86] What was required for a covenant or reconciliation, therefore, was a second party (creation), an estrangement (fall), and an eternal mediation (redemption through Christ). The covenant of grace follows as a perfectly logical consequence of the eternal double decree.

Second, the relationship of the covenant to the nonelect in the visible Church is both broader and clearer than scholars in the past have supposed. Diestel, Schrenk, and Baker understood the relationship too narrowly ("The covenant in Olevianus has to do only with the elect"[87]), and Berkhof too imprecisely ("The question remains unanswered, whether and in how far the nonelect are covenant children also in the sight of God"[88]). De Jong's contention that for Olevianus the nonelect in the visible Church "sustain some relationship to the covenant and its promises"[89] is actually nearest Olevianus's mature position, though still somewhat vague. It is a relationship only to the external administration of the covenant through the Word and sacraments, not to the substance or real benefits of the covenant administered internally by the Holy Spirit. The nonelect bear the marks of the covenant in their flesh but not in their hearts.

Signs of the Covenant

Three Senses

When he discusses the signs of the covenant, Olevianus uses the terms *signa, sigilla,* and *testimonia foederis* interchangeably but not always in the same sense. He usually has in mind either: 1) a signification of the substance of the covenant; 2) a signification of the mutuality of the covenant; or 3) the signs as covenants themselves. We shall examine each of these three senses in turn.

We find a clue to the first meaning already in the titles to Part II of *De substantia,* the only place in Olevianus's works where the sacraments are treated in comprehensive, systematic fashion. On the title page of *De substantia,* Part II is called *De mediis, qui-*

---

86. *De substantia,* 30–1.
87. Schrenk, *Gottesreich und Bund,* 61.
88. Berkhof, *Systematic Theology,* 285.
89. De Jong, *Covenant Idea,* 25.

bus ea ipsa substantia nobis communicatur, but on the first page of the section itself (p. 247) it is entitled *De testimoniis foederis gratuiti.* By placing these two titles side by side, we have Olevianus's first definition in a nutshell. A covenant sign or *testimonium,* he suggests, is first of all something that testifies to or calls our attention to the substance of the covenant, something that designates where God's offer of reconciliation can be found. God enters into covenant or fellowship with the Church at a prearranged place or by certain preestablished means, namely, the ministry of the Word and sacraments.[90] It is here that the covenant as the promise of reconciliation is transformed into the covenant as reconciliation itself; here, to use Olevianus's terms, the *substantia* or benefits of the covenant promise are administered to and realized in the lives of believers. It is not, in the case of the sacraments at least, that the covenant *signa* or *media* possess in themselves any special power to justify. The example of the penitent thief on the cross is sufficient, Olevianus believes, to show that in certain circumstances one can be saved quite apart from the sacraments. Nevertheless, they are the means which God has ordained as the *loci* or channels of His grace, and willfully to disregard (*contemnere*) them is to disregard the covenant itself.[91]

The signs of the covenant in the Church, says Olevianus, are of two sorts—*testimonia audibilia* and *testimonia visibilia.*[92] The oral witness is the Word of the covenant of grace, the covenant promise; the visible testimonies are the sacraments of baptism

90. ". . . de testimoniis, quibus Deus de hac ipsa substantia foederis testatur." *De substantia,* 247. "Init foedus sive *koinonian* cum Ecclesia per ministeriam Verbi & Sacramentorum." *Expositio,* 36.

91. "Quorsum igitur Sacramenta? Non ut iustificent, sed ut sint signa atque sigilla iustitiae fidei, quibus . . . Deus nobis iustitiam in Christo crucifixo gratis offert." Comm. on Gal. 2:21, p. 37. "Dicimus autem ex scripturis sanctificationem omnem signorum, hoc est, separationem eorum a rebus profanis ad usum sacrum, hunc nimirum ut sint testimonia visibilia gratiae a Deo in Christo crucifixo promissae, ex ordinatione Dei ad illum usum pendere, & non esse qualitatem aliquam signis impressam." *De substantia,* 412–13. "Deus quidem non ita alligavit se ad Sacramenta, quin etiam absque iis foedus contrahat seu efficaciter vocet, ut latronem in cruce (hinc illa distinctio apud veteres, Baptismus flaminis, sanguinis, fluminus) sed nos alligavit ut nemo ea contemnere possit absque contemtu foederis." Ibid., 422. Cf. also 309.

92. "Testimonia autem divina ordinaria in Ecclesia . . . sunt partim audibilia, partim etiam visibilia. . . . Audible testimonium est verbum foederis gratuiti. . . . Sacramenta [sunt] visibilia testimonia." Ibid., 250, 311.

and the Lord's Supper. Although Olevianus devotes by far the greater part of his space to a discussion of the sacraments, he still claims that the principal means (*praecipuum*) by which the benefits of the covenant are offered is the proclamation of the *promissio Evangelij*.[93] In the first place, it is in conjunction with the preaching of the Word that the Holy Spirit creates faith in the elect. To ask, he says, whether it is possible to be given faith apart from the external hearing of the Word—that is, in some other kind of revelation—is to ask whether one can live without breathing or without food. But along with faith one also receives, initially and then in greater measure, the object of faith: Christ Himself clothed with the promises of forgiveness and renewal. The substance of the covenant, then, may never be separated from the witness of the Word,[94] for it is through the proclamation of the promise that the content of the promise is offered.

The sacraments, or *testimonia visibilia foederis,* are annexed to this oral proclamation of the gospel as *appendices* of the covenant promise.[95] They, too, are covenant signs in Olevianus's first sense of the term, for they signify or identify the covenant of grace by confirming and underscoring the promise of reconciliation.

Baptism, first of all, is a testimony to our incorporation into the covenant of grace, that is, to our entrance into communion with Christ and His benefits of forgiveness and new life. The washing with water signifies our purification both from the guilt

93. "Praecipuum ergo quo Deus substantiam foederis gratuiti nobis seminique nostro coniunctim offert, est promissio Evangelij solenniter promulgati." Ibid., 309. Cf. also 311.
94. "Placet enim Deo testificatione verbi velut medio, non modo fidem semel creare, sed etiam conservare & augere, ac per eam foederis quoque illam substantiam electis universis non tantum semel communicare, sed etiam quotidie & in finem usque semel inchoatam *koinonian* suis velut gradibus promovere, nempe in annunciatione poenitentiae & remissionis peccatorum in nomine Christi . . . seu quotidiana vocatione per doctrinam Evangelij, qua nobis offertur Christus vestitus foedere gratiae seu promissione remissionis peccatorum & donationis Spiritus." Ibid., 248. "Quaeritur, an non possit dari fides sine externo auditu verbi, scilicet per revelationem sine verbo? Respondeo, Idem est, ac si roges, an homo nequeat vivere sine respiratione, sine cibo?" Comm. on Rom. 10:14, p. 538. ". . . igitur Deus substantiam illam foederis a testimonia verbi . . . non vult esse separatam. . . . Nunquam enim remissio peccatorum & Spiritus sancti communicatio separanda est a testimonia verbi." *De substantia*, 249.
95. ". . . sacramenta eius sunt appendices ceu *sphagides* promissionem obsignantes." Ibid., 309.

of sin and, in some measure, from its corruption.[96] Olevianus is always insistent, of course, that baptism is not a cause but only a sign of this double benefit of the covenant.[97] It is the Holy Spirit who purifies, not the water. But he will go so far as to say that the water of baptism is more than mere water (*schlect wasser*), for the water is so bound to the promise of God that the physical cleansing becomes if not the instrument at least the occasion for the spiritual cleansing. In every baptism there are two parallel baptizers, two baptizands, and two washings. As the outer self is washed with water by the minister, the inner self is washed with the blood of Christ by the Holy Spirit. Physical baptism is still only a sign or outward testimony of spiritual baptism, but the two events do coincide and are bound together in the relationship between promise and sign. That is what Paul meant in Titus 3:5, says Olevianus, when he referred to Holy Baptism as "the bath of rebirth and renewal by the Holy Spirit."[98]

If baptism is the means whereby we are incorporated into the covenant of grace, the Lord's Supper is the means whereby that covenant bond is renewed and confirmed. In baptism our *Ge-*

96. "Baptismus enim insitionem nostram in foedus gratuitum, eiusque Mediatorem Christum testificatur & obsignat, atque ita imputatam iustitiam & regenerationis initium." Ibid., 334. "Primum, enim pro accepto Baptismi testimonio, cum cruenta Christi victima *koinonias* initio . . . laetis animis gratiae agimus." Ibid., 355. ". . . testimonio Baptismi sumus in Christo gratis adoptati & regeniti & eiusmodi gradibus ad complementum deducitur." Ibid., 356. "Ipsa enim tinctio quae sit aqua mundationem notat Act.22.v.16. Ea sit partim remissione, partim renovatione Ephes. 5." Ibid., 332.
97. "Non est causa iustificationis Baptismus, sed signum sacrum eius iustificationis, quam per fidem in sanguinem Christi habet Ecclesia & singula eius membra." Comm. on Gal. 5:6, p. 109.
98. "Der Tauff ist . . . nicht schlect wasser, sonder ein wasser in Gottes gebott verfasset und mit Gottes verheissung verbunden, nemlich . . . dass das blut Jesu Christi, des Sohns Gottes, uns reiniget von allen unsern Sünden, und dass er uns durch den heiligen Geist . . . ernewern wölle zum ewigen leben. . . . Wasser thuts freylich . . . nicht, sonder der heilig Geist . . . durch die verheissung, so mit unnd bey dem wasser ist. . . . Dann ohn das wort der verheissung ist das wasser schlecht wasser und kein Tauff, aber mit der verheissung Gottes ists ein Tauff des lebens unnd ein bad der Widergeburt im heiligen Geist, wie S. Paulus sagt zum Tito am 3.cap." Reu, "Fürschlag," 1319, 1321. "Im H. Tauff sind zu betrachten zweierley waschung, zweierley Prediger oder ausspender des Tauffs, zweierley Menschen, so getaufft werden. Der eusserlich Mensch wirdt mit dem eusserlichen Tauffwasser begossen vom eusserlichen diener oder Prediger. . . . Der innerlich mensch wirt in dem blut Christi gewaschen durch den H. Geist." Reu, "Kurtzer Underricht," 1328.

meinschaft (communion) with Christ and His *duplex beneficium* is begun; in the Lord's Supper it is increased. The supper is the place where the marriage vows between Christ the Bridegroom and the Church His Bride are repeated and where the relationship between them is strengthened.[99] It is here, as in the proclamation of the Gospel, that Christ communicates Himself and that the believer grows in communion with Him by feeding on His crucified body and blood.[100] Although one is incorporated only once into Christ and thus need only be baptized once, to *develop* in faith and fellowship with Christ, one has to feed frequently at His table.[101]

Covenant signs for Olevianus, then, are first of all testimonies to the place or means that God has chosen to communicate the substance of His covenant promise. But they are also, in the second place, testimonies to the *mutuality* of the covenant between God and us.[102] We know that for Olevianus the covenant in the

---

99. "Wozu dann noch das hl. Abendmahl? . . . Dass durch diese öffentliche und fröhliche Handlung der Bund zwischen Christo dem Breutgam und der Kirchen seiner Braut erneuert und also die Gemeinschaft der Kirchen mit ihrem Breutgam vermehret werde." Sudhoff, "Abendmahlpredigten," no. 2, 196. Cf. his reference to this relationship as a "solenni contractu ceu sponsalibus." *De substantia*, 316. See also *Gnadenbund*, 320–21, and *De substantia*, 362–63.

100. "Wie in der täglichen Verkündigung des hl. Evangeliums die Seele mit dem gekreuzigten Sohn Gottes Jesu Christo als dem einigen wahren Himmelsbrot gespeiset wird, und also zunimmt in der Gemeinschaft des Liebes und Blutes Christ. . . : Also ist es auch gewiss, dass wann wir mit wahrem Vertrauen die Gedächtniss des gekreuzigten Leibes und vergossenen Blutes Christi halten im hlgn. Abendmahle, dass die Gemeinschaft seines Leibes und Blutes in unseren Herzen durch den hl. Geist zunimmt." Sudhoff, "Abendmahlpredigten," no. 5, 214.

101. "Postremo Baptismum repeti fas non est. Quia, cum Baptismus sit Sacramentum adoptionis & regenerationis, ut semel tantum adoptamur atque renascimur, non saepius; ita testimonium eius non iteratur. Sacrae Eucharistiae alia est ratio, quia semel renati in celebratione beneficiorum frequentes esse debent, & in Christo crescere; ideoque testimonium celebrationis & augmenti *koinonias* saepe ab iis usurpari." *De substantia*, 333.

102. "Iam ad visibilia illa testimonia quod attinet, primum videndum an ea immediate annexa sint corpori & sanguini Christi, an vero promissioni seu mutuo foederi. Respondeo, non corpori & sanguini immediate, sed mediate sunt sigilla promissionis de unica oblatione corporis Christi pro omnibus & solis fidelibus, & una applicatione eorumdem per fidem & Spiritum Sanctum atque ita mutui foederis gratuiti." Ibid., 407–8. ". . . atque ita actiones illae sigilla sunt mutuae confoederationis inter Deum & nos." Ibid., 408. ". . . actio illa est Testimonium foederis mutui inter Deum & nos." Ibid., 411. ". . . Sacramentum seu testimonium mutui foederis." Ibid., 414.

narrower sense cannot be realized in us without a covenant in the broader sense: the unilateral promise of reconciliation demands a bilateral commitment to its terms. God may offer peace, but we must pledge to keep it. God may write the treaty, but we must sign it if its provisions are to be put into effect. This, in Olevianus's view, is precisely what happens in the sacraments. The sacraments represent not merely the substance of the covenant but an *act of mutual covenanting* by which that substance is offered and received. It is here that both parties come together and ratify the pact of reconciliation.

In signifying the mutual covenant of grace, the sacramental ceremony itself takes on a covenantal structure for Olevianus. All the features of an ordinary covenant are there—promises, conditions, responses, and seals. The two main divisions in the administration of a sacrament are the *administratio doctrinae* and the *administratio signi,* each with its own "covenantal" elements.[103] The first part, the administration of doctrine, is the proclamation of the Word or divine *oblatio* of grace in the promises of the gospel. This *oblatio* always carries with it God's command or condition of faith, our need to recognize that we are wholly dependent on the grace offered in the gospel. "He who *believes* and is baptized will be saved," Olevianus quotes from Mark 16, "but he who does not believe will be condemned."[104] He makes clear, however, that this is not a *legalis conditio,* one which we can fulfill in our own strength, but an *Evangelica conditio,* one which God fulfills in His elect when He awakens faith through the preaching of the Gospel.[105]

The second main part of the sacramental-covenantal ceremony is the administration of the signs, whereby the oral prom-

---

103. "Duo itaque sunt in administratione cuiusque Sacramenti, doctrinae administratio & signi." Ibid., 323.

104. "Ita gradus tres sunt in administratione sigillorum. 1. Oblatio foederis totiusque eius substantiae, per praedicationem Evangelij in articulis fidei comprehensae: cuius summatia repetitio sit in promissione & comminatione, institutione cuiusque Sacramenti posita ut in Baptismo: Qui crediderit (scilicet Evangelio) & baptizatus fuerit salvus erit; qui non crediderit condemnabitur." Ibid., 329.

105. "Qui tamen modus, quo fruitio victimae ad nos pervenit . . . non est legalis conditio; quia non impletur ex nostris viribus, sed Deus mandando efficit in electis id ipsum quod mandat. Ideoque si modus conditio vocanda est, Evangelica vocetur necesse est. Cum autem promissio proponatur sub conditione Evangelica, seu eo modo ut fide accipiatur." Ibid., 410–1.

ises between God and us are visibly ratified or sealed. The *administratio signi* is a public reenactment of the private agreement between God and the believer reached in the *administratio doctrinae,* but with one major difference: God switches roles with us. In the *administratio doctrinae* it is God who promises and we who respond; here it is we who first promise and God who responds: we, in the binding (*obligatio*) of our consciences or our assent of faith to the promises offered in the Gospel; and He, in the sealing (*obsignatio*) of the content of those promises in our hearts.[106] Through the *testimonia visibilia,* both parties to the covenant bind themselves to the articles or promises of the covenant proposed by God. We seal our faith in them; God seals His faithfulness to them.

God's visible *obsignatio* of his oral *oblatio* takes place only after our visible *obligatio* to His oral *conditio.* This order of the administration, Olevianus feels, is of the utmost importance. In the first place, it has an ancient biblical precedent. In establishing the covenant of grace with Abraham, God began with the gospel promise, then added His command of faith and repentance, and finally introduced the sign of mutual ratification, circumcision.[107] But the order of this and every administration of the covenant has ultimately to do with the purpose of God's eternal decree. The goal of the decree was to communicate the benefits of the covenant to the elect and to remove all excuse from the reprobate, so that through both His mercy and His justice God might receive glory. By placing the command of faith and the warning about unbelief before the seal of the promise of grace, God removes Himself from the awkward position of having to impart His blessings to those who

---

106. "2. Conscientiae obligatio, quod consentiat per Dei gratiam, seu stipulatio assensus conscientiae in oblatum foedus totamque eius substantiam in Christo; aut si mentiatur, quod iure a tota substantia foederis excludatur, & condemnetur. 3. Obsignatio ex parte Dei erga conscientiam sic affectam per ipsius gratiam, iuratum foedus eiusque totam substantiam ratum ei fore in aeternum nec esse periculum mutationis sententiae, aut si eius non memor fuerit, se non fore sanctum Deum Psalm 89." Ibid., 329–30. "In administratione vero mutuae attestionis per visibile signum, attestatio assensus nostri seu stipulatio fidei in propositos articulos Dei obsignationem velut ipsius manu imprimeda . . . antecedit." Ibid., 325. Cf. also 311–13, 326–27.

107. Ibid., 313–15.

refuse to believe. It ensures, in other words, that He binds Himself only to those who, by His grace, first bind themselves to Him.[108]

In the case of baptism, Olevianus sees this covenantal structure reflected already in the baptism of John (Matt. 3:1ff). First, the Father offers His Son through John's preaching of the Gospel, promising forgiveness and eternal life to those who repent and threatening with eternal death those who do not. Second, He instructs each person to be baptized as a sign of acceptance of the grace He has offered. Finally, He seals internally the blessings already promised the believer externally.[109] Baptism here and throughout the New Testament, then, is a sign of the mutuality of the covenant. God not only offers Himself to us, but we also outwardly engage and bind ourselves to Him. Without a corresponding inward pledge, however, we really perjure ourselves in our baptismal vows and thereby store up for ourselves greater damnation.[110]

108. "Scopo seu fini consilij divini forma haec solemniter contrahendi foedus est accommodata. Scopus enim consilij divini cum sit omnibus & solis electis foedus gratiae efficaciter communicare, quo glorificetur in immensa sua misericordia etiam in hac vita tam in anima quam in corpore electorum; reprobis vero omnem excusationem adimere, quo glorificetur in sua longanimitate & iustitia, sapientissimo consilio in eadem invitatione ad suam gratiam, quia multi hypocritae ad eam se ingerunt mandatum promissioni vult antiere in solemni foederis contractu, ut sicut electis misericorditer largitur idipsum quod mandat, ita reprobis mandatum ipsius contemnentibus se non obstringat." Ibid., 315. Cf. also 318–9.

109. Ibid., 330–31. On this Reformed attitude toward John, see David C. Steinmetz, "The Baptism of John and the Baptism of Jesus in Huldrych Zwingli, Balthasar Hubmaier and Late Medieval Theology," in *Continuity and Discontinuity in Church History,* eds. F. Church and T. George (Leiden: E. J. Brill, 1979), 169–81.

110. "Unnd dieweil wir zu keines andern leibs glidern als zu des leibe Christi, welcher sich von Johanne hat tauffen lassen, . . . getauffet seind: Ists gewiss, dass wir uns in unserm Tauff mit dem leib, welcher im Jordan getaufft ist, verlobt und verbunden haben. Unnd wann wir ein ander haupt annemen, dass wir in dem gelübd unsers Tauffs meineydig und brüchig werden." "Abendmahlpredigten," no. 2, *Gnadenbund,* 348. "Wo nun kein wahre buss unnd Glaub folgt in denen die zu ihren tagen kommen, und also von dieser Welt scheiden, dienet das eusserliche bundzeichen der heiligen Tauff nur zur grösserer verdamnis, dieweil sie den bund Gottes durch unglauben und Gottloses leben entheiliget, unnd also das leiden Jesu Christi verstossen und verachtet, ja das Blut des Testaments verunheiliget haben, Heb. 10." Ibid., no. 1, 275.

So too with the Lord's Supper. It, too, bears witness to the mutual covenant between God and us.[111] There, too, as Olevianus puts it, "Christ and we swear together, with hearts and hands united."[112] Again, all the components of a covenant are present. At the Last Supper Christ first promised that He would sacrifice His body and blood in our stead and on our behalf, that He would put that sacrifice on eternal display before the Father in heaven, and that He would strengthen the mystical bond between Himself, the Head, and us, the members of His body.[113] To this promise He joined a command, namely, that we accept this promise in faith. Olevianus does not overlook the fact that in the biblical accounts of the Last Supper the command ("Take, eat, . . . drink . . .") actually precedes the promise (". . . this is the New Testament . . ."), but he argues that according to their meaning the two are reversed. It is as if Christ had said: *Because* I promise, *therefore* believe."[114] He also admits that there is no *expressed* promise of union with Christ in the words of institution. He does suggest, nonetheless, that in the command to take, eat, and drink, a union with the Offering is implied. In the same way in which a promise of spiritual circumcision is implicit in the command to be circumcised and a promise of spiritual rebirth in the command to be born again, a promise of union with Christ through spiritual eating and drinking is included in the command to eat and

111. ". . . actio visibilis sit testimonium mutui foederis inter Deum & nos." Ibid., 409.

112. Reu, "Bauern Catechismus," 1313.

113. "Was seinds dann für wort der verheissung, in welche er diss brot und wein verfasset? Erstlich verheisst er damit, dass er seinen leib fur uns und also an unser statt geben wil und sein blut fur uns lassen vergiessen. Zum andern, dass er mit dem opffer seines leibs und bluts fur uns wil im Himmel erscheinen (Heb. 8:1). Zum dritten, dass er sich mit uns durch seinen heiligen Geist wil vereinigen, als das haupt mit den glidern." Reu, "Fürschlag," 1323.

114. "Neque est quod ordinem syllabarum aucupemur. Etsi enim mandatum videatur praete[n]dere, ACCIPETE, EDITE, & promissionem sequi, HOC EST CORPUS MEUM, certum tamen est, in sensu promissionem anteire; mandatum, ut eam amplectamur, sequi, ac si diceret: Quoniam corpus meum, me pro vobis traditurum, & sanguinem meum pro vobis effusum iri promitto, ut vester sit cibus & potus, agite fideli & grato animo ranto dono fruimini." *De substantia*, 339–40.

drink the bread and wine.[115] Promise and command, then, are intimately bound together in the Lord's Supper, so intimately, in fact, that to accept or reject the command is to accept or reject the promise as well. It is only when we obey the command of faith that the promise is actually sealed and the mutual covenant ratified.[116]

Since Olevianus understands the *administratio signi* as a visible ratification of the covenant made in the *administratio doctrinae*, it should come as little surprise that he sometimes speaks of *signi foederis*, in the third place, as covenants themselves.[117] One finds this kind of covenant language more often in his discussion of the eucharist than of baptism and more often to describe the divine *obsignatio* than the human *obligatio*, but it occurs frequently enough to merit special attention.

Olevianus describes baptism, first of all, as God's "visible oath" (*sichtbaren Eyd*) and "sure pledge" (*gewisses pfand*) that we are reborn and forgiven just as surely as we are washed with the baptismal water. Baptism is more than a sign or symbol of the covenant; it is itself a covenant—a "divine token" (*Gottlich warzeichen*) or mark that we "wear on our bodies till the grave."[118] He

115. "Deinde promittentia unionem cum eadem semel oblata victima ad vitam aeternam; quae unionis promissio in verbis, HOC EST NOVUM TESTAMENTUM deserte testimonio Ieremiae expressa: mandato vero accipiendi, edendi, bibendi per analogiam inclusa est. Sicut enim mandato circumcisionis inclusa erat iuxta analogiam promissio circumcisionis spiritualis . . . & mandato Christi oportere omnino nos renasci Ioan. 3. promissio regenerationis spiritualis, seu gratuitae adoptionis propter victimam Christi & renovationis Spiritus Sancti, qui cum eam nos unit; ita & mandato accipiendi, edendi, bibendi, secundam analogiam inclusa est promissio unionis & ex parte Dei per Spiritum, ex parte nostra per fidem ab ipso datam, cum eadem victima." Ibid., 385–86.

116. "Etenim ita sunt unita promissio & mandatum sicut in verbi praedicatione, ita in Sacramentis, ut nemo fiat particeps rei promissae qui testimonium contemnit." Ibid., 421–22. ". . . ita nec e victima cruenta Christi vitam aeternam quisquam percipit nisi qui Spiritu & fide cum ea uniatur . . . ita victimae pro omnibus oblatae unio erga singulos sit propria quam Dominus cuique largitus est fide." Ibid., 393, 394.

117. "Sciendum duas esse partes foederis, promissionem & repromissionem. Signum autem vocatur foedus, nempe testimonium & signum visibile. Ergo quemadmodum in verbo sive foedere audibili, non promittit nisi sub conditione, ita nec in verbo visibili; id est, signo, aliter promittit." Comm. on Rom. 2:17, p. 108.

attaches a much wider variety of covenantal labels to the eucharistic signs: *offentlich zeugnus, Eid, sichtbarer Eid, sichtbare Eydspflicht, Pfand, gewisses Pfandt, sichtbares Pfand, Brief und Siegel, sichtbares Siegel,* and *Siegel und gottliches Pfand.* Once again these almost always refer to God's covenant promises, not ours. The bread and wine are visible pledges on God's part that His Son has suffered His bloody death for us who believe, that we are eternally pardoned from our sins, that through the Holy Spirit He renews us and accepts us as members of Christ, and that our union and fellowship with Christ will continue to increase until it is perfected in eternity. In short, the sacramental signs are God's visible affirmation that He keeps His covenant.[119]

That the Lord's Supper is indeed a *sichtbarer eyd Gottes* can be demonstrated, Olevianus believes, from the words of institution themselves. Christ claimed that the cup (or more accurately the wine in the cup) was the New Covenant in His blood which would be poured out for many for the remission of sins. It is clear, however, that when Scripture uses the terms *Bund*

118. "Im heiligen Tauff bezeuget uns Gott, als mit einem sichtbaren eyd, dass wir so gewiss durch das blut und Geist Christi von allen unsern sünden gewaschen seind, so gewiss wir mit dem Tauffwasser gewaschen oder begossen seyn." "Abendmahlpredigten," no. 3, *Gnadenbund,* 352. ". . . wirdt auch darumb der Tauff die abwaschung der sünden unnd das bad der widergeburt genennet, dass der eusserliche Tauff ein gewisses pfand und Gottlich warzeichen ist, dass wir so gewisslich durch das blut unnd geist Christi newgeboren unnd vergebung der sünden haben, als wir mit dem eusserlichen Tauffwasser getaufft seyn." Reu, "Kurtzer Underricht," 1328. ". . . usque in sepulchrum gestamus testimonium gratiae & fidei sive foederis inter Deum et nos in nostro corpore, & illud foedus est. Galatae post Baptismum peccaverant, revocat tamen eis Baptismum in memoriam." Comm. on Gal. 3:27, p. 81.

119. ". . . ein offentlich zeugnus sey, das Gott seinen eyd und bund gehalten, und uns von den sünden und ewigen todt durch das opffer des leibs und bluts Jesu Christi erlöset habe." "Abendmahlpredigten," no. 8, *Gnadenbund,* 435. ". . . dass nemlich der heilig Wein . . . darumb das vergossen Blut Christi genant wirdt, dass er dir eine erinnerung und gewisses pfandt sey, dass . . . für dich zur vergebung aller deiner sünden, das Blut Christi einmal am creutz vergossen sey." Ibid., no. 1, 286. ". . . hat auch Christus das heilig gebrochne Brod und Wein zu unserm Troste eingesetzt, dass sie uns ein sichtbarer Eid Gottes sein sollen, dabei uns Gott schwört, dass der ewige Friede zwischen ihm und uns gemacht sei, und dass er uns durch den hl. Geist erneuere und zu Gliedern seines Sohnes angenommen . . . habe . . . , und [dass wir] je länger je mehr ihm eingeleibt werden und endlich ihm gleichformig sein werden in der ewigen Klarheit." Sudhoff, "Abendmahlpredigten," no. 8, 195.

Gottes or *Testament Gottes*, it always means an *Eid Gottes* with which God promises His grace and binds Himself to us. Since the wine at the Last Supper is called the *Bund Gottes*, and since we should always read *Eid* for *Bund* in Scripture, it follows, Olevianus concludes, that the wine itself is a visible *Eid* or *Bund* of God by which He reaffirms His promises of grace.[120] The believer can be confident that as surely as the bread is broken and the wine poured out before his eyes, Christ's body was broken and His blood shed for his soul[121]—as surely, in fact, as if God were swearing an oral oath from heaven. Olevianus even implies that it would be preferable if God did speak to us directly but that like the Old Testament Israelites we could not bear the sound of His voice. God has, therefore, accommodated Himself to our weakness and resorted to nonverbal oaths instead. In lieu of His actual voice He has chosen the elements of the Supper to serve as "covenants" of His covenant.[122]

Olevianus does not hold, however, that the eucharistic elements are exclusively *divine* pledges or covenants. To the extent that they signify a mutual act of covenanting, they become, in his eyes, human covenants as well. Participation in the supper is the means by which we, as it were, sign a promissory note (*syngrapha*) binding ourselves (or rather having ourselves bound) to God.[123] The supper becomes for us, as it

120. "Nu aber ist es gewiss, dass wo die heilig Schrifft von dem bund Gottes . . . meldung thut so verstehet sie den eyd Gottes, damit er uns seine gnad verheisset, unnd sich also uns verbindet. . . . Darauss schliss ich, dieweil der sichtbar wein der Bund Gottes genant wirdt, und als der Bund eben der eyd Gottes ist, so muss folgen, dass der heilig sichtbar wein uns ein sichbarer eyd Gottes ist, damit er seinen Bund der gnaden mit seinen gläubigen vor ihren augen erfrischet, besigelt und in statiger gedächtnis behelt." "Abendmahlpredigten," no. 8, *Gnadenbund*, 313–14.
121. Sudhoff, "Abendmahlpredigten," no. 5, 214–15.
122. "Wir halten und glauben auch, dass die Gabe, so uns Christus durch das sakramentliche Brot und Wein an Eides Statt lässt vor Augen stellen . . . uns durch den Glauben wahrhaftig mitgetheilt werde, eben so gewiss, als wenn uns Gott einen Eid aus dem Himmel schwüre. Denn dieweil er nicht täglich aus dem Himmel mit uns reden und uns schwören will, wie wir denn auch seine Stimme nicht erdulden könnten, hat er unserer Schwachheit zu Gutem die Sakramenta an Eides Statt verordnet." Ibid., no. 8, 227.
123. ". . . sed visibili etiam testimonio velut data syngrapha singulis fidelibus id promissum confirmare, & vicissim huic duplici beneficio summo & quidem gratuito, eos subscribere, ac vicissim ipsa actione se redemtori obstringere aut potius ab ipsomet redemtore eos sibi obstringi voluit." *De substantia*, 392.

is for God, a visible oath of obligation, an oath by which we swear our total dependence on the righteousness of Christ, our gratitude to Him for His gift of redemption, and our resolve to live a life according to His commandments. Public ingestion of the elements is, in sum, our pledge or our covenant that "as He wholly belongs to us, we wish also wholly to belong to Him."[124]

Unbelievers

We are able to deal now with the question of the "Lutheranness" of Olevianus's sacramental doctrine, particularly as it relates to the participation of unbelievers in the Lord's Supper. As was mentioned in Chapter I, Otto Ritschl claimed in his *Dogmengeschichte* that on the matter of the "objective character" of the Lord's Supper, Olevianus moved away from Calvin's position that unbelievers partake only of empty figures or signs to the more Lutheran view that the elements retain their sacramental character even for those who misuse them.[125]

An examination of the sources will show that Ritschl seriously misunderstood Olevianus. The only evidence that he cited in support of his claim was a passage in *De substantia* where Olevianus writes that "they are sacrments even for those who abuse them."[126] Olevianus's point here, however, is that as a visible *witness to God's grace*, a sacrament remains a sacrament regardless of the disposition of the participant. Baptism and the eucharist testify to God's gracious promises not because of any inherent power in the signs, or even because of the faith of the believing communicant, but because they have been so or-

124. "Sie werden auch zu unterscheiden wissen die sichtbare eydspflicht, so durchs Sakrament geschieht, von dem das damit geschworen, unnd zu beyden seyten gehalten wirdt, nemlich, dass . . . wir solche wolthat mit höchsten danck annemen." "Abendmahlpredigten," no. 8, *Gnadenbund*, 495. "Was hulden und schweren wir herwiderumb dem Herrn Jesu Christo in seinem H. Abendmahl? Zwey ding. Erstlich, dass wir all unser gerechtigkeit und leben ausserhalb unser in Christo als dem wahren himmelbrot suchen wöllen. Zum andern, dass wir durch seine gnade einen ernstlichen fürsatz haben, nach allen seinen gebotten zu leben. Und in summa, wie er gantz unser, also wir auch gantz sein eigen seyn wollen." Reu, "Bauern Catechismus," 1313.
125. See Chapter I, n. 65.
126. *De substantia*, 413.

dained by God. The belief or unbelief of the participant does not alter their role as covenant testimonies.[127]

More than that, Olevianus's entire doctrine of the Lord's Supper is clearly anti-Lutheran in tone and emphasis. In his "Abendmahlpredigten" in particular he spares no words in attacking the Lutheran doctrines of ubiquity, corporal presence under the species of bread and wine, and oral manducation.[128] To be sure, he does hold that in the supper we feed on the *verus Christus*, the "true, natural, and crucified body and blood of Christ."[129] But he emphasizes just as strongly that this body and blood of Christ are joined not to the bread and wine but to the promise of God that accompanies the elements. As such, the body and blood can only be received by the soul in faith, not by the hand, the mouth, or the stomach. To teach otherwise, he says, is to confuse the *testimonium* and the *res testata*.[130]

While sign and signified may not be confused, however, neither may they be completely separated. The physical eating and spiritual eating in the eucharist are temporally parallel activities. As in the sacrament of baptism, there are two corresponding administrators, two recipients, and two kinds of elements

127. "Dicamus autem ex scripturis sanctificationem omnem signorum, hoc est, separationem eorum a rebus profanis ad usum sacrum, hunc nimirum ut sint testimonia visibilia gratiae a Deo in Christo crucifixo promissae, ex ordinatione Dei ad illum usum pendere, & non esse qualitatem aliquam signis impressam, quae vel in ipsa actione eis insit . . . vel post actionem etiam reliqua maneat, ut proptera conservari debeant. . . . Non enim fides utentis facit sacrum sigillum seu Dei testimonium, sed voluntas Dei." Ibid., 412–13.

128. See esp. Sudhoff, "Abendmahlpredigten," no. 1, 192; no. 2, 200–3; no. 4, 206–8; no. 8, 228–29; and no. 9, 203–4. Cf. also *De substantia*, 356–58, 370, 401–5.

129. ". . . ut verum etiam Christum ita in cibum accipiamus. . . ." *De substantia*, 343. "Non Sacramentale corpus, aut quod signum sit seu figura nobis promitti & praestari, sed verum & naturale corpus pro nobis crucifixum." Ibid., 399–400.

130. "Haec de testimonio audibili in coena, scilicet promissione & eius unione cum re testata. Nam corpus quod pro nobis traditur, coniungitur promissioni immediate, non pani. Pani autem non nisi mediate seu secundario, quatenus scilicet panis fractio & tota illa actio visibilis ut sigillum annexum est promissioni obsignandae." Ibid., 407. "At vero pane nobis annunciat, se in crucem pro nobis velle se dare in victimam, non in pane; & quidem in victimam inferendam in coelum, non in os; fide applicandam in menti, non ventri." Ibid., 358. ". . . in latebra hac latet confusio testimonii cum re testata & tota analogia tollitur." Ibid., 402.

involved in the supper. As the physical mouth receives the bread and wine offered by the minister, the spiritual mouth (the soul by faith) receives the body and blood of Christ offered by the Holy Spirit.[131] In that sense Olevianus will go so far as to say that the body of Christ is "mediately" (*mediate*) attached to the bread, since the bread and the promise to which the body is "immediately" attached are always offered together.[132]

It is only in this context that Olevianus's view of the partaking by unbelievers can be properly understood. For while the bread and the body are always offered together, they are received together only if the recipient believes. Both believer and unbeliever bring their physical mouths to the Holy Meal, and both receive the physical elements. But since only true believers are capable of spiritual eating, only they actually receive the body and blood of Christ. Unbelieving participants add to their damnation not, as Ritschl implied, because they have partaken unworthily of the body of Christ but because they have not partaken of it at all—because, in fact, they have repudiated the offer of that body in the promise.[133] Paul does not say, "Whoever eats the *body* in an unworthy manner" but "Whoever eats the *bread*."[134]

Olevianus is not driven, then, as Ritschl suggested, to a Lutheran doctrine of the eucharist by the logic of his Reformed doctrine of the covenant. His understanding of the Lord's Supper is quite consistent both with the Calvinist tradition before him and with the rest of his own covenant theology. God applies His covenant promise of reconciliation only to those who covenant

131. Reu, "Kurtzer Underricht," 1329; Sudhoff, "Abendmahlpredigten," no. 1, 194–95 and no. 7, 222.

132. See n. 130 above.

133. ". . . quod testimonia visibilia in usu sacrae Eucharistiae non accipiantur nuda seu avulsa a promissione. Hac adeo verum est, ut etiam hypocritae non possint nudum panem edere in sacru Eucharistia, sed talem qui est annexus promissioni (ideoque fiunt rei non panis, sed corporis Christi in promissione ipsis oblati; ab ipsis vero spreti atque contempti I. Cor. 11:28, 29)." *De substantia,* 414. "Dieweil die gotlosen das gläubige hertz nicht haben, können sie auch die himmlische speiss unnd tranck nicht empfangen und werden also schuldig an dem leib Christi, eben darumb, dass sie jhn nicht empfangen, sonder durch ihr unglaubiges hertz jhn verstossen unnd verachten." Reu, "Kurtzer Underricht," 1329.

134. Sudhoff, "Abendmahlpredigten," no. 4, 209.

with Him in faith. His offer of the *res testata* must be believed to be received—around the Word, in the baptismal font, at the Lord's table. Otherwise, he insists, the *testimonium*, while still a *testimonium*, is spiritually worthless.[135]

Infant Baptism

That the covenant promises must be believed to be received raises the question of how Olevianus can consider infants of believers to be covenant members, since at their age they are incapable of the faith and obedience that God works in adults to meet the conditions of the covenant. His response here is somewhat perplexing, because it is not clear whether he considers children to be part of the covenant of grace by virtue of their baptism or by virtue of their birth to covenant parents. In several places in his "Abendmahlpredigten" he seems to suggest the former. When a baby is baptized in the name of Jesus Christ, the parents should be assured that just as certainly as the water cleanses his or her body, so certainly does the Father through the Holy Spirit seal in his or her heart *gemeynschafft* with the body and blood of Christ and, through that communion, the double benefit of the covenant—the forgiveness of sins and the beginnings of righteousness and holiness.[136] As the apostle Paul testifies in Ephesians 5, *gemeynschafft* with the true body of Christ is actually communicated (*mitgetheilet*) in baptism. There the *Verbindung* of Christ and us takes place (*geschicht*).[137] What this amounts to really is covenant membership through a

135. "'Qui crediderit, inquit, & baptizatus fuerit, salvabitur; Qui vero non crediderit condemnabitur.' Nec enim iuvabit eum testimonium si re testate careat." *De substantia*, 353.

136. ". . . wenn dein kind in den namen Jesu Christi getaufft wirdt, solen gewiss seyn, dass der Himmlisch Vatter durch den H. Geist, der die wurzel des Glaubens ist, es in seinem hertzen versigelt, dass es gemeynschafft hat an dem gecreutizigten leib, und vergossenen blut Jesu Christi, und dardurch hat die abwäschung, das ist, die vergebung seiner sünden, wahre gerechtigkeit und heiligkeit, so gewiss als es mit wasser, welches die leibliche unreinigkeit pflegt abzuwäschen, getaufft ist, und dass er durch den H. Geist ein wahres glied des wahren leibs Jesu Christi ist." "Abendmahlpredigten," no. 5, *Gnadenbund*, 405.

137. "Wie der Apostel dise gemeinschafft des wahren leibs Christi, so im Tauff versigelt unnd mitgetheilet wirt, bezeugt an die Ephes. im 5. cap. Da er die Verbindung Christi unnd unser, so im heiligen Tauff geschicht." Ibid., 406–7.

kind of baptismal regeneration: in baptism "the Holy Spirit joins the heart of the child with that of Jesus Christ and renews it to eternal life."[138] It is not, Olevianus quickly adds, that the body and blood of Christ are physically (*leiblich*) present in either the water or the child. Christ has ascended to and remains in heaven.[139] But the physical and spiritual ablutions in baptism so closely parallel each other that it is "as if the water were the blood of Christ and the washing away of sin itself." How else could little children be saved, he asks, if they did not have true communion with the body and blood of Christ, which is sealed and confirmed in them in their baptism?[140]

In some of his later writings, however, Olevianus stresses that the promises of the covenant pertain to children of believing parents by virtue of the parents' faith. Parents who hear the gospel should keep in mind that what is entrusted to them is the promise not only of their own salvation but also of the salvation of their children, who ought then to be brought up as heirs of that promise. Just as the apostle Paul assured the Philippian jailor that by believing in Christ he *and his house* would be saved, so, too, can Christian parents today be confident that their children are Christians—*nati Christiani*, in fact—on the basis of the covenant promise, "I will be a God to you and to your seed."[141] In these contexts Olevianus tends to minimize the role of baptism. Baptism does not make a child a Christian, he maintains; it only visibly seals or confirms promises made to the child already in the

138. Ibid., 407.
139. "Und hie disputirt man nicht, ob der leib und das blut Christi leiblich in oder unter das wasser komme, oder ob Christus leiblich in das kind komme . . . sonder man glaubt . . . dass Christus auffgefahren ist gen Himmel. Unnd dass er dennoch durch seinen H. Geist das kind zum wahren glid seines leibs . . . anneme." Ibid., 406. Cf. also 407.
140. "Abendmahlpredigten," no. 6, *Gnadenbund*, 427. Ibid., no. 5, 406.
141. "Et parentes audientes Evangelium, non tantum sibi concreditas esse propriae salutis promissiones statuant, sed etiam salutis ipsorum seminis, seu liberorum, ut & ipsi in fide Christi educentur velut eiusdem promissionem haeredes. Ideo Paulus & Barnabas in Actis cap. 16. vers. trigesimoprimo, Commententariensi interroganti, quomodo servandus esset, respondent, Crede in Dominum Iesum Christum, & servaberis tu & domus tua. Et sic liberi nostri sunt sancti propter foedus gratuitum ex ipsius foederis formula, Ero Deus tuus & seminis tui. Vide I.Cor.7. vers. 14." *De substantia*, 307. "Filij mei non sunt ex Gentibus peccatores, sed natura, id est, nati Christiani." Comm. on Gal. 2:15, p. 28.

womb.[142] To be sure, these children are conceived in sin, but even before their baptism they are justified by the power of the covenant promise.[143] Salvation, therefore, is not by baptism but solely by grace (the promise of the covenant) and by faith (the parents' belief in the promise). If parents do not believe, their children, as infants at least, cannot be received into the covenant.[144]

In still other passages in his writings, however, Olevianus concedes that not every child of believing parents is a member of the covenant of grace. In a discussion in the *Expositio* of the two spiritual kingdoms for instance, he says that the Kingdom of Christ is made up of believers and their children, *unless* when these children grow older, they reject the covenantal blessings through infidelity. The Kingdom of Satan, by the same token, includes on the one hand those who have not repented, believed, and been baptized and, on the other, those who have been baptized but have remained impenitent. The latter are joined in baptism to the visible Church but remain in the Kingdom of Darkness until such time as they might believe.[145] All

142. ". . . non satis est certo statuere in Baptismo offerri promissiones foederis liberis nostris (ut quidem existimant Baptismum esse primum salutis limen, in eoque solo ac primum salutem eis promitti, atque ita excludant priores promissiones Evangelij ipsis factas in utero)." *De substantia*, 307.

143. "Non quod non concepti in peccato, sed tectum peccatum satisfactione Christi. Ideo 1.Cor.7 [:14]. Sancti dicuntur Christianorum liberi, etiam ex uno parente fideli geniti. Ergo Baptismus non facit ex Ethnico Christianum, sed promissionem, quae iam ante ad infantem pertinet, obsignat. Nam mullius Turcae filium licet Baptizare, quia promissio ad ipsius patrem non pertinet. Ideoque liberi fidelium ante baptismum iustificati sunt per Christum vi promissionis." Ibid. In his Comm. on Rom. 5:12–6 (p. 208) Olevianus goes so far as to say that "in utero matris fidelium infantes sunt peccatores, sed propter promissionem, peccatum eis non imputatur, sive textum est."

144. "[Sigilla] . . . hoc ipsum visibiliter obsignant, quod in Evangelio fidelibus ipsorumque semini coniunctim promittitur. . . . Cum itaque Parentes foedus oblatum respuunt, ipsorum infantes haudquaquam in foedus recipiuntur." *De substantia*, 307–8.

145. "Duo esse regna spiritualia, etiam in hoc mundo, certum est: . . . Regnum Christi, in quo revera sunt quicunque resipiscunt, & credunt, & in eius nomen baptizati sunt; ipsorumque adeo liberi, nisi ubi adoleverint, infidelitate oblatum beneficium reiiciant. Alterum vero regnum Satanae & tenebrarum, in quo ii sunt omnes, qui non resipiscunt, & non credunt in Christum: hi partim non baptizati, sed aperti contemptores baptismi . . . , partim quidem baptizati, sed tamen impoenitentes & infideles; hi etiam si baptizati sint & adiungant se visibili Ecclesiae, manet tamen tantisper revera in regno & potestate tenebrarum, dum convertantur & credant." *Expositio*, 1–2.

covenant parents, Olevianus adds in *De substantia*, are, of course, entrusted with bringing up their baptized children in the way of the Lord. At a child's baptism the parents make their own *pactum* with God to raise that child in the fear of the Lord in response to His covenant promises. When these children reach maturity, however, parents who have been faithful in their duty are no longer responsible if their children persist in unbelief.[146]

In his Romans commentary, finally, Olevianus claims that baptized infants can be "cut out" (*excinduntur*) of the covenant if they reject its promises upon reaching the age of discretion.[147] This is especially surprising since earlier in the commentary he had stated that infants of believers are justified already in the womb.[148] Here, too, he argues that infants who die before receiving the sign of baptism are saved by virtue of the promise to their parents. If they die after their baptism but before they reach adulthood, they also remain in the covenant, because they have not yet reached an age where they could refuse to believe the promise confirmed in their baptism. But if they reject the covenant once they are mature, they are cut out. This implies, of course, that they once *were* members of the covenant. To understand how this could be, we must realize that Olevianus has in mind here a distinction similar to the one implied in *De substantia* between the general outer *administratio* of the covenant

146. "Qui igitur id non praestant profanant nomen Dei, cui id in Baptismo voverunt, quodque super infantes invocatum est hoc pacto: Domine sis secundum promissionem foederis tui gratuiti infanti meo propitius pater in Christo; & ego ex tuo mandato voveo me eum tibi educaturum. Infantes vero ubi adoleverint, si institutioni & correctioni Domini se non submiserint, profanant nomen Dei, quod super eos invocatum est; sed si parentes fecerint officium liberaverint se voto; sanguis vero qui perit, erit super caput filiorum contumacium, qui Deo eripiunt, quod semel ei fuerat consecratum." *De substantia*, 199–200.

147. "In his comprehenduntur fidelium infantes, pueri, qui excinduntur e foedere, si verbum contemnant: Si moriantur ante signum acceptum, habent promissionem, & antequam repellerent, mortui sunt. Sic post signum foederis ante aetatem adultam si pueri moriantur, id est, post confirmatam promissionem, & inscriptam ipsorum corporibus, non excinduntur, quia promissio Dei per se firma & per ipsos infirmari non potuit, quia ad eam aetatem non pervenerunt, ut eam incredulitate potuerint repellere. Quod si autem ubi ad aetatem venerint promissionem infidelitate reiecerint, excinduntur e foedere." Comm. on Rom. 11:17–18, p. 574.

148. See n. 143 above.

promise and the special inner *administratio* of the *substantia* of that promise. Earlier in this same passage in the Romans commentary, he asserts that there are two external and two internal bonds by which our attachment to the covenant is secured. The external *vincula* are God's *vocatio* through the Word and signs of the covenant and our *approbatio* in the profession of our faith and participation in the sacraments. The internal *vincula* are God's gracious election and the Holy Spirit. The internal bonds, says Olevianus, can never be broken; the external bonds can.[149] If we carry Olevianus's argument on through, to be cut out of the covenant as an adult must mean that the ties to the covenant as an infant were only external, that the individual in question never was elect and never did receive the gift of the Holy Spirit.

Olevianus's whole discussion of infants and the covenant, then, leaves us with many more questions than answers. Are infants members of the covenant by virtue of their baptism or by virtue of the promise to their believing parents? We have found support in his writings for both possibilities. It may be that there is not really an inconsistency here but that Olevianus has in mind, once again, the difference between the covenant promise and the effectual administration or realization of that promise in the individual. In that case, as he implies in the Romans commentary, a child would be saved by the promise before baptism, but in baptism this promise would be realized or actually applied to the heart.

But that would still not answer the question of how a baptized infant of covenant parents could grow up impenitent. If the child becomes an heir of the promise before baptism and a participant in the riches of the promise in baptism, how could he or she wind up in the Kingdom of Satan? Those whom God has chosen, Olevianus stated earlier, He has chosen to an *inseparable* union with Him. The justification and sanctification sealed in baptism are benefits of an *eternal* covenant. The inter-

---

149. "Porro quemadmodum insitio surculorum in stipites certis sit mediis & vinculis, ita & haec insitio in foedus Domini promissum Abrahamo in semine benedicto. Duplica autem sunt vincula huius insitionis. Duo externa: Vocatio externa per verbum & signa foederis, & eiusdem vocationis externa approbatio sive professio doctrinae & sacramentorum participatio; interna vincula insitionis etiam duo: electio gratuita & Spiritus fidei; haec vincula non possunt abrumpi, illa possunt." Comm. on Rom. 11:17–18, p. 574.

nal bonds to the covenant can *never* be broken. How then could an infant, joined to the heart of Jesus Christ and renewed unto eternal life in baptism, fall away? Apparently, Olevianus means to distinguish here between elect and nonelect children: what really happens in baptism depends on the ultimate destiny of the child. Elect children—that is, those who either die in infancy or bear the fruit of faith in adulthood—receive the internal benefits of the covenant in baptism, while nonelect children receive only the external sign. In that case, of course, the significance of any given baptism could be determined only after the fact: by how long the child lived, first of all, and, if the child did reach adulthood, by the spiritual tenor of his or her life.[150] But to parents present at their child's baptism, this could hardly provide the kind of assurance of which Olevianus speaks in the "Abendmahlpredigten." We can only conclude that he leaves unclear the precise temporal relation of "inner" to "outer" baptism in infants. At times he seems to suggest that inner baptism precedes outer baptism; at other times, that it occurs simultaneously with outer baptism; and at still others (in nonelect infants), that it does not take place at all.

Conclusion

The key to Olevianus's doctrine of the covenant of grace is to be found in three distinctions he frequently makes: 1) an explicit distinction between the *substantia* and the *administratio* of the covenant; 2) a further, though implicit, distinction between the outward *administratio* of the covenant promise to all within the visible Church and the inward *administratio* of the *substantia* of

150. In one passage in *De substantia* (pp. 327–28) Olevianus admits that one's election can never be presumed from the reception of the sign of baptism: ". . . tamen singulis baptizatis salus sine praecedente attestatione certo promittitur: quam promissionem saepe carere effectu, ipsa experientia testatur. . . . Neque enim omnes illi sunt electi. . . . Nec vero a Sacramentis ad conditionem electionis fas est homines religare. . . . quatenus nimirum a fideli sensu conscientiae, Sacramentorum usurpatione obfirmato, Deoque obstricto, ad vocationem efficacem, inde ad electionem immutabilem ascendimus: tantum abest ut sigilla fidem nostram a conditione arcanae electionis in eorum usurpatione suspendat. Quod necessario fieret, si certitudo salutis a certitudine externae obsignationis, quae electis cum reprobis est communis, primum omnium aestimaretur."

this promise to the elect; and 3) an implicit distinction between the covenant as a divine testament or promise, on the one hand, and as a mutual binding of wills, on the other. The first two of these are particularly helpful in solving some of the problems we encountered in the older research on Olevianus's covenant theology. For example, the relationship of the nonelect in the visible Church to the covenant is actually very clear (vs. De Jong, Berkhof, Schrenk, Diestel): they are included in the external administration of the covenant through the Word and sacraments but not in the internal administration of the substance or benefits of the covenant through the Holy Spirit. For the same reason, Olevianus's view of the *manducatio infidelium* cannot be characterized as "Lutheran" (Ritschl). Unbelievers at the Lord's table partake only of the signs by which Christ and the substance of the covenant are offered, not of these benefits themselves.

The closest Olevianus comes to acknowledging the third distinction, that between a unilateral and bilateral dimension to the covenant of grace, is in his discussion of the first two. The "substance of the covenant" is the substance strictly of the divine *promise* of forgiveness and renewal; the administration always involves one's response to this offer of grace. This latter distinction provides the categories by which to explain the interplay of divine initiative and human response in the Abrahamic covenant, the "new covenant" of Jeremiah 31, the Kingdom of God, the mystical union with Christ, the covenantal function of the Creed, and the sacramental administration of the covenant. It is curious that Olevianus himself never mentions this distinction; it is perhaps the single most important assumption in his doctrine of the *foedus gratiae*.

4

Covenant or Covenants?

Pretemporal Covenant

In the nineteenth and early twentieth centuries three prominent historians of theology—Heppe, Schrenk, and Ritschl—claimed that Olevianus speaks not only of a covenant of grace but also of a pretemporal *sponsio* by the Son whereby He placed himself under obligation to the Father to carry out His work of redemption. Ritschl did not share Heppe's and Schrenk's view that Olevianus actually identifies this *sponsio* as a *foedus* or *pactum*, but he did find in this "Vereinbarung Christi mit dem Vater" at least the rudiments of what later theologians would describe as a more formal intertrinitarian covenant.[1]

These three historians were certainly correct in calling attention to the importance of the *sponsio* concept in Olevianus's theology. Frequently in *De substantia* (Part I) Olevianus refers to Christ as the *sponsor* ("guarantor")[2] and to His promise as the

---

1. Heppe, *Dogmatik des deutschen Protestantismus* 2:218: "Hieraus erhellt, dass die Erlösungslehre Olevians ihren eigentlichen Schwerpunkt in der Lehre von dem *pactum* und *consilium salutis* des Vaters und Sohnes und von der darauf beruhenden *insitio* der *electi in Christum* oder *in corpus Christi mysticum* hat." See also 215–16. Schrenk, *Gottesreich und Bund*, 61: ". . . zumal jene Verknüpfung von *foedus* und *sponsio*, von *foedus* and vorzeitlichem *pactum*, die sich bei Olevianus bereits deutlich findet." Ritschl, *Dogmengeschichte*, 3:419: "Und zwar stellt Olevian diese beiden Tätigkeiten des Bundesmittlers unter den leitenden Gesichtspunkt einer *Sponsio*, durch die sich Christus Gott dem Vater zu ihrer Durchführung verpflichtet habe. Damit hat er zuerst den Gedanken einer dem Gnadenbund vorangehenden und ihn begründenden transzendenten Vereinbarung Christi mit dem Vater ins Auge gefasst, wenn auch nicht schon er selbst, sondern erst Spätere diese Übereinkunft als ein förmliches *foedus* oder *pactum* dargestellt haben."

2. *De substantia*, 52, 62, 76, 124.

eternal *sponsio* ("guarantee")[3] or *fideiussio* ("surety," "bail")[4] that by His sacrifice He would justify the elect and by His Spirit renew them in the image of God. The covenant overtones here cannot be missed; it is a task to which He had bound (*sponpondit*)[5] or obligated Himself (*se obligarat*).[6]

Furthermore, while Olevianus never explicitly identifies this pretemporal *sponsio* as a *foedus*, the two terms are often closely linked by implication. First of all, in similar passages in the "Abendmahlpredigten," the *Notae in Evangelia*, and the commentary on Romans, he asserts that Christ "ratifies" (*macht . . . fest, erigit, sanciverit*) "His covenant" (*foedus suum*) or "the eternal covenant between God and the Church" in two directions— *erga Patrem* and *erga nos*. *Erga Patrem* He offers up His body and blood to the Father on behalf of the Church in order to redeem her from the bondage of Satan and the wrath of God. *Erga nos* He effects in us true faith through the Word and sacraments and unites us to Himself.[7] There is, to be sure, no mention here of a *sponsio* or the pretemporality of this covenant, but it is reasonable to infer that behind the two-directional *ratification* of the covenant made in eternity Olevianus sees a two-directional *promise* of the covenant, or what he elsewhere refers to as the eternal *sponsio* of the Son. The Son could hardly have fulfilled *erga Patrem* what He had not promised *erga Patrem* from all eternity.

This inference is substantiated in various places in *De substantia* where Olevianus points out the correspondence of the twofold *sponsio* of the Son to the *duplex malum* committed by humanity in the fall, the twofold mandate received from the Father, and the twofold benefit of the *foedus gratuitum* bestowed upon the elect. In obedience to the Father's mandate, Christ had committed Himself to the work of satisfaction for sin and renewal according to God's image. This twofold redemptive work would remove the offense against God and the corruption of humanity brought on by the fall and provide the elect with the cov-

---

3. Ibid., 23, 24, 39, 48, 63, 75, 86, 106, 118, 123, 134, 157.
4. Ibid., 24.
5. Ibid., 62, 76, 124.
6. Ibid., 134.
7. "Abendmahlpredigten," no. 2, *Gnadenbund,* 320–21; *Notae in Evangelia,* 12; Comm. on Rom. 11:27, p. 589.

enant blessings of justification and sanctification.[8] While Olevianus may not refer explicitly to the *sponsio* as a *foedus* here, the two concepts are intimately related: in committing Himself to the role of mediator of the covenant imposed upon him by the Father, the Son becomes the *sponsor foederis*.[9] What is referred to elsewhere as the ratification of His *foedus* with respect to the Father is described in *De substantia* as the fulfillment of the *sponsio* made to the Father. Indeed, the content of the two corresponds so closely that Olevianus sometimes uses the terms interchangeably in the discussion of a single theme.[10]

The connection, then, between *sponsio* and *foedus* in Olevianus is probably less clear than Schrenk implied but certainly more developed than Ritschl supposed. The same is true of the connection between *sponsio* and *pactum*. In the broader contexts in which the *sponsio* language occurs, Olevianus considers the promise of the Son as part of a wider pretemporal redemptive agreement between the Father and the Son, but only once does he actually call the agreement a covenant (*pactum*). In this arrangement the Father gives the Son a command, the Son promises to obey it, and the Father then accepts the Son's obedience.[11]

8. "Prout autem homo duplex malum commiserat: nam & inobedientia Deum offenderat, & peccando semetipsum corruperat sive opus Dei destruxerat: ita & Filius Dei mediator foederis a Patre constitutus spondet pro duabus rebus, primo se satisfacturum pro peccatis omnium quos Pater ei dedit. Ioan. 17: & ab aeterno per Christum in filios adoptare decrevit, Ephes. 1. Secundo se etiam effecturum ut sibi insiti pace conscienti fruantur atque indices renoventur ad Dei imaginem, quo Deus scopum primae creationis in ipsis consequatur." *De substantia*, 23. "Ad utramque foederis partem & sponsionis Christi pro nobis." Ibid., 106. ". . . ad utramque foederis gratuiti & sponsionis Christi partem faciat." Ibid, 118. ". . . utramque tum mandati a Patre accepti, tum sponsionis suae partem." Ibid., 123.

9. Ibid., 76.

10. In his treatment of the offices of Christ, for example, Olevianus seeks to show the relationship of the offices to "utraque pars sponsionis suae" (p. 124) or, as he says later, "ad utramque foederis partem" (p. 131). Cf. also the interchange of terms in his discussion of the Last Judgment (pp. 155, 157).

11. "Ad formam vero sacrificij propitiatorij requiritur mandatum personae impositum (Ioan. 6. Quem Pater signavit. Et Psal. 110, Heb. 10) spontanea erga id obedientia (Ioan. 12) cum intercessione ut a Patre nobis accepta feratur illa obedientia . . . & detur Spiritus Sanctus. . . . Formalis itaque causa & scopus superiorum proximorum articulorum est, quod *eo pacto* Filius Dei incarnatus semel se in victimam propitiatoriam onustam omnium electorum peccatis obtulit." *De substantia*, 63 (italics added).

First, the Father enlists the Son in the service of His redemptive purposes. By decree,[12] by oath[13] (Ps. 110:4), and by command[14] He ordains the Son as an eternal priest who is to make a complete offering for sin and preserve its efficacy forever. The Son in reply promises by His double *sponsio* that He will fulfill the command of the Father. He accepts the mandate. His will is obedient to the Father's decree.[15] Finally, the Father assures the Son by a *promissio* of His own that He accepts the *sponsio* of the Son and approves His *perpetua voluntas servandi*.[16]

"Agreement" may not be the best choice of terms here, for when Olevianus discusses this pretemporal arrangement between the Father and the Son, his emphasis is often on the initiative and activity of the Father and on the passivity of the Son. Initially, the Son is not a participant at all. It is the Father who decrees to demonstrate His love toward us—by *giving* His Son.[17] The Son is part of the plan but not part of the planning. Moreover, when in eternity the Son is recruited for this redemptive task, his role is always passive, as is borne out in the voice of the verbs Olevianus uses. The Son is determined (*ist geordnet*)[18] by the Father for His mediating work, ordered (*verordnet sey*)[19] to set up an eternal priesthood, established (*constitutus*) as mediator of the covenant,[20] ordained (*ordinatus*),[21] anointed (*unctus est*),[22] sealed (*obsignatum*),[23] and finally sent (*gesandt*)[24] and displayed (*exhibitus*)[25] by the express command of

---

12. *Expositio*, 72–73; *De substantia*, 24–25, 69, 124.

13. Sudhoff, *Fester Grund*, 1590 ed., 57–58; *Expositio*, 70, 72–73; *De substantia*, 134, 125–26.

14. Reu, *Vester Grundt*, 1567 ed., 1356; Sudhoff, *Fester Grund*, 1590 ed., 52, 57–58; *Expositio*, 70–71, 94; *De substantia*, 23–24, 31, 62–63, 98, 123.

15. "Utrumque sponsionis seu fideiussionis partem & mandati a Patre accepti ut impleret Mediator." *De substantia*, 24. ". . . voluntate Mediatoris obediente huic decreto Patris." Ibid., 69.

16. "Porro Christi sive uncti cognomine utraque pars sponsionis exprimitur, & promissio quoque quod Pater sponsionem acceptet." Ibid., 68.

17. "Etenim quia coelestis Pater infinitam suam dilectionem nobis reipsa testatam facere decreverat donatione Filij." Ibid., 24.

18. Sudhoff, *Fester Grund*, 1590 ed., 57–58.

19. Ibid., 52; Reu, *Vester Grundt*, 1567 ed., 1356.

20. *De substantia*, 23.

21. *Expositio*, 70.

22. Ibid., 70, 72–73.

23. Ibid., 71.

the Father. Both the Father's orders and the eternal priesthood itself are laid upon His shoulders (*impositum*).[26]

It is true, as Ritschl pointed out and as we have seen, that with respect to the *sponsio* itself it is the Son who is the actor: He performs an act of binding Himself to the Father. But even in some of the contexts in which the term *sponsio* appears, Olevianus's focus is trained not on the activity of the Son but on the activity of the Father through the Son. In his treatment of the names of Christ in *De substantia,* for example, he states that in the title "Christ" or "Anointed" both parts of the *sponsio* are expressed. How? Because by the name of Christ or Messiah it is taught that this Person came *with the command of the Father* and was *ordained by God* both as a Priest who would sacrifice for sin and as a King who would instill in us a zeal for righteousness.[27] Olevianus's attention has quickly shifted from what the Son does to what the Father does to and through the Son. A short while later he asserts that the two parts of the *sponsio* can better be understood when one considers the form and purpose (*formam & scopum*) of Christ's humiliation—His offering for sin and satisfaction for sin, respectively. But the form of this sin offering first required a command placed upon His person (*mandatum personae impositum*) and then voluntary obedience to the command (*spontanea erga id obedientia una*).[28] Other examples could be cited,[29] but these should suffice to show that Olevianus considers the *sponsio* as the Son's response to the decisions and initiative of the Father. If this can be termed an

24. Sudhoff, *Fester Grund,* 1590 ed., 52.

25. *Expositio,* 70.

26. *Expositio,* 72–73; *De substantia,* 62–63, 124.

27. "Porro Christi sive uncti cognomine utraque pars sponsionis exprimitur. . . . Primum enim Christi seu Messiae appellatione docetur hanc personam venisse cum mandato & Patris, a Deo ordinate esse, ut sit Sacerdos aeternus, qui pro nobis sacrificet & intercedat; & sit Rex noster qui efficiat seu generet in nobis odium peccati & studium iustitiae." *De substantia,* 23.

28. "Habemus nunc quomodo sponsor noster priori sponsionis suae parti satisfecerit; tum etiam quemadmodum impletionem alterius partis inchoarit. . . . Utrumque melius intelligetur ubi formam scopum tantae humiliationis attente consideraverimus. . . . Ad formam vero sacrificij propitiatorij requiritur mandatum personae impositum . . . [&] spontanea erga id obedientia una." Ibid., 62–63.

29. Cf. Ibid., 24–25, 123, 134–35.

agreement, it is at most an agreement between master and servant: the Father decrees and commands; the Son obeys.

What we have in Olevianus, then, is a pretemporal "covenant" at two levels or in two different senses, roughly comparable to the narrower and broader senses of covenant that he uses elsewhere. The first is a unilateral promise or *sponsio-foedus* by the Son to the Father that He will justify and sanctify the elect. The second is a bilateral redemptive arrangement (*pactum*) between the Father and the Son, of which the *sponsio* is but one element. Olevianus refers to the latter as a covenant only once and often portrays the Son as only a passive, submissive participant. But the outlines of a pretemporal *pactum salutis* or counsel of redemption are clear. The *mandatum* (Father)-*sponsio* (Son)-*promissio* (Father) sequence is bound together by a mutual resolve on the part of Father and Son, by a perfect harmony of wills. The Father wills or decrees that the Son save us; the Son wills to obey the Father; the Father wills to accept the intention of the Son to save for all eternity.[30] The covenantal idea is present; only the fully developed covenantal terminology is lacking.

Covenant of Creation

Olevianus uses the term *foedus creationis* only three times in his writings (all in *De substantia*) and never in such a way that its meaning is clear from the immediate contexts:

> 1) We say all this to show the shamelessness and blindness of those who by denying this truth [concerning the different persons in the Godhead] allow themselves to be led away from the true God and a covenant of redemption. It was by the affirmation of truth—an affirmation confirmed by the mouth of God but twisted to an evil purpose—that in the beginning Satan led mankind away from God, and the *creationis foedere*.[31]

---

30. "Ac simul est perpetua voluntas servandi in hoc Mediatore consentiens cum voluntate Patris acceptante pro aeterna reconciliatione semel oblatum sacrificium & approbante hoc studium servandi in Mediator." Ibid., 125. See also Sudhoff, *Fester Grund,* 1590 ed., 123–5, and *Expositio,* 154–5.

31. "Haec ideo tantum, ut appareat eorum impudentia & excaecatio qui a negatione illius veritatis a vero Deo redemptionisque foedere se obducti patiuntur, cuius affirmatione, Dei ore comprobata, in perversum tamen finem detorta Sathan initio hominem a Deo & creationis foedere abduxit." *De substantia,* 9.

2) An incarnate Son was necessary not only to make expiation *pro dissoluto creationis foedere* and to bring about its renewal but also that that expiation once made might be of lasting effect and the restoration to the law fuller and more excellent. . . .[32]

3) At the beginning of the human race that old serpent led humanity away from the word of the law, and thus *a creationis foedere*, by a false interpretation. . . . The summary of this law shining forth in the image of God was that he love the Lord his God with all his heart . . . and as a testimony of this love refrain from eating from the one tree.[33]

The most we can deduce from these three references is that the covenant of creation was something the human race abandoned in the fall through Satan and regained in redemption through Christ. There are hints that it is related to the law (*ius, lex*) and to the *imago Dei.* But what exactly this covenant was is not clear.

The meaning of the *foedus creationis* becomes apparent only when we turn to the synonyms Olevianus uses for the term: *primum foedus,*[34] *foedus naturale,*[35] and most often (especially in his earlier writings) *ius creationis.*[36] Each of these terms refers to the relationship in Paradise between God and humanity, the original union (*coniunctio*) that existed between the Creator and His first image bearers.[37] It was a relationship, says Olevianus, of perfect conformity: a conformity of holiness and righteousness between Creator and creature (the *imago Dei*) and a

32. "Requirebatur, inquam, Filius incarnatur, ut non tantum pro dissoluto creationis foedere fieret expiatio, & eiusdem instauratio: sed etiam expiationis semel factae perpetua esset duratio, & restitutio in ius amplius & excellentius." Ibid., 26.
33. "In ipso generis humani exordio serpens ille antiquus a verbo legis, atque ita a creationis foedere false interpretatione hominem abduxit . . . cuius legis in imagine Dei lucentis summa erat, ut diligeret Dominum Deum ex tota anima . . . & in testimonium dilectionis illius ab unius arboris usa abstineret." Ibid., 270.
34. Ibid., 9.
35. Ibid., 251, 254.
36. Comm. on Gal. 3:2, p. 40; 3:21, p. 75; Comm. on Rom. 1:18, p. 30; 8:12–13, p. 341; Comm. on Phil. 3:9–10, pp. 42, 43; *De substantia*, 12–13, 22, 90, 251, 294, 313.
37. ". . . primum foedus seu coniunctionem, quae inter Deum & hominem conditum ad Dei imaginem intercedebat." *De substantia*, 9.

conformity of the human mind, will, and affections, of all faculties and all actions to that image.[38] The *foedus creationis* was a *foedus naturale,* he seems to suggest, because it was a relationship in which Adam and Eve were "naturally," i.e., by nature as bearers of God's image, conformed to their Creator.

Like the covenant of grace later on, however, the covenant of creation was not a relationship devoid of human responsibility. God had revealed Himself to Adam both internally (in His image) and externally (in His handiwork), and in return He expected that Adam pledge to Him full allegiance, honor, and glory.[39] He had shown to Adam His favor and endowed him with His image—the spiritual gifts of knowledge, righteousness, and holiness—but all on the condition of obedience.[40] The *naturale foedus,* therefore, was a relationship of *conformitas cum Deo* but at the same time a *naturalis obligatio* on Adam's part to maintain that conformity. Time and again Olevianus describes the *foedus creationis* as a *ius creationis,*[41] an obligation to the Creator inherent in humanity's status as crea-

---

38. ". . . foedere naturali inter Deum et nos seu conformitate illa cum Deo, quae lucebat in ipsius imagine." Ibid., 254. "Quid sit imago Dei, ad quam homo est conditus? . . . Erat conformitas sanctitatis & iustitiae inter creatorem & hominem." Comm. on Col. 3:10, pp. 160–61. ". . . talem iustitiam, quae sit conformitas in ratione nostra, voluntate, affectibus, omnibus denique facultatibus & actionibus inde ortis, cum lege divina seu imagine ad quam eramus conditi." Comm. on Phil. 3:9–10, p. 43.

39. ". . . ostendanto quod fuerit naturale foedus seu naturalis obligatio inter Deum quatenus est Creator & homines ad ipsius imaginem conditos: hoc nimirum, ut quemadmodum Deus ipsis patefecerat partim interne in seu imagine, partim externe in speculo opificii huius mundi, ita vicissim ab ipsis honoraretur & glorificetur." *De substantia,* 251.

40. ". . . ut quemadmodum primus Adam ea conditione favorem imaginemque Dei acceperat, ut sibi, haberet ac posteris, si in obedientia erga Deum perstitisset . . . Sicut enim primus Adam ea lege favorem Dei & spiritualia dona acceperat, ut sibi ea haberet ac posteris si in obedientia perstitisset." Ibid., 79, 80. "Quid sit imago Dei ad quam homo est conditus? . . . Atqui hic renovari iubet ad cognitionem Dei, & ad Ephes. 4, ad iustitiam & sanctitatem veram." Comm. on Col. 3:10, pp. 160–61. Olevianus seems to think of the image in both an ontological and a relational sense (see n. 38 above).

41. For example: ". . . conformitas . . . cum lege divina seu imagine ad quam eramus conditi, quam conformitatem Deus iure creationis a nobis requirit." Comm. on Phil. 3:9–10, p. 43. "Sic etiam Deus Legem nobis proponit veluti syngrapham eius obedientiae quam ipsi iure creationis debemus." Comm. on Gal. 3:21, pp. 75–76. See also the references to *ius creationis* listed in n.36 above.

ture. God had bound not only Himself to humanity but also humanity to Himself. As the beneficiaries of His image and His favor, we had been placed in His debt. We were, so to speak, His vassals.[42]

God bore witness to this relationship of conformity and obligation, Olevianus continues, in the law of nature or natural law (*lex naturae*,[43] *ius naturae*,[44] *vox naturae*,[45] *ius divinum*,[46] *ius Dei naturale*[47]), i.e., His holy will implanted in our natures, written in our hearts, and inscribed on our minds.[48] This natural law was a natural knowledge (*notitia*) of God concerning His justice, His holiness, and His hatred of sin,[49] and as such, he implies, a part of the *imago Dei* itself. At creation the law of nature manifested itself in the image of God; as an expression of God's will, it was an expression also of that righteousness and holiness represented in His image. Conformity to the one, therefore, was conformity to the other.[50]

Olevianus also closely associates the *lex naturae* with the conscience. Usually he speaks of the conscience as the *place* in which the law of nature holds its court, but at one point he goes so far as to define the conscience itself as the *notitia Dei* which

42. "Tota vita nostra debetur Deo iure creationis, ut eius gloriae serviat, & nulla pars diabolo aut vitiis. Haec est una obligatio ius creationis, quo nos tanquam vasalli Deo, als dem leben herrn zu dienen schuldig sein." Comm. on Rom. 8:12–13, p. 341.

43. *Expositio*, 6; Comm. on Rom. 1:18, p. 30; 1:29–31, pp. 58, 59; 1:32, pp. 64–65; 2:12–14, p. 99; 7:5–7, pp. 273–74; *De substantia*, 3, 195–96, 251, 298, 301.

44. Comm. on Rom. 1:32, pp. 64–65.

45. Ibid.

46. Ibid.

47. Ibid.

48. "Das Gesetz ist eine solche lehr, die Gott der natur eingepflantzet . . . hat." Reu, *Vester Grundt*, 1567 ed., 1337. ". . . opus legis natura in cordibus scriptum." *Expositio*, 6. "Huius naturalis obligationis testimonium Deus extare voluit partim in lege naturae inscripta mentibus." *De substantia*, 151.

49. "Ius Dei est ius naturae, sive noticiae, quas & Creator homini indidit . . . ut essent testimonia de Deo & de iudicio Dei; & certe sciremus hac voce naturae commonefacti, Deum vere & horribiliter irasci omnibus facientibus contra has noticias divinitus nobis insitas." Comm. on Rom. 1:32, pp. 64–65.

50. ". . . legis in imagine Dei lucentis." *De substantia*, 207. "Lex . . . est expressio imaginis Dei. . . . Cum ergo Deus sanctus sit, iustus & bonus, lex qua nobis sui imaginem exprimit, non potest non esse iusta, sancta, bona. Exprimit in ea sanctum & immutabilem suam voluntatem, quales non esse velit, & punit quicquid ei non est conforme." Comm. on Rom. 7:12, p. 290.

impels one toward the good and judges that which is wicked.[51] At any rate, it is important to note here that he does not *equate* this natural law with the covenant of creation. The *lex naturae* testifies to our obligations in and by the *ius creationis,* but it is not that covenant relationship itself.

What, then, happened to the *foedus creationis* in the fall? As a relationship of conformity, Olevianus seems to suggest, it was annulled, but as an obligation to conformity it remained in effect. In the fall humanity deserted (*defecisse*) the Creator and the *ius creationis.*[52] Satan led them away (*abduxit*) from the covenant of creation[53] and thus destroyed (*everteret)* this *primum foedus seu coniunctionem* between Creator and creature.[54] There was a loss (*amissio)* of the image.[55] The *foedus creationis* was dissolved (*dissoluto).*[56] Our debt of loyalty to God, however, was not cancelled. By the *ius creationis* we were still bound to obedience or, as sinners now, to the punishment that befit our disobedience. Like borrowers in debt beyond their means to repay, we no longer had anything to give, but that did not mean we were no longer obligated to give it.[57]

If Olevianus makes very clear that our covenant obligation after the fall is still in force, however, he is less clear about the status of our internal witness to that obligation, the *lex naturae.* He leaves no doubt that the image of God was lost in the fall, and his implication earlier that the *lex naturae* (as natural knowledge) was a part of that image is supported in his statements that that "word of the law" was wrenched (*ereptum)* out

51. " . . . clamor legis in conscientia." *De substantia,* 298. ". . . quid sit conscientia, nempe notitia Dei impeliens ad quaedam opera bona & iudicans recte facta & malefacta." Comm. on Rom. 2:12–4, p. 99.

52. *De substantia,* 313.

53. Ibid., 9, 270.

54. Ibid., 9.

55. Comm. on Col. 3:10, p. 161.

56. *De substantia,* 26.

57. ". . . Deus Legem nobis proponit veluti syngrapham eius obedientiae vel ad poenam." Ibid., 251. ". . . Deus Legem nobis proponit veluti syngrapham eius obedientiae quam ipsi iure creationis debemus, addita quidem hac conditionali promissione, si feceris haec quae iure creationis debes, vives; non tamen eo consilio, quod existimet nos solvendo esse, multo minus quod velit nos fiduciam in opera desigere, sed potius eo consilio, primo ut omnibus nostris quaerimoniis praescindat." Comm. on Gal. 3:21, pp. 75–76.

of the hearts of our first parents,[58] the light of the law of love extinguished (*extincta*),[59] and the law of nature obliterated (*oblit-eratae*).[60] But at other times, strangely enough, his appraisal of the effects of the fall is not quite so pessimistic. The law of nature, he says, was weakened (*labefacta*) by a corrupted nature,[61] hampered (*impeditur*) by the violence of the passions,[62] engulfed by doubt and darkness,[63] but not completely erased. Sparks of the knowledge of God remain.[64] And, as much as we refuse to heed it, we retain a *naturalis sensus* in our consciences that God hates sin and will exact a punishment for it. This *clamor legis in conscientia* could not be silenced nor the dread of God's wrath removed without the intervention of the death of Christ. Only within the context of our reconciliation with God could this witness to our obligations under the covenant of creation be appeased and our consciences set at rest.[65]

It would seem, then, that past studies of Olevianus's covenant theology have claimed for his *foedus creationis* either too little or too much. Obviously, he does not understand the covenant as strictly a covenant of grace (Barth)[66] or as strictly postlapsarian (Diestel).[67] One could even argue with Otto Ritschl's assertion that Olevianus treats the *foedus creationis* and its synonyms "nur an wenigen kurzen Stellen."[68] But it is just as misleading to suggest that we find in Olevianus "a distinctly federal system, making clear and extensive use of the double covenant idea" (McCoy),[69] or that he regards the covenant of works "schon ganz in derselben Weise . . . wie Cocceius" (Heppe).[70] Not only does Olevianus never use the term *foedus operum* but there are

---

58. *De substantia*, 272.

59. Ibid.

60. Comm. on Rom. 1:29–31, p. 58.

61. Comm. on Rom. 7:5–7, pp. 273–74.

62. Ibid.

63. Comm. on Rom. 1:18, p. 59; 1:32, pp. 64–65.

64. "Tantum enim singulis relictum est scintillarum cognitionis Dei." *De substantia*, 318.

65. Ibid., 195–96, 298, 269–70; Comm. on Col. 3:15, p. 174.

66. Barth, *Church Dogmatics*, 4/1:59.

67. Diestel, *Geschichte des Alten Testaments*, 288.

68. Ritschl, *Dogmengeschichte*, 3:418.

69. McCoy, "Covenant Theology of Cocceius," 76.

70. Heppe, *Geschichte des Pietismus*, 211, n. 1.

several major features of that doctrine in its more developed (Cocceian) form that are missing in his *foedus creationis:* First of all, Olevianus does not describe the covenant of creation, as Murray thought, as "the eternal rule of righteousness *to which . . . is annexed the promise of life on the fulfillment of perfect obedience."*[71] He nowhere speaks of the promise of eternal life as the reward of Adam's obedience. He refers to obedience as an obligation *iure creationis,* a testimony of love to God, and a condition for bearing the divine image, but never as the stepping-stone to eternal life. *Coniunctio* or *conformitas* with God, he implies, was reward in itself.[72] Second, he never explicitly identifies the garden prohibition in Genesis 2:16,17 (". . . but of the tree of the knowledge of good and evil you shall not eat, for in the day that you eat thereof, you shall surely die") as the condition of the *foedus creationis.* He talks in a general way about obedience as the *conditio* of the image, the favor, and the spiritual gifts of God[73] and even about obedience to the garden command as a *testimonium* of the love required in the (natural) law,[74] but the links among *conditio, abstinentia,* and *foedus creationis* in his discussion are, at most, weak and indirect. Third, unlike Cocceius and the Puritan covenant theologians of the seventeenth century, Olevianus does not treat the covenant of creation as the biblical-historical or theological foil for the covenant of grace. Never once does he directly compare or contrast the two. There are, to be sure, occasional hints that the two covenants are related. In the breaking of the *foedus creationis* the image of God is lost; in the *foedus gratiae* it is restored.[75] The second Adam, the foundation of the covenant of grace, makes amends for the dissolution by the first Adam of the covenant of

71. Murray, *Encyclopedia of Christianity,* s.v. "Covenant Theology" (italics added).

72. He does say that eternal life is the reward of obedience in the *legal* covenant (see n. 57 above and *De substantia,* 13), and to the extent that the covenant of creation is reflected in the legal covenant one might infer that what is explicitly stated about the latter is implicit in the former. But the connection is certainly not clearly drawn.

73. *De substantia,* 79–80.

74. See n. 33 above.

75. "Imago Dei in eo consistit, ut mens ipsa & internae facultates mutentur." Comm. on Rom. 12:2, p. 614. ". . . redderetque eis imaginem Dei." *De substantia,* 12.

creation.[76] And the law engraved on human hearts in the *foedus gratiae* is really a reiteration of the original law of nature. But once again the connections here are few and far between and never more than implicit. Fourth, as Vos pointed out,[77] Olevianus does not consider Adam the federal or representative head of the human race in the covenant of creation. Adam's guilt is not directly imputed to his posterity; his guilt, along with his corruption, is inherited.[78] We, his descendants, fell with him in his fall because we were then present in his loins; we were part of him and thus part of his sin.[79] Finally, as Vos also noted, Olevianus does not clearly express "the way in which the covenant of works was to be distinguished from the natural relationship in which man as creature stands to God."[80] Vos appears to fault Olevianus on this score but in so doing really misses Olevianus's point. For Olevianus the covenant of creation *was* the relationship in which Adam stood with God by virtue of his creation—a relationship of dependence, conformity, and obligation. Inherent in Adam's status as a bearer of the image given at creation was the obligation to live up to that image or suffer the consequences. The absence of a distinction here is not an oversight in his doctrine of a prelapsarian covenant but its central point.

What we find in Olevianus, then, are neither just the faint outlines nor a highly developed form of the Reformed covenant of creation/works. The outlines of the doctrine are clear: the covenant of creation has its parties, its conditions, its benefits, its penalties. But it is an idea without an assigned place in Ole-

76. In his statement in *De substantia,* 26, "Requirebatur . . . Filius incarnatus, ut non tantum pro dissoluto creationis foedere fieret expiatio, & eiusdem instauratio," Olevianus clearly implies that the work of Christ brings about the renewal of the covenant of creation. But he nowhere makes clear the relationship of this restored *foedus creationis* to the *foedus gratiae.* Cf. also Ibid., 23, 74.

77. "Covenant in Reformed Theology," 237–38.

78. Lex (quatenus est foedus), quae eum [the old man] totum vitamque eius totam peccati & damnationis convincit, quicquid, inquam, ex naturali vita Adami emanat ut imputatio defectionis ac reatus, & corruptio cum suis fractibus." *De substantia,* 100. Olevianus does refer here to the *imputatio reatus* ("the imputation of an accused state") but it is an imputation that flows *ex naturali vita Adami,* i.e., from a natural, not judicial, relationship to Adam.

79. Reu, *Vester Grundt,* 1567 ed., 1384–85; Sudhoff, *Fester Grund,* 1590 ed., 117; Sudhoff, "Abendmahlpredigten," no. 5, 210; *Expositio,* 182; Comm. on Rom. 5:12–16, pp. 195, 201, 203; *De substantia,* 10, 11, 86, 253.

80. "Covenant in Reformed Theology," 238.

vianus's theology. His references to a *foedus* or *ius creationis* are scattered throughout his works and usually appear as incidental to the discussion of other theological topics. The doctrine occurs frequently enough not to escape notice, but in Olevianus's covenant thought as a whole it plays at most a minor role.

Covenant with the Devil

While Olevianus never directly compares or contrasts the covenant of grace with the covenant of creation, he does distinguish the covenant of grace from what he terms the "covenant with the Devil" (*verbundnuss mit dem Teuffel*,[81] *foedus cum Diabolo*,[82] *nefarium foedus*,[83] *foedus Satanae*[84]) made by humanity in the fall. The parallels he draws between these two covenants are striking: 1) He understands the covenant with the Devil—like the covenants of creation and grace before and after it—as a relationship, an allegiance, a bond of mutual commitment. In the fall, says Olevianus, humanity separated itself from its union with God and bound itself (*sich . . . verbunden*) to the Devil.[85] Adam switched loyalties, sold himself (*se manciparat*) to a new master.[86] He was no longer a vassal of God but a captive and a slave of Satan.[87] 2) The first Adam had been the *fundamentum* of our defection from God and the covenant with the Devil in much the same way that the second Adam became the *fundamentum* of our reconciliation with God and the covenant of grace.[88] 3) We

81. Reu, *Vester Grundt,* 1567 ed., 1355.
82. *Expositio,* 89 (twice).
83. *De substantia,* 10. Ritschl (*Dogmengeschichte,* 3:418) and Murray (*Encyclopedia of Christianity,* s.v. "Covenant Theology") both make a brief reference to this term in Olevianus.
84. *De substantia,* 253.
85. "Nuhn hat sich aber der mensch durch die sünde, der Gott feind ist, von Gott abgesündert und sich mit dem Teuffel verbunden." Reu, *Vester Grundt,* 1567 ed., 1355.
86. ". . . nefarium illud foedus, quo homo se manc[i]parat Sathanae." *De substantia,* 10.
87. ". . . captivum Satanae." Comm. on Rom. 8:28, p. 376. "Erstlich macht [die sünd des ersten Adams], das wir an leib und seel eigene knecht des Sathans seind." Reu, *Vester Grundt,* 1567 ed., 1384.
88. "Quemadmodum igitur certa persona fuit, per quam peccatum intravit in mundum, & per peccatum mors, atque ita causa & veluti fundamentum extitit defectionis a Deo, & foederis cum Diabolo; ita etiam certam personam a Deo constitui oportuit, quae fundamentum & causa esset reconciliationis." *Expositio,* 89.

entered the *foedus Sathanae* through faith in the mendacious promises of Satan ("You will not die; you will become like God");[89] we enter the *foedus gratiae* through faith in the sure promises of Christ. 4) Those in covenant with Satan are citizens of the Kingdom of Satan/Darkness; those in covenant with Christ are citizens of the Kingdom of Christ/Light.[90] Unless and until we transfer citizenship once again, we remain under Satan's rule (*Herrschaft*),[91] his power (*Gewalt, potestas),*[92] and his tyranny (*tyrannis).*[93] 5) Under the impious covenant (*nefarium foedus*) we are by nature members (*glidmassen)* of Satan; under the gracious covenant we become not merely members of Christ but participants in His divine nature.[94] 6) Finally, in those who through faith are engrafted into Christ, the *imago Sathanae* is covered over or concealed (*tegitur)* and the *imago Dei* restored.[95]

According to Olevianus, one remains in this covenant of bondage to Satan until one is reconciled to God in the covenant of grace. It is in the law that we first learn how to "flee" the covenant of Satan and take possession of the covenant of grace.[96]

89. ". . . nefarium illud foedus, quo homo se manc[i]parat Sathanae, eius mendacibus promissis fidem habens, quod transgrediendo divinum mandatum, eoipsi aequalis futurus esse." *De substantia*, 10.

90. "Duo esse regna spiritualia, etiam in hoc mundo, certum est: Regnum nimirum Tenebrarum, & regnum lucis; atque omnino necesse est ut quilibet hominum in alterutro horum sit dum hic vivit. . . . Alterum vero regnum Satanae & tenebrarum, in quo ii sunt omnes, qui non resipiscunt, & non credent in Christum." *Expositio*, 1–2. Cf. also ibid., 71; Sudhoff, *Fester Grund*, 1590 ed., 54–55, 57–58, 165–66; Comm. on Col. 1:12–13, pp. 79–81.

91. Sudhoff, *Fester Grund*, 1590 ed., 54–55.

92. Ibid; Comm. on Gal. 5:1, p. 103; Comm. on Col. 1:12–3, p. 81.

93. *De substantia*, 140.

94. ". . . die wir von natur glidmassen des Satans waren, auss genaden nit allein zu wahren glidern [Christi] leibs annimt, sonder auch theilhafftig machet seiner Göttlichen natur." "Abendmahlpredigten," no. 6, *Gnadenbund*, 423. Cf. also *Expositio*, 81–82.

95. "Quotquot enim vere Christo per fidem sumus insiti, praeter illud beneficium remissionis, quo tegitur imago Sathanae: alterum simul incipimus possidere, nempe instaurationem imaginis Dei, quae constat veteris hominis mortificare, & vivificatione Spiritus, ad Rom. 6." *Expositio*, 184. It is not possible to determine what exactly Olevianus means here by the "image of Satan." Unfortunately, this is the only passage in his writings where this phrase is found.

96. ". . . Lex . . . docens & quid peccatum & quantum malum sit: quo foedus Satanae fugere, gratiae vero foedus & semel aditam reconciliationis posses-

Then, in our reunion with God we are set free from our slavery to Satan, redeemed from his power, and liberated from his kingdom.[97] In short, we are no longer captives of Satan, but *captivi . . . Jesu Christi,* no longer in *Gemeinschaft* with Satan but in eternal *Gemeinschaft* with Christ.[98]

Legal Covenant

The *foedus legale* for Olevianus is a postlapsarian renewal or re-iteration of that dimension of the *foedus creationis* by which humanity was under obligation from the time of creation to conform to the righteousness and holiness of the Creator. This *pactum,* he says, was established at Mount Sinai following Israel's deliverance from Egypt and obligated the people of God to perfect observance of the law through the exercise of their own moral powers. Those who kept the commandments were promised eternal life; those who did not stood under the wrath of God's curse.[99] As such, the *lex scripta* (or Decalogue) stood in the same relation to the *foedus legale* as did the *lex inscripta* (or law of nature) to the *foedus creationis,* namely, as a testimony

---

sionem magni facere discamus." *De substantia,* 253. Olevianus's expression "to flee the covenant of Satan" is reminiscent of a statement in one of his earlier works that under the influence of sin "wir Gott fliehen." Reu, *Vester Grundt,* 1567 ed., 1384.

97. ". . . eosque [Christus] vindicando a tyrannide & servitute Satanae." *De substantia,* 140. ". . . von der Gewalt des Teufels erlöst." Sudhoff, *Fester Grund,* 1590 ed., 54. ". . . a potestate regno diabolo nos liberat." *Expositio,* 4.

98. *De substantia,* 168: "Darumb, dass obschon sie eusserlich von dem heiligen brot am Tisch des herrn assen, so wurden sie doch nit theilhafftig des wahren himmelbrots, nemlich der gemeynschaft und bluts Christi, dieweil sie noch verhaften in der gemeynschaft des Teuffels unnd nicht buss theten." "Abendmahlpredigten," no. 4, *Gnadenbund,* 381.

99. "Qui cum tales sint, nolle se, ait Dominus, eiusmodi foedus cum iis percutere, cuius vel minima pars in ipsorum viribus fundata sit, quale illud fuerat, quod percusserat cum patribus eorum, cum educeret eos ex Aegypte. Rationem assignat: Quia non servarunt illud. Cur autem non servarunt? An quia non debebant? Imo iure creationis debebant: deinde etiam ex pacto. Foedus enim legale erat pactum solemniter confirmatum, quo obligabatur populus ad praestandam propriis viribus (Mat. 22.) perfectam obedientiam Legi, cum sit aeterna norma iustitiae in mente divina; cui vult omnes rationales creaturas esse conformes ac a Deo promittebatur vita aeterna perfecte servantibus; maledictio vero denunciabatur transgredientibus." *De substantia,* 12–13.

to one's obligation to perfect obedience.[100] The one is inscribed on human hearts, the other on tablets of stone, but both bear witness to the same *ius creationis,* to the same guidelines for discerning good and evil, and to the same sentence of judgment.[101] Like their respective covenants, the law given at Sinai was really the law given at creation "widerholet und verneuwert."[102]

Why was a renewal of the covenant of creation and its attendant witness necessary? First of all, because of the damage done to the *lex naturae* in the fall. As we have already mentioned, Olevianus sometimes goes so far as to say that the law of nature was extinguished or obliterated in the fall. At the very least it was weakened, impeded in carrying out its judicial task by a nature now enslaved to its passions. The human mind (*mens),* the seat of this internal witness, was enshrouded in doubt and moral murkiness; an evil fog had set in. Therefore, he concludes, it was necessary that the law first implanted in our natures at creation be restated.[103] Our obligation to God had not changed, but the chief witness to that obligation had been virtually stilled and God wished for it to be heard once again.

---

100. We quite agree with Verhoeven's conclusion ("Olevianus," 52) that "het is nl. niet zo, dat Olevianus het wettisch verbond en het natuurlijk verbond geheel identificeert. Ook zegt hij nergens, dat het wettisch verbond een hernieuwde instelling of een voortzetting van het natuurlijk verbond is. . . . Hoewel Olevianus het dus niet expliciet zegt, suggereert hij wel heel sterk, dat her wettisch verbond een vernieuwing van het natuurlijk verbond betekent. Hij stelt nl., dat de Dekaloog, die het wettisch verbond karakteriseert, in het verlengde ligt van de wet der natuur die het verbond der schepping karakteriseert."

101. "Una quidem fuit lex moralis omnium temporum cordibus hominum inscripta, & deinde literi consignata; hoc est, inde ab Adamo sciverunt homines quales esse, quae mala vitare, contra quae bona facere debuerint." Comm. on Rom. 1:2, pp. 2–3. "Ius Dei naturale & ius Dei scriptum, sive decalogus, idem est." Comm. on Rom. 1:32, p. 65. "Quod lex sive naturae, sive scripta (nam eadem est lex quoad sententiam)." Comm. on Rom. 1:29–31, p. 59.

102. Reu, *Vester Grundt,* 1567 ed., 1337.

103. "Gravissimae sunt causae cur ius [naturale] illud scribi voluerit. Primum enim post lapsum hominis in mentibus multum est dubitationum & tenebrarum. Paulatim mala exempla augebant caliginem. Ergo repeti & describi fuit necesse; interim vero idem ius est." Comm. on Rom. 1:32, p. 65. "Decalogus adea spiritualis est, referens naturam legislatoris, ut non solum externa & crassa peccata, sed etiam malum intus latens prodat. Id lex naturae, labefacta a natura corrupta, non ita potest prodere." Comm. on Rom. 7:5–7, pp. 273–74.

The goal of the legal covenant and its commandments, however, was to produce not only knowledge of moral obligation but also knowledge of sin. God placed the law before us like a promissory note of the obedience we owed Him *iure creatione,* not because He expected that we could pay our due but precisely because He knew that we could not and would have to turn to Him for help.[104] The law exposes but does not remit sin. It comes with accusations rather than promises. It condemns us; it does not save us. But in its condemnatory role the law points us beyond itself to the gospel and thus serves as a preparation for salvation. In its diagnosis of our illness, it compels us to flee to Christ, the *verus medicus.*[105] For only when we are emptied of all confidence in ourselves are we able to take hold of the promises of the covenant of grace.[106]

This transition from the *foedus legale* to the *foedus gratuitum* has both a historical-redemptive and a personal dimension. We shall deal with the question of the legal covenant as a historical dispensation later in this chapter, but it can be noted here that for Olevianus every individual believer makes the passage from the former covenant to the latter. He understands Paul to say in Romans 7:14 that the life of the Christian always consists of two parts, two stages: one before conversion, the other after; one *sub lege,* the other *sub gratia;* one in

---

104. ". . . finis legalis foederis agnitio peccati." Comm. on Rom. 3:21–23, pp. 134–35. "Sic etiam Deus legem nobis proponit veluti syngrapham eius obedientiae quam ipsi iure creatione debemus, addita quidem hac conditionali promissione; si feceris haec quae iure creationis debes, vives; non tamen eo consilio, quod existimet nos solvendo esse, multo minus quod velit nos fiduciam in opera desigere, sed potius eo consilio, primo ut omnibus nostris quaerimoniis ansam praescindat." Comm. on Gal. 3:21, p. 76.

105. "Lex veluti Syngrapha est qua ostenditur quid debeas Deo iure creationis, sed non habet promissionem remissionis peccatorum & novae instaurationis ubi eam semel transgressus fueris, ideo terret tantum." Comm. on Gal. 3:2, p. 40. "Scopus enim praeceptorum omnium est Christus in iustitiam omni credenti: Ut tibi caeco & arroganti ostendat peccata tua, & tibi aegroto, neque id agnoscenti, ostendat morbum tuum, ut ad verum medicum Christum confugias." Comm. on Rom. 10:4, p. 495.

106. "In his mors a peccato per legem inflicta, praeparatio est recipiendam gratiam. Nisi enim vacui simus ab omni confidentia propriarum virium & persuasi simus nostram sapientiam esse inimicitiam adversus Deum, non sumus capaces ipsius gratiae." Comm. on Rom. 7:9, pp. 285–6.

the legal covenant, the other in the covenant of grace.[107] All people, of course, are by nature under obligation to conform to the divine standards of righteousness expressed in the law, but when we take the step of faith from the legal to the gracious covenant, we are suddenly freed from that obligation by Him who fulfilled the law perfectly in our stead.[108] That does not mean that the law disappears from the Christian life. With respect to the "old man" in us and our "animal" or "natural life," the law continues to convict us of sin and condemnation. But with respect to that part of us that has been reborn by the Holy Spirit, the law serves as a guide, not a judge; as a *regula gratitudinis*, not a *legalis custodia*. In fact, says Olevianus, inasmuch as the law in the New Covenant is engraved by the Holy Spirit on human hearts to restore them to their original obedience, it is itself a part of the covenant of grace.[109]

107. "Totam igitur hominis vitam in duas partes dividat: unam ante conversionem, alteram post conversionem; sive duplicem facit hominis statum, unum, sub lege, id est, quamdiu non est renatus, alterum sub gratia, id est, postquam coepit renasci." Comm. on Rom. 7:1–4, p. 267. "Nec etiam impedit novi foederis promissio, quo minus infideles ut Turcae, Iudaei, & hypocritae inter Christianos, qui adhuc sunt sub lege tam naturae quam scripta, tantipser sub ea maneant, & quia utriusque transgressores sunt . . . donec transeant ad foedus novum, sive donec fiat reconciliatio per fidem in Christum, Rom. 1:v.12,14; Gal. 3:v.12; 2 Cor. 5:ver.20,21." *De substantia*, 252–53.

108. "Docet solutam esse Legis vim tam damnandi quam exigendi ex nostris viribus, quia sit soluta obligatio nostri ad foedus legale." *De substantia*, 90. "Etsi autem nolit amplius foedus legale nobiscum percutere ut deserte testatur Ierem. 31, id tamen non impedit quin naturalis obligatio praecedat ad perfectam obedientam ex propriis viribus praestandam vel ad poenam, donec per Christum novo initio foedere obligatione illa liberemur." Ibid., 252. "Christus se offerens in mortem crucis, praestat & solvit pro fratribus quod Lex requirebat, hoc est, illa obedientia Filij, qua nostram maledictionem in se transfert, aequipollet plenae observationi Legis, quam nos debeamus," Serm. on Luke 2:41–52, *Notae in Evangelia*, 54. Cf. also the Comm. on Rom. 7:1–4, p. 267.

109. "Atque ad hunc veterem hominem & totam vitam naturalem [earlier: animalem] seu *psuchikeen* pertinet Lex (quatenus est foedus), quae eum totum vitamque eius totam peccati & damnationis convincit . . . ; non autem id quod ex vivifica vi Spiritus Christi proficiscitur." *De substantia*, 100. "Postquam ad Christum veniamus, regula est gratitudinis. . . . In summa Deus vult inchoari in hac vita novam obedientiam & nos proficere donec per ipsius Spiritum prorsus imago Dei instauretur in nobis." Comm. on Gal. 3:19, p. 71. "Atque sic lex pars est foederis gratuiti, quatenus per Spiritum inscribitur cordibus, eiusque inscriptionis organum ceu calamus est concio resipiscentiae." *De substantia*, 295.

Covenant with Creatures

It is hardly surprising that past research on Olevianus has made no mention of a covenant between believers and other creatures in his writings. Of all of Olevianus's uses of the term "covenant," this *foedus cum creaturis* is the least often mentioned (four times)[110] and the most difficult to understand. The common link among all four references is his citation of Hosea 2:18: "And I will make for you a covenant on that day with the beasts of the field, the birds of the air, and the creeping things of the ground; and I will abolish the bow, the sword, and war from the land; and I will make you lie down in safety" (RSV). Even this clue is not very helpful, however, unless we first have in view the close relationship Olevianus sees between the covenant of grace and divine providence.

The doctrine of providence, he asserts, is really a part of the doctrine of the covenant.[111] This is so because God governs the universe not merely by a "general reason and motion" (*ratione motu universali*) but also by a "particular" (*particulari*) rule which extends even to the least of sparrows and the very hairs of our heads.[112] This special control, moreover, is directed toward the benefit of those who are reconciled or in covenant with God. God has so reconciled Himself to us in Christ that it is impossible for Him to send anything our way that is not for our good.[113] By His covenant promises He has bound Himself to us and taken us under His special care. That is why believers are reminded of

110. Reu, *Vester Grundt*, 1567 ed., 1353; *Expositio*, 49, 64; Serm. on Luke 2:21, *Notae in Evangelia*, 42.

111. "Ut doctrina de Dei providentia in cordibus nostris fixam sedem habeat, necesse est, ut includatur in doctrinam de foedere." Serm. on Mt. 6:25–34, *Notae in Evangelia*, 248.

112. "... Deum eadem omnipotentia, qua singula condidit, etiam ea tueri & conservare, atque admirabili sua providentia gubernare ... idque non ratione aliqua & motu universali duntaxat, sed etiam particulari, & quidem qui ad minimos usque passerculos & vilissimos capitis nostri pilos ... extendatur." *Expositio*, 50.

113. "... die Verheissung des Evangelii, dass Gott, der sich uns zum Vater gegeben hat, so vollkommen mit uns in Christo versöhnet ist, dass er uns unmöglich zuschicken kann, was nicht zu unserm Besten dienet." Sudhoff, *Fester Grund*, 1590 ed., 12.

God's covenant when they reflect on His providence. The two can never be separated.[114]

The two main benefits of this special providence or care for His *confoederati* are God's provision and His protection. The former is clearly set forth in Matthew 6:25ff., where Jesus distinguishes between the sons of the heavenly Father (those who have been adopted into the covenant) and the *gentes* or *infideles* (those outside the covenant). It is the *gentes*, says Jesus, who are forever worrying about what they shall eat, drink, and wear. The *confoederati* know that they need not concern themselves about such matters, for God is an ever-present help to them.[115]

The second benefit is divine *defensio*[116] against other creatures,[117] sin, the Devil,[118] and fear itself.[119] This was made clear already in God's covenant with Abraham when He proclaimed, "I am El Shaddai [God Almighty]" (Gen. 17) and earlier in Genesis 15, "Fear not, Abraham, I will be thy shield."[120] God pro-

---

114. "Non solum omnia Dei dispensatione fieri statuendum est, sed etiam in nostrum bonum omnia & singula fieri; ideoque certus eris, quemlibet eventum tibi fore salutarem: Primum, quia se tibi licet indigno in Christo obligavit, dum promisit." *Expositio*, 54. ". . . & ut dum cogitas de Dei providentia, simul etiam cogites, Deum iureiurando tibi confoederatum esse . . . doctrinam de providentia Dei nunquam separandum esse a foedere adoptionis gratuito." Serm. on Mt. 6:25–34, *Notae in Evangelia*, 248.

115. "Christus discernit inter Patris coelestis filios, hoc est, confoederatos iure adoptionis, & inter gentes, hoc est, infideles, qui sunt extra foedus, quos hac nota insignit Christus, quod dicat, Quid edemus, quid bibemus, aut quo amiciemur? Omnia ista gentes requirunt. Quo docet Christus, doctrinam de providentia Dei nunquam separandam esse a foedere adoptionis gratuito, quo nobis eius constet utilitas." Ibid.

116. "Quae bona promittuntur in hoc foedere? . . . Corpus anima recipiuntur in tutelam Dei." Serm. on Luke 2:21, *Notae in Evangelia*, 42. Cf. also Reu, *Vester Grundt*, 1567 ed., 1351; Sudhoff, *Fester Grund*, 1590 ed., 128; *Expositio*, 166; Comm. on Rom. 8:34, p. 398; Comm. on Col. 1:14, pp. 81–82.

117. Reu, Vester Grundt, 1567 ed., 1345; Sudhoff, *Fester Grund*, 1590 ed., 128; *Expositio*, 48–49, 54–56.

118. Sudhoff, *Fester Grund*, 1590 ed., 57.

119. ". . . so wirdt dann allererst das hertz von aller angst und forcht, ja auch von aller sorgen gefreiet und entlediget, wenn ihm das liecht der vorsehung Gottes durch die gnade des H. Geysts im hertzen auffgangen ist." Reu, *Vester Grundt*, 1567 ed., 1353.

120. Comm. on Phil. 1:28, p. 15; *Expositio*, 48.

tects His special people with special care.[121] Because we are in covenant with the Creator, we have nothing to fear from His creation, for the Creator has everything under complete control. It is as easy for Him to bring something again to nothing, if need be, as it was to create it out of nothing in the first place.[122] Even the devils, who try to sabotage the salvation of the elect, cannot so much as move without divine permission and are, in fact, compelled to perform His will.[123] Nothing, therefore, not even devils, can separate us from the love of God (Rom. 8:38,39). No one can snatch God's sheep out of His hand (John 10:28).[124]

This does not mean, Olevianus always adds, that God's *confoederati* never experience adversity. But if or when it happens, it is always for their ultimate good, always beneficial (*salutaris*).[125] Since it is also part of the covenant with the Creator that He will remember their sins no more, they can be assured that hardship is not an expression of God's anger or the severity of His justice against their personal sin. It is rather a means that God uses to bring the other promise of the covenant to fruition: by His loving correction He renews them, sanctifies them.[126] As the pledge (*pignus, pfand*) of all His promises, moreover, God has given them Christ Himself—in death (Rom. 8:32). With Him as their pledge—Him with whom they are coheirs and by whom all other creatures are governed—all things must be

---

121. ". . . sed proprio sanguine eos a potestate tenebrarum redemit, sibi in peculium acquisivit, neque acquisivit modo, sed acquisitos etiam peculiari cura protegit." Ibid., 83.

122. ". . . quia creatori aeque facile est eas destruere, & in nihilum redigere, atque facile fuit semel ex nihilo creare." Ibid., 48.

123. "Diabolos vero, Electorum insidiantes, licet spiritu suo non ut Angelos gubernat, potestate tamen sua tanquam freno ita coercet, ut ne movere quidem se possint, nisi quoad ille permittit, & voluntati ipsius reluctantes etiam invitos & praeter consilium eam cogit exequi. Job 1, Luke 22, Rom. 16, I Cor. 10." Ibid., 57.

124. Ibid., 164; Reu, *Vester Grundt*, 1567 ed., 1345.

125. *Expositio*, 54, 165; Sudhoff, *Fester Grund*, 1590 ed., 12; *De substantia*, 19.

126. "Cum igitur foederis caput unum sit, quod Dominus peccatorum nostrorum nolit recordari amplius, certum est etiam res adversas non ab irato Deo . . . seu a rigore ipsius iustitiae nobis immitti, neque esse signa animi a nobis alienati. . . . Sed cum & altera foederis pars non minus a Deo servanda sit de inscribenda sua lege in corda, non mirum si absque, amore vere paterno suos castiget . . . ut filij sui porro reddantur cautiores & sanctiores." *De substantia*, 19–20.

working for their good, even when the contrary appears true.[127] Whatever befalls the believer, then, must be interpreted as beneficial to his salvation. To question providence is to question the covenant itself, to call into question the reality of one's own reconciliation.[128] If God is for us, Olevianus quotes (Rom. 8:31), who can be against us? And God *is* indeed *pro nobis*—by His eternal covenant.[129]

It is against the background of this close bond between covenant and providence that Olevianus's four references to a "covenant which the faithful . . . also have with creatures" must be understood. It has been mentioned that in all four instances Olevianus cites as biblical evidence of this covenant Hosea 2:18, where God promises a covenant with the beasts of the field and birds of the air, that they not harm His chosen people. God pledges to direct His providential rule toward the favor of His *confoederati*. What Olevianus apparently means by *our* covenant *cum creaturis*, then, is that by virtue of our covenant with the Creator we become the beneficiaries of the *Creator's* covenant with His creatures. It was, after all, in our interest that God made a *foedus cum creaturis* at all. We are therefore in covenant with these creatures indirectly or by extension, i.e., only because we share in the benefits of God's providence that accrue to us in the covenant of grace. God has a covenant with creatures; we have a covenant with God; therefore, we also have (i.e., share in the blessings of) a covenant with creatures. As Olevianus himself puts it, "Whatever we experience at the hands of creatures is sent our way by God and indeed for our own good,

127. "Qui igitur fieri potest, ut ulla creatura tibi noceat, quae absque praesenti operatione Filij Dei, qui pignus tuum est ne movere se quidem potest? Imo qui fieri potest, ut non omnes creaturae per & propter filium, in quo consistunt, & quo gubernantur cuiusque tu cohaeres es, necessario cogantur tibi inservire & cooperari in bonum, etiam tum cum maxime tibi videntur adversari?" *Expositio*, 56.

128. "Quaecunque igitur sive publice sive privatim inciderint tam laeta tam tristia, non nisi beneficia & quidem Dei beneficia, quaeque certo saluti sint, habeat oportet, quicunque persuasus est, Deum sua providentia sapientissime omnia administrare, sibique plene in Christo reconciliatum esse. Nisi igitur sapientia nostra carnis soli sapienti Deo resistere, & in Christum blasphemi esse velimus ut qui Patrem non plene nobis reconciliarit." Ibid., 61.

129. "Insiste mediatatione, Deus est foedere aeterno pro nobis, Prov. 21." Comm. on Rom. 8:31, p. 378.

because of our constant and everlasting covenant with the Creator, and *per consequens* with all creatures."[130]

To say, then, that we have a covenant *cum creaturis* is really only to say that we experience the benefits of God's covenant *cum creaturis*. By virtue of our special relationship to Him, we stand in a special relationship to them: they can do us no ultimate harm; they can only work for our good.[131]

Old Covenant—New Covenant

One important question remains in this examination of other covenants in Olevianus's theology: how can he refer to the same *foedus gratiae* as both an "old" and a "new" covenant? Does he consider them to be two distinct covenants?

We must begin by emphasizing that Olevianus regards the covenant of grace as a single redemptive thread woven through all of biblical history. There has always been but one *foedus aeternum gratuitum seu Evangelium*[132] and one means (faith) by which the benefits of this covenant are appropriated. Adam, Eve, Abel, Seth, and their descendants obtained the same righteousness and rebirth through the same faith in the same Mediator as we do in the Church today.[133] Abraham was not saved any more by merit or any less by grace than we are. By faith he,

---

130. ". . . statuendum est, quae per creaturas nobis immittuntur, a Deo immitti, & quidem in nostrum bonum, idque propter constans & aeternum foedus cum Creatore, & per consequens cum omnibus creaturis." *Expositio*, 49.

131. "Ad haec cum constans & aeternum foedus cum Creatore habeamus, necesse est, etiam omnes creaturas nobis cooperari in bonum (Hos. 2:18)." *De substantia*, 19.

132. Ibid., 295.

133. "Darauss kanstu nu leichtlich sehen dass Adam, Eva, Abel, Seth und andere ire nachkommen, die ir vertrauen auff die verheissing Gottes von dem leiden Christi gesetzt haben, die haben auch durch denselbigen Glauben auff das zukünfftige leiden Christi vergebung der sünden, wahre gerechtigkeit und ewiges leben, in ihren hertzen gehabt, eben so wol, als wir haben durch den Glauben und vertrauen auff das leiden Christi, das nun vor tausent, funffhundert und mehr jahren geschehen ist." "Abendmahlpredigten," no. 1, *Gnadenbund*, 260–61. "Ideo in semetipsis perditi reconciliationem quaerebant in eodem Mediatore, quo nos prout in omnibus sacrificiis in ipsius sacrificium respiciebant . . . & per eundem eodem quo nos Spiritu adoptionis donabantur . . . qui eandem iustitiam fidei in [pro-] missa Christi victima . . . eandemque regenerationem ex fide in ipsis operabatur, quam in nobis, eandemque spem & expectationem haereditatis coelestis ab eodem semine benedicto, in quo sicut & nos fide censebantur." *De substantia*, 231.

too, was engrafted into Christ.[134] All believers from Adam on, therefore, make up one body through the Holy Spirit and are members of the one Head, Jesus Christ.[135]

When Olevianus does use the terms "old covenant" and "new covenant," then, what he usually has in mind are two "dispensations"[136] or "economies"[137] of this one covenant of grace, separated chronologically by the redemptive work of Jesus Christ. This historical division of the covenant corresponds, in his view, to the division of the Scriptures into the Old and New Testaments, so that he usually uses the phrases *sub veteri/novo foedere* and *sub veteri/novo testamento* interchangeably.[138]

What set these old and new administrations of the covenant of grace apart from each other were not essential differences in the promise, condition, or benefits of the covenant but differences in the tense and clarity of the promise and in the enjoyment of the benefits. In the first place, the covenant promise of reconciliation through Christ did not change in content, only in tense. The promise to Adam and Eve, repeated in the covenant agreement with Abraham[139] and later renewed with David,[140] al-

134. ". . . a parte Abrahami & nostrum omnium nihil esse, quod mereatur gratiam." Comm. on Gal. 3:18, p. 68. "Observandum etiam etsi Abraham vitam fere Angelicam viveret, tamen non ideo remissionem peccatorum accepisse, sed fide, qua inserebatur in illud semen, in quo & ipse & omnes Gentes erant benedicenae." Comm. on Gal. 3:5–9, p. 44.

135. ". . . gleichwie nur ein Haupt der Kirche ist, nämlich Christus, also auch alle Gläubigen von Adam an bis zum Ende der Welt, sind seine Gleider, und ein Leib durch den heiligen Geist, sind alle durch ein Haupt erlöset, einem haupt eingeleibt und werden an einem Haupte erhalten durch den Glauben an ihn." Sudhoff, *Fester Grund,* 1590 ed., 160.

136. Comm. on Rom. 8:15, p. 345.

137. Comm. on Col. 2:14, p. 144.

138. See, e.g., the Sermon on Mark 7:31–37, *Notae in Evangelia,* 239; Serm. on Luke 10:23–38, *Notae in Evangelia,* 241; Comm. on Col. 2:14, pp. 141–45; Comm. on Rom. 8:15, pp. 345–46. Occasionally, Olevianus uses the term *foedus vetus* synonymously with *foedus legale* (see, e.g., his Comm. on Gal. 4:19–26, pp. 98–99). This represents only the assignment of different meanings to the same word in different contexts, however, and is not an attempt to identify through a common term the legal covenant with the Old Testament covenant of grace.

139. ". . . ab initio mundi facta est gratuita promissio de benedicto semine mulieris . . . & deinde eadem fuit repetita sub forma foederis gratuiti percussi cum Abrahamo." *De substantia,* 230.

140. "Etenim foedus salutis cum Abrahamo percussum, renovatum fuit cum Davide, eique promissus Rex aeternus, ex ipsius semine, qui esset huius foederis Mediator." *Expositio,* 76.

ways pointed to the future: "The seed of the woman *will* crush the serpent's head" (Gen. 3:15); ". . . through your offspring all nations on earth *will* be blessed" (Gen. 22:18); "I *will* raise up your offspring to succeed you, who *will* come from your own body, and I *will* establish His kingdom" (2 Sam. 7:12). In the New Covenant, however, the focus is always trained backward: "God, *having raised up* his Son Jesus, sent him to bless you" (Acts 3:26).[141] That is the first major difference Olevianus sees between the two economies of grace: the promises of the Old Covenant always looked to what *would* happen in Jesus Christ, the promises of the New Covenant to what *has* happened in Jesus Christ. Adam and Eve exercised the same faith as we do today, but it was directed toward the future, not the past, suffering of Christ.[142] Sins in David's day were forgiven in the same way as sins today but by a confidence and trust in the sacrifice of Christ yet to come, not already come.[143]

Olevianus recognizes the difficulty in affirming that the patriarchs participated in the blessings advertised in the covenant promise long before that promise was actually fulfilled in the death of Christ. He argues, however, for the efficacy of Christ's death from eternity on the premises 1) that the power of His passion, like Christ Himself, is the same yesterday, today, and forever (Hebrews 13:8),[144] and 2) that the names of the elect "are written in the Book of Life of the Lamb which was slain from the beginning of the world." On that basis, he concludes, it can be argued that the sacrifice of Christ, though still an event in the future, had always been present and efficacious before the face of the Father.[145] One's temporal relation, therefore, to

141. Comm. on Rom. 11:27, pp. 586–88.
142. See n. 133 above.
143. "Derhalben zu Davids Zeiten, ehe Christus noch gelitten hat, wurden die Sünden vergeben durch den Glauben und das Vertrauen auf das zukünftige Opfer, gleichwie sie uns vergeben werden durch den Glauben oder das Vertrauen auf das Opfer Christi, das doch schon vollbracht ist." Sudhoff, *Fester Grund,* 1590 ed., 98.
144. "Origo autem erroris de Lymbo est, quod putarunt multi, & adhuc putant, non ante remissa esse peccata, quam Christus sit passus. Atqui Christi passio vim suam ab aeterno habuit. Christus enim heri & hodie, & idem quoque in secula, Hebr. 13 vers. 8." *Expositio,* 117.
145. "Die Leiden Christi haben vor dem Angesicht Gottes zu Adams und Evas Zeiten, ja von Ewigkeit her seine Kraft gehabt, wie in der Offenbarung

the fulfillment of the promise poses no obstacle to one's sharing in its benefits.

It is more than the tense of the promise that distinguishes the old administration of the covenant from the new. The quality of its revelation and the quantity of its benefits also differ. First of all, the Mediator of the covenant is both revealed (by God) and perceived (by us) with greater clarity *sub novo foedere*. The Old Testament church caught a glimpse of the redemptive work of Christ but only through the shadows of figures and types and only from a great historical distance.[146] The deliverance from Egypt, for example, stood as a *Vorbild* for the Israelites of the eternal deliverance through Christ from the stranglehold of Satan.[147] The land of Canaan served as God's pledge of Israel's heavenly inheritance still to be purchased;[148] the sacrifices for sin as *figura* of the coming sacrifice of the Messiah;[149] and the blood sprinkled on both the people and the Book of the Law as a *typus* of the blood to be shed one day on the cross.[150] Even the twelve precious stones (representing the twelve tribes of Israel) worn on the breast of the High Priest when he entered the tabernacle symbolized the true Israel secured in the heart of Christ as He sits today in the presence of His Father in the heavenly sanctuary.[151] But these were only hints of a redemptive drama far off in the future—a mere flicker of light, he suggests, when compared with the bright blaze of revelation in the New Covenant. For us in the New Testament Church the light is better: the Mediator has come, has spoken, has died, has risen. And because the light is better and the shadows dispelled, our vision is

---

Johannis geschrieben steht, dass die Namen der Auserwählten geschrieben sind im Buche des Lebens, des Lammes, so geschlachet ist vom Anbeginn der Welt. Daraus zu sehen ist, dass der Tod Christi, der noch zukünftig war, allzeit vor dem Angesichte Gottes gegenwärtig und kräftig gewesen sei." Sudhoff, "Abendmahlpredigten," no. 1, 186.

146. "In veteri testamento minor erat patefactio Christi eiusque cognitio . . . quia Christum . . . minus perspicue cognoscebant, sed eminus tantum per figuras venturum intuebantur." Comm. on Rom. 8:15, p. 347.

147. Sudhoff, *Fester Grund*, 1590 ed., 138.

148. Comm. on Gal. 3:15–17, p. 64; *De substantia*, 115–16.

149. Expositio, 107; *De substantia*, 65.

150. Comm. on Rom. 3:31, pp. 155–56.

151. Sudhoff, *Fester Grund*, 1590 ed., 127–28.

greatly improved. We see, as it were, in the glass clearly what our Old Testament forebears saw only darkly.[152]

The grace of the covenant comes to us of the New Testament age not only in greater clarity but also in greater abundance.[153] First of all, in the New Testament age the Holy Spirit and with Him the riches of the covenant are poured out in more copious measure than in the Old.[154] This is not to say, of course, that either the Spirit or the gifts He bears were absent *sub veteri testamento*. The Holy Spirit worked in the fathers of old the same righteousness of faith and the same rebirth that He works in us.[155] But Olevianus makes a distinction here between *possessing* and *enjoying* the benefits of the covenant. All believers possess the whole Christ and in Him the whole substance of the covenant, but the extent to which they experience or enjoy that possession is proportional to the measure of the Holy Spirit in their lives. The stronger the presence of the Spirit, the stronger the experience (*sensus*) of faith; the stronger the experience of faith, the stronger the union with Christ; the greater the enjoyment of His covenantal gifts.[156] While it is true, then, that the Old Testament faithful enjoyed the same kind of *koinonia* with Christ as we do, they did not enjoy it to the same degree. The Holy Spirit, the bond of this union, had yet to be given in fuller effusion.

152. "Illi in sacrificiis Christum moriturum eminus conspicabantur, quem nos mortuum & excitatum in Evangelio tanquam in speculo retecta facie cernimus." *De substantia*, 295.

153. "Feliciorum esse statum fidelium sub novo foedere, quam sub vetere. Quia subiectum circa quod versatur foedus, nempe Christus . . . non tantum clarius nobis sit manifestatus, sed etiam cum donorum suorum plenitudine exhibitus." Serm. on Luke 10:23–38, *Notae in Evangelia*, 241.

154. "Discrimen novi & veteris testamenti hic observandum, quod in duabus rebus consistit. In pleniore revelatione gratiae, & maiore copia Spiritus. . . . Ad haec, illis [OT believers] quoque datus fuerat Spiritus sanctus, sed idem maiore copia in novo testamento est effusus." Ibid.

155. *De substantia*, 231 (quotation in n. 133 above).

156. "Nam cum fides virtute Spiritus Sancti sacrae huius unionis sit vinculum prout ea crescit, crescit & unio. . . . Non quod in Deo sit variatio, aut substantia foederis in se crescat, aut minuatur: quod absit . . . , sed ad fidei nostrae sensum hoc referendum est. Etsi enim fides totum Christum gratuito Dei dono communiter cum omnibus fidelibus possidet ceu communem fontem . . . fruitur tamen eo in hac vita secundum donatam mesuram fidei." Ibid., 229–30.

Second, believers *sub novo testamento* enjoy a greater measure of the grace of the covenant because they are no longer in bondage to the law. Olevianus does not at this juncture abandon his position that the old administration of the covenant was a covenant of *grace*. Even in the Old Testament, gospel—not law—was the *maior et principalior doctrina*.[157] He suggests, however, that between the first statement of the promise in Eden and its final confirmation on Calvary the law (as a witness to the legal covenant) intervened to pave the way toward the fulfillment of the promise. The moral law convicted the Israelites of sin; the ceremonial law pointed toward final redemption from sin through the blood of the perfect Lamb.[158] The law, therefore, did not eclipse the covenant of grace; it supplemented it. It served as a signpost to the promise, a tutor coaxing its pupils toward the truth. But it was a harsh teacher—ever threatening, cursing, and frightening its subjects, ever placing on their backs a heavy ceremonial burden.

We in the New Covenant have it much easier. We are no longer faced with the impossible task of keeping the law perfectly nor with the difficult regimen of the Mosaic ceremonies. As our ransom, Christ bore the curse of the moral law, and as the perfect Sacrifice He fulfilled forever the ceremonial law.[159] That is the "new" covenant Jeremiah was talking about: not the forgiveness of sins itself, since forgiveness was present already in the "old" covenant, but Christ's full payment for sin on the cross and the Holy Spirit's soothing of our consciences with the *finality* of forgiveness; not regeneration itself, since the Old Testament fathers were also regenerated, but the Holy Spirit's en-

157. Comm. on Rom. 5:20, p. 225.
158. "Lex autem obiter ingressa est (Gal. 3.v.17) non quae oboleret promissionem, seu mutaret Dei consilium, sed quae viam sterneret executioni promissionis, hoc est, quae convinceret peccati & sic a se ad Christum ablegaret, & typis suis testimonium daret confirmationi venturae, atque ita ad fundamentum foederis gratiae Patres duceret, mortem, inquam, testatoris seu unicam victimam in cruce semel oblatam." *De substantia*, 296.
159. Fideles qui natura sunt sub lege, eximuntur tam stricto domino gratia fideiussoris. Nam Fideiussor factus est pro iis *lutron* placens iram Dei, ut lex non possit maledictionem instigere." Comm. on Rom. 6:13, p. 256. ". . . sic intelligendum est, quod illud regimen Mosaicum & ceremoniae & maledictio finem habeant in Christo uti deinde, volente Deo, plenius ostendetur." Comm. on Gal. 3:19, p. 72.

graving of the law on our hearts as an instrument of that renewal.[160] Where formerly there was a mixture of faith and fear, now there is only faith; where formerly a mixture of freedom and bondage, now only freedom.[161] After Christ, the covenant of grace and its covenanters move forward unfettered by the covenant of law.

The continuities and discontinuities that Olevianus finds in the transtestamental covenant of grace are reflected in his understanding of the signs of this covenant, the sacraments. Both the Old Testament sacraments (circumcision, Passover, sacrifices) and New Testament sacraments (baptism, Lord's Supper) are signs and seals of the same covenant of grace, of the same promise of union with Christ, and of the same obligation of faith and repentance.[162] Both serve also as a *testificatio mutua* of commitment between God and us—as mutual oaths themselves, as it were.[163] And finally, neither the sacraments of the Old nor of the New Testament are of themselves efficacious. The tendency to confuse the sign with the thing signified has always existed: e.g., the confusion of circumcision with God's gracious disposition, burnt offerings with reconciliation, and the sacramental bread with the benefits of the crucified body of Christ. But in both testaments it was always the thing to which the sign bore witness and not the sign itself that was to serve as the focus of faith. In the case of physical circumcision, it was only as the Israelites looked forward in faith to the One who would bear God's curse in their stead that they were also spiri-

---

160. "Confirmat [Christus] enim eam [i.e., legem] non modo dum veritatem ceremoniarum implet sua morte . . . & gratuitam veniam conscientiis affert prout supra in confirmatione foederis gratuiti expositum est . . . sed etiam quatenus Legem moralem ipsam inscribit cordibus." *De substantia*, 269.

161. Comm. on Rom. 8:15, p. 347.

162. "Ergo nostri infantes illi oleae signo foederis incorporandi seu inserandi sunt, prout & illorum infantes inserebantus tanquam teneli surculi: hoc tantum est discrimen quod signa incorporationis diversa: Illis erat circumcisio, nobis Baptismus. Usus & gratio eadem ad. Col. 2." Comm. on Rom. 11:17–18, p. 570. "Ergo verus usus Sacramentorum initiationis tam Circumcisionis quam Baptismi, ut obligent nos ad poenitentiam fidem ac vicissim poenitentibus & credentibus obsignent gratuitam promissionem *koinonias* cum Christ." Comm. on Rom. 2:25–28, p. 111.

163. "Abendmahlpredigten," no. 1, *Gnadenbund*, 264–65; *De substantia*, 395–97.

tually circumcised. In the sacrifice of a lamb, it was only by faith in the future sacrifice of the perfect Lamb that the Old Testament faithful obtained God's acceptance. Finally, in eating the bread of the New Testament Supper, it is only in believing that Christ has offered up His body as a sacrifice on our behalf that we receive spiritual nourishment.[164] No special grace inheres in the elements or in the acts themselves.

The differences in the two dispensations of the covenant of grace are also reflected in the respective sacraments. First of all, while the sacraments of both eras direct the attention of their participants to the same historical event, the death of Christ, they do so from different standpoints in history. The bloody sacrifices of the Old Testament, from Abel's offering to the Passover, all looked ahead to the forgiveness and righteousness that would one day be secured in the sacrifice of the Lamb of God.[165] Circumcision signified the promise of the blessings to be displayed in the coming of the seed of Abraham.[166] The Lord's Supper, however, the New Testament counterpart to the Passover, looks back to the sacrifice of Christ as an event once and for all time completed.[167]

Second, the two sets of sacraments differ in the degree of light they shed on the cross as the decisive event in redemptive history. The Old Testament ceremonies pointed believers to the sacrifice of Christ but not nearly so clearly or directly as did the ceremonies of the New Testament.[168]

164. *De substantia*, 401–5.

165. "So stell dir für die Augen das opffer Abels, da er ein lämblein Gott dem Herrn schlachtet. Diese übung war ihm ein gewisses Sacrament, das ist, so ein heiliges gewisses warzeichen . . . dabey Abel solt verstehen, vertrauen und gedencken, dass er . . . durch den Glauben unnd vertrauen auff das leiden Jesu Christi, gewislich vergebung seiner sünden her, unnd gefreyet were vom ewigen todt." "Abendmahlpredigten," no. 1, *Gnadenbund*, 264–65.

166. ". . . circuncisio non erat simpliciter sigillum iustitiae fidei, sed iustitiae exhibendae in venturo semine Abrahae." Comm. on Phil. 3:3, p. 36.

167. ". . . dass er eben diess heilige Sakrament gleich vor seinem Leiden . . . hat eingesetzt und zwar an Statt des Osterlammes, welches auf das zukünftige Leiden Christi wiess, wie das hl. Abendmahl auf das schon vollbrachte." Sudhoff, "Abendmahlpredigten," no. 1, 189.

168. "Nam typi illi & umbrae ducebant eos ad sacrificium Christi, quanvis obscurius, quo nostra Sacramenta nos ducant clarius." Comm. on Gal. 4:1–5, p. 86.

Finally, the sacraments of the Old Covenant bound the Old Testament church to the legal as well as the gracious covenant, whereas the sacraments of the New Covenant are free of all ties to the *foedus legale*. Circumcision in particular underscored the obligation of the circumcised to the perfect observance of the law *propriis viribus,* to which, of course, they were already bound *iure creationis.* Nevertheless, the function of circumcision as a rite of initiation into the legal covenant was merely *accidentalis.* Its primary or deeper (*proprius*) purpose was to initiate Abraham and his seed into the covenant of grace. That, Olevianus concludes, is why circumcision was abolished at the coming of Christ.[169] The promised seed that it had anticipated had now arrived.[170] The legal taskmaster to which circumcision had bound the Church in a covenant of law had completed its work.[171] The Holy Spirit was now about the task of transferring the law from tablets of stone to the tablets of human hearts.

It ought to be pointed out, finally, that Olevianus distinguishes between what we might call an objective and a subjective dimension to the covenant of grace in each of its two dispensations. Objectively, or what he calls "meritoriously," the covenant of grace was ratified in repeated sacrifices in the Old Testament and in the one Sacrifice in the New Testament. But subjectively, or what he calls "efficaciously," the covenant promises are not ratified until they are actually applied to the people, until the sacrificial blood is sprinkled on the congregation (Old Covenant) or the promises are sealed in our hearts by the Holy Spirit (New Covenant).[172] Or again, (and here Olevi-

169. Comm. on Rom. 2:25–28, pp. 114–15. Cf. also Comm. on Phil. 3:3, pp. 36–37: "Secunda ratio cur circumcisio cesset, quia non tantum erat signum iustitiae fidei, sed aliquid in eo erat legale, Quatenus scilicet volebat Dominus eo signo obligare Iudaeos ad obedientiam totius legis."

170. "Nam ipsius [Dei] voluntas fuit, ut [circumcisio] duraret duntaxat usque ad exhibitum Messiam, utpote quod de eo in carnem mittendo testaretur." Comm. on Col. 2:11, pp. 134–35.

171. "... sub qua legali custodia [Deus] eos continere volebat, donec veniret illud promissum semen (ad Galat. 4) cuius custodiae legalis veluti sera, & ingressus erat circuncisio." Comm. on Phil. 3:3, p. 37.

172. "Dupliciter foedus hoc erigitur: 1. Merito Christi. Idem est Iehova qui condit testamentum, & qui morte illud confirmat ad Hebr. ca.9. . . . 2. Illud testamentum seu foedus efficacia ipsius Christi in nobis quoque ratum fieri

anus's use of this distinction is more implicit), objectively the covenant of grace is promised in a statement of what God would do (Old Testament) or has done (New Testament) *in history*: "I will crush/have crushed the head of the serpent." Subjectively, however, the covenant is promised in a statement of what God will do (if one is still in the legal covenant) or has done (if one is already in the covenant of grace) *in us*: "If you believe what I will do/have done in history, you are forgiven and renewed."

This double dimension to the covenant is of utmost importance to Olevianus's picture of the twofold economy of the covenant of grace. It explains, for example, why the legal covenant could be abrogated in the death of Christ objectively and yet not abrogated subjectively until an individual, even after Christ's death, enters the covenant of grace. It explains, too, why the covenant of grace was ratified in the death of Christ objectively and yet ratified subjectively even before His death in the lives of believers *sub veteri foedere*. It was only in the objective abrogation of the legal covenant and the objective ratification of the gracious covenant that a personal abrogation and ratification became possible. But Olevianus does not see the objective redemptive-historical dimension to these covenants as placing any historical *limits* on the personal dimension. The legal covenant holds sway in the lives of human beings long after its redemptive-historical abolition, and the gracious covenant long before its redemptive-historical confirmation.[173]

Conclusion

The sharp differences of opinion in the past about the presence and number of other covenants in Olevianus's theology stemmed

---

oportet. Hoc fit cum fide illud obsignat cordibus nostris. . . . Sic in confirmatione veteris Testamenti sive foederis: 1. Effundebatur sanguis, id est, fiebat sacrificium. . . . 2. Moses sanguine aspergat librum legis & populum. . . . Ergo meritum ibi notatur. . . . Etiam applicatio ad populum." Comm. on Rom. 11:27, pp. 586, 589.

173. Verhoeven ("Olevianus," 115) may be correct in stating that Olevianus never explains "hoe het te verstaan is, dat het wettisch verbond ook na de komst van Christus is blijven voortbestaan," but this distinction between the *heilsgeschichtlich* and personal dimensions of the covenant of grace is certainly the place to begin.

in large part from a cursory reading of the sources. Barth, for example, in insisting that in Olevianus "the covenant is described uniformly, unequivocally, and exclusively as the covenant of grace,"[174] overlooked completely Olevianus's references to five additional covenants: a *foedus creationis, foedus Sathanae, foedus legale,* and *foedus cum creaturis,* as well as a pretemporal *pactum* between the Son and the Father. It was just as misleading, however, for Schrenk to claim that a pretemporal covenant "is already *clearly* found in Olevianus"[175] or for Heppe to assert that Olevianus understands the covenant of works "in entirely the same way"[176] as Cocceius fifty years later. While Olevianus mentions these other covenants, he does so infrequently and does not discuss them at any length. Only the first outlines of the later Reformed doctrines of a *pactum salutis* and *foedus operum* can be detected. One ought to be careful, therefore, to claim neither too little nor too much for these other covenants in Olevianus's theology. His covenant theology is dominated by, though not restricted to, the *foedus gratiae.*

174. Barth, *Church Dogmatics,* 4/1:59.
175. Schrenk, *Gottesreich und Bund,* 61 (italics added).
176. Heppe, *Geschichte des Pietismus,* 211, n. 1.

5 Olevianus's Covenant Theology in Historical-Theological Perspective

In the two previous chapters we have been examining Olevianus's covenant doctrine from a largely theological point of view. We have seen how he understands the nature of the covenant of grace and its relation to other key doctrines such as predestination and the sacraments, and we have also discovered and discussed a variety of other covenants in his writings. We are now at the point, therefore, where we can return to the historical questions raised in Chapter I concerning the place and significance of Olevianus in the history of covenant theology. We shall look first at his role in the development of continental Reformed covenant thought and then at his place in the broader history of this doctrine.

Continental Reformed Context

First Covenant Theologian?

As we saw in Chapter I, a number of scholars in the past have identified Olevianus as the first Reformed covenant theologian, that is, the first to use the covenant idea as the organizing principle of a theological system.[1] This thesis is all the more worth

1. "Bei Olevian tritt überhaupt der Bundesbegriff zum ersten Male als constitutives und gestaltenes Prinzip des ganzen Systems auf." Heppe, *Geschichte des Pietismus*, 211. "In dieser Schrift [*De substantia*] dient der Gedanke des Bundesschlusses Gottes zum ersten Mal als gestaltendes Prinzip der Dogmatik." Bizer, "Historische Einleitung," xxxviii. "Though Bullinger is credited with the first complete treatise on the subject and though Calvin makes the covenant idea primary in his understanding of the church, none of the early Reformers

considering because the very same distinction has been accorded to Heinrich Bullinger (1504–1575). Both Von Korff and Schrenk concluded early in this century that Bullinger was the first to employ the covenant idea as a constitutive dogmatic principle,[2] an accomplishment that, in Von Korff's words, distinguished him as "der erste eigentliche Föderaltheologe."[3] Van't Hooft and Fast described the covenant as the "Kern" and "Kernstück" of Bullinger's theology.[4] And more recently, Baker has argued that the covenant became the "first principle" and the "key interpretive motif of Bullinger's theology, the principal formative and organizing factor in his thought."[5]

In our judgment, however, the weight of the evidence rests on the side of those who have argued that the covenant is but one doctrine among and alongside others in Bullinger's theological system.[6] Bullinger was indeed the first in the Reformed tradi-

---

were strictly covenant theologians, in the sense that the covenant became the organizing principle of their thought. Not until the 1580's was a form of covenant theology developed by Zacharius Ursinus and Caspar Olevianus at Heidelberg." Priebe, "Covenant Theology of Perkins," 30–31. "Olevianus . . . employed the idea of a divine covenant for the first time as an organizing principle for dogmatics." Stoever, "Covenant of Works," 30–31, n.15. Presumably, this is also what Sudhoff meant when he claimed that Olevianus "wird durch dieses Werk [*De substantia*] der eigentliche Gründer der Föderal-Theologie." *C. Olevianus,* 460.

2. "So machte er den Bundesbegriff zum bestimmenden Ausgangspunkt und zum beherrschenden Gedanken seines ganzen Lehrsystems." Von Korff, *Die Anfänge der Föderal-theologie und ihre erste Ausgestaltung in Zürich und Holland* (Bonn: Emil Eisele, 1908), 16. ". . . wird hier zum ersten Male der Versuch gemacht, den Bundesgedanken als konstitutives dogmatisches Prinzip zu benutzen." Schrenk, *Gottesreich und Bund,* 44.

3. Von Korff, *Anfänge der Föderaltheologie,* 15.

4. According to Peter Walser (*Die Prädestination bei Heinrich Bullinger im Zusammenhang mit seiner Gotteslehre* [Zurich: Verlag, 1957], 234–35), "Van't Hooft bezeichnet den Bund Gottes als den Kern von Bullinger's Theologie." Heinold Fast (*Heinrich Bullinger und die Täufer: Ein Beitrag zur Historiographie und Theologie im 16. Jahrhundert* [Weierhof: Mennonitischen Geschichtsverein, 1959], 132–33) comments: "Er war damit nicht originell, sondern übernahm die Gedanken Zwinglis. Doch baute er sie in zielsicherer Weise aus und machte sie zu einem Kernstück seiner Theologie."

5. Baker, *Bullinger and the Covenant,* 10, 14.

6. "Erstens ist der Bund ein Begriff unter und neben andern, jedoch kein Hauptbegriff (etwa gar im Sinne eines Centraldogmas). . . . Gerade für einen Traktat wie diejenigen von 1534 eignet sich das Bundeswort ganz besonders, um die evangelische Lehre volkstümlich zu machen. . . , aber er hat die Einordnung

tion to devote an entire treatise to the subject of covenant, his monograph *De testamento seu foedere*, published in 1534. Furthermore, as Baker has convincingly demonstrated, the covenant notion helped to shape his perspective on history, Christian society, and ethics.[7] But it never penetrated his theology to the extent that it became an organizing principle—at least explicitly. In the most detailed systematic exposition of his theology, the *Summa Christlicher Religion* (1556), only two of the ten books, "God and His Works" (Book II) and "The Sacraments" (Book VIII), even mention the word "covenant." What is more, there is no discussion of covenant where one might most expect it: in the sections on the Bible (Book I), the Law (Book IV), grace and justification (Book V), faith and the gospel (Book VI), and good works (Book IX).[8] The same is true of his Second Helvetic Confession (1566), where mention of the covenant is limited almost entirely to the chapters on the Church and ministry, the sacraments, and baptism (Chapters XVII–XX). There is no indication in these more systematic works that the covenant serves as the structural principle for Bullinger's dogmatics. Covenant does not even appear, on the surface at least, as the dominant motif or unifying theme of his theology.[9] Aside from *De testamento*, references to covenant in Bullinger's writings are, as

---

des Bundesbegriffs in die Gesamttheologie trotz der Lektüre der Dekaden nicht erarbeitet." Walser, *Prädestination bei Bullinger*, 248. "The covenant is not the sole ground or central structure of Bullinger's theology. It points to and is fulfilled in the work of Christ. The covenant serves to guarantee the centrality of Christ. . . . Both Bullinger and Musculus developed complex covenantal soteriologies in which the motifs of grace, election, covenant, faith, and justification all point to the central motif of the Mediator and his work." R. Muller, "Predestination and Christology," 150, 183.

7. *Bullinger and the Covenant*, especially chapters 3–5.

8. *Common Places of Christian Religion [Summa Christlicher Religion]*, trans. John Stockwood (London: Tho. East and H. Middleton, 1572). According to Walser, Van't Hooft still claims that "es klar geworden sein dürfte, dass die Bundesgedanke, obschon nicht überall ausgesprochen, doch wie ein roter Faden durch das ganze Buch gehe." *Prädestination bei Bullinger*, 234–35.

9. Baker admits that "perhaps it is too early to call Bullinger a covenant theologian" and that "the covenant was not a dogmatic principle in the later Reformed scholastic sense" (*Bullinger and the Covenant*, 9, 48), but he still insists that covenant was "the cornerstone and organizing principle of his thought" (p. 48). What Baker understands as the difference between "organizing principle" and "dogmatic principle in the later Reformed scholastic sense" is not clear.

Walser puts it, "like the pearls on a long string—but with large spaces in between."[10]

We should also consider the suggestion by August Lang that Olevianus's colleague Zacharias Ursinus (1534–1583) employed the covenant as the organizing principle of his *Summa theologiae* (often called the *Catechesis maior*), composed in late 1561 or early 1562. Lang claimed that the major divisions of the catechism (Faith, Law and Prayer, Ministry of the Church) correspond exactly to the three parts of the covenant of grace (promise, obligation, seals).[11] Lang's argument, however, was somewhat incautious. Ursinus does state that the whole of Christian doctrine can be divided into four parts: the sum of the divine law, or the Decalogue; the sum of the gospel, or the Apostles' Creed; the invocation of God, or the Lord's Prayer; and the institution of the ministry of the Church.[12] But while he explains the significance of each of these topics for the covenant, he nowhere intimates that the divisions are themselves *suggested* by the covenant. It is more likely that he patterned the *Catechesis maior* after Calvin's Genevan Catechism of 1542, which is also essentially a brief exposition of the Creed, the Law, and the Lord's Prayer.[13] Furthermore, Ursinus is just as concerned in the first section of the catechism (*De fide*) with the *fides qua*, which he identifies as a covenantal *obligation*, as with the *fides quae*, the content of the covenantal promise.

---

10. "Wie die Perlen an einer langen Schnur—jedoch mit grossen Zwischenräumen—taucht das Bundeswort immer wieder auf." *Prädestination bei Bullinger,* 249. Walser does not believe Bullinger lacked the theological skills to develop such a dogmatic system but that it was "ein Vorzug der Theologie Bullingers, dass er ähnlich wie Melanchthon in massvoller, umsichtiger und wohlabgewogener Weise ein Lehrstück neben das andere fügt, immer als Auslegung der heiligen Schrift, welche auch keine Centraldogmen aufstellt. Die Einseitigkeit ist gerade nicht Bullingers Art." Ibid., 248.

11. *Der Heidelberger Katechismus und vier verwandte Katechismen* (Leipzig, 1907), LXIVff.

12. *Catechesis, summa theologiae per questiones et responsiones exposita* in *D. Zachariae Ursini . . . opera theologica,* ed. Quirinus Reuter (Heidelberg: John Lancellot, 1612), 10 (Qs. 8 and 9).

13. Interestingly, Lang himself recognized that "in jener Reihenfolge . . . berührte sich Ursin gerade nicht mit Bullinger, weder in dessen Summa noch Catechesis, sonder mit Calvins Katechismus." *Heidelberger Katechismus,* LXVI.

If it was not Bullinger or Ursinus, then, was it Olevianus who first used covenant as an organizing principle? The claim of primacy for Olevianus begs the question, of course, of whether he employed the covenant as an organizing principle at all, and that is an assumption that, as in the case of Bullinger, cannot be granted. To be sure, the covenant does serve as the foundational concept, the basic motif, even the unifying theme of Olevianus's theology. In the *Expositio* and *De substantia* (Part I), both of which are expositions of the Apostles' Creed, Olevianus states at the outset that the articles of the Creed about to be explained are really a summary of the covenant of grace—the articles, as it were, of the eternal peace established between God and the human race.[14] The four major divisions of the Creed correspond respectively to the first party (Father), the Mediator (Son), the Applicator (Holy Spirit), and the second party (Church) of the covenant.[15] Even the individual articles of faith ought to be regarded as promises of the covenant, which God has fulfilled in Christ and gives to those who profess this faith.[16] In the *Expositio* and *De substantia*, and to some extent already in *Vester Grundt*, he conducts a painstaking examination of each of these secondary articles of the Creed in their relation to the double promise of the covenant—forgiveness and internal renewal. That Christ was "conceived by the Holy Spirit," for example, ensured both the purity of his human nature necessary for our justification and the unity of divinity and humanity necessary for our sanctification.[17] That He "suffered under Pontius Pilate, was crucified, and died" made possible both our justification before God and the daily *Absterbung* of sin within us by

---

14. *Expositio*, 10–11: "Adhaec quemadmodum in foederibus humanis certa quaedam capita, quae articulos nominant, proponi solent, quibus utrinque iuratis pax ineatur atque colatur: sic etiam divinum illus foedus, quo nos Deus aeternum sibi reconciliat, certis quibusdam capitibus, sive articulis continetur, quae sacrae huius reconciliationis sunt fundamenta, & quibus aeternam pacem inter se & credentes vult constitutam. . . . Ideoque sciendum est, articulos fidei [i.e., the Apostles' Creed] summam continere, & veluti capita illius foederis, quod fide inter Deum & nos constat." Cf. also *De substantia*, 4.

15. *Expositio*, 16.

16. Ibid., 17.

17. *De substantia*, 39.

the power of His death.[18] His burial, as an extension of His death, served further to confirm the testament ratified in His death.[19] In His resurrection the *duplex beneficium* shone forth in full certainty and glory; in His session it is preserved in the presence of the Father; and in His return in judgment it will be brought to perfection in the lives of those in whom it has been applied.[20] In sum, the covenant in Olevianus is not just one theological locus situated alongside others but a comprehensive concept which embraces his entire theology. One can with good reason speak not just of Olevianus's covenant *doctrine* but of his covenant *theology*.

Nevertheless, the covenant does not serve as the *organizing* principle of Olevianus's dogmatics. His method of organization is still basically creedal, not covenantal. Covenant for him does not suggest covenantal *categories* by which to arrange his dogmatic material—neither biblical categories (such as the covenant with Abraham, covenant with Moses, Old Covenant, and New Covenant) nor dogmatic categories (such as the pretemporal covenant, covenant of works, covenant with the Devil, and covenant of grace). As we have seen, his major systematic works, *Vester Grundt*, *Expositio*, and *De substantia* are first of all

18. "Q: Erkläre mir den Nutzen, den wir aus dem Tode Christi bekommen, etwas weitläufiger. A: Der erste Nutzen ist, dass der Gehorsam des Todes Christi unsere Gerechtigkeit vor Gott is. . . . [Der andere ist] die Absterbung der Sünden: dass die Christgläubigen, welche die Kraft des Todes Christi durch den heilgen Geist empfinden, nunmehr der Sünden täglich absterben." Sudhoff, *Fester Grund*, 1590 ed., 92–94. Cf. also *De substantia*, 48, 63.

19. "Ergo quemadmodum mors, ita & eius progressus sanctionem testamenti in se continet. . . . Est [His burial] enim continuatio seu progressus mortis." *De substantia*, 58.

20. ". . . elucet tamen in eius resurrectione plena ipsius satisfactionis & exhibitae promissionis certitudo atque gloria." Ibid., 76. ". . . those that are in league with God so reap from thence this consolation: that they know that this covenant of grace, by the intercession of this mediator kept and maintained everlastingly [in His session] . . . might continually be in force." *Exposition*, 270 (Latin text illegible here). Cf. also *De substantia*, 124–25. "Primus itaque finis reditus Christi ad iudicium est, ut Filius Dei in vera sua natura humana in qua passus est ut maleficus, declaretur iustus in conspectu omnium Angelorum & hominum. . . . Hic igitur finis ad priorem foederis gratuiti partem facit. . . . Huc accedit finis alter plena renovatio seu glorificatio Ecclesiae Phipp. 3. Conversatio nostra in coelis est, unde etiam Servatorem expectamus Dominum nostrum Iesum Christum, qui transformabit corpus nostrum humile." *De substantia*, 158–59.

commentaries on the Apostles' Creed, and while Olevianus takes great pains to point out the covenantal implications of every part of the Creed, his treatment of covenant is still largely shaped and limited by the twelve articles. It is no accident, for example, that he devotes very little attention in his dogmatic works to the function of the sacraments in the covenant until *De substantia* (Part II), which was originally composed as a separate treatise but was appended to his major commentary on the Creed (*De substantia* [Part I]) when it was published in 1585. The Creed nearly always forms the boundaries within which his discussion of the covenant is enclosed.

Still, although Olevianus employs the covenant only as the unifying, not the organizing, principle of his theology, one could argue that he was the first to do this. To be sure, covenant is a pervasive theme in Bullinger's social and political thought, but it does not dominate or permeate his systematizations of doctrine. Covenant does dominate Ursinus's *Catechesis maior*, which appeared in print at least a year before Olevianus began his first major treatise (*Vester Grundt*), but the covenant suddenly and mysteriously receded into the background in Ursinus's later theological works and played no major role in his mature theology.[21] In Olevianus's writings, on the other hand, the

21. Already in his abbreviated catechism (the so-called *Catechesis Minor*, 1562), composed just a matter of months after the *C. maior*, the term *foedus* had virtually dropped out of sight. Lang states (*Heidelberger Katechismus*, LXXVIII) that Ursinus mentions *foedus* only twice in this smaller catechism (Qs. 63, 71) but it also appears a third time in Q. 55. Ursinus still refers to remission of sins, righteousness, and eternal life as the benefits of salvation (Qs. 12, 25, 26, 58, 60, 62, 65) but no longer as covenantal benefits. Subsequently, the covenant appears again only in a few scattered places in Ursinus's *Loci* (1567) and commentary on the Heidelberg Catechism (first published in 1584) and in one comparatively short excursus on "The Covenant of God" under Q. 18 in the commentary. We find nothing in the commentary to support Heppe's contention that "durch das ganze System der christlichen Lehre durchgeführt erscheint dieselbe dagegen in Ursins *Explicationes catecheticae*. Alle einzelnen Sätze des Katechismus sind durchaus im Geiste der Föderaltheologie entwickelt." *Dogmatik des deutschen Protestantismus*, 1:189–90.

No one has yet satisfactorily explained this sudden turnabout. According to Lang, some have seen it as an attempt by Ursinus to bring his doctrine of the sacraments into closer alignment with the *Confessio Augustana variata* by eliminating any chance that the "signs of the covenant" might be misinterpreted as the bare sacramental signs of Zwinglianism. One wonders, though, whether the entire catechism would have had to be altered to avoid confusion in only one

covenant becomes increasingly more prominent. One need only note how it is unmentioned in the title of *Vester Grundt*, added to the subtitle of the *Expositio Symboli Apostolici (in qua summa gratuiti foederis aeterni inter Deum & fideles breviter & perspicue tractatur)*, and finally used in the main title of *De substantia foederis gratuiti*. Ursinus may have been the first to employ the covenant as the unifying theme of his theology in a single document, but Olevianus was the first to do so throughout a lifetime of theological reflection and a corpus of theological works.

Synthesizer of Bullinger and Calvin?

Past scholarship has also assigned Olevianus a special place in the history of Reformed covenant theology for synthesizing Bullinger's covenant doctrine with some of the central themes in Calvin's thought. In Verhoeven's words, "Olevianus was a disciple formally of Bullinger, materially of Calvin."[22] That Olevianus was influenced to some extent by both Bullinger and Calvin is indeed quite likely. He had gotten to know Bullinger well during his visit to Zurich in the late 1550s and remained in correspondence with him until Bullinger's death in 1575. In a letter to Bullinger in 1563 Olevianus explicitly acknowledged his debt to the Zuricher: "Indeed, if there be any clarity in [these catechisms that we have just composed], we owe it in large measure to you and the clear geniuses of the Swiss."[23]

---

of its parts. Lang himself suggested that "das wichtigste Motiv weshalb Ursin das foedus zum Zentralgedanken von Ma[ior] gemacht hatte, war die Betonung des Gesetzes als der unveränderten göttlichen Lebensnorm auch für den Bekehrten. Nun hatte aber Ursin selbst schon anerkannt, dass doch auch dem Gesetz als Zuchtmeister auf Christum Rechnung getragen werden müsse, und zu diesem Zweck in der Einleitung von Ma das foedus naturale eingeführt. Es hätte indes seltsam zugehen müssen, wenn diese völlig singuläre Vorstellung den Kritikern von Ma nicht befremlich erschienen wäre. So weit sich überhaupt etwas vermuten lässt, war sicherlich das foedus naturale ein Hauptstein des Anstosses." *Heidelberger Katechismus*, LXXIX. But Lang himself admitted that this was only a "hypothetische Erklärung." Perhaps the question that needs to be addressed first is the one raised by Wilhelm Neuser (following Lang's lead)— whether Ursinus wrote the *Catechesis minor* at all. "Die Väter des Heidelberger Katechismus," *Theologische Zeitschrift* 35, no. 3 (May/June 1979):178–9.

22. Verhoeven, "Olevianus," 114.

23. "Certe si qua in iis est perspicuitas, eius bonem partem tibi et candidis ingeniis Helvetiorum debemus." Letter from Olevianus to Bullinger (April 14, 1563) reprinted in Sudhoff, *C. Olevianus*, 482–83.

So far as Calvin's influence is concerned, we know that one of Olevianus's chief preoccupations following the boating accident in 1556 was his study of Calvin's works.[24] Less than two years later he spent almost a year in Geneva studying theology with Calvin in person, and the two continued to correspond after Olevianus's departure in 1559.[25] Years later, in his post at the newly founded academy in Herborn, Olevianus based his lectures in dogmatics on Calvin's *Institutes* and in fact edited his own compendium of the *Institutes* in 1586.[26] When he died in early 1587, he was hard at work on a German translation of Calvin's sermons on Job.[27] Not surprisingly, more than one scholar has noted that Olevianus became the most significant of Calvin's students on German soil.[28]

Furthermore, it is very well possible that a number of themes in Olevianus's covenant theology can be attributed to Calvin's direct influence. Even a partial list of parallels in their thought is fairly lengthy: the twofold benefit of salvation, remission of sins (or justification) and inner renewal (Calvin: regeneration), which one finds mentioned in tandem in Calvin as early as his *Genevan Confession* of 1536;[29] the *imago Dei* consisting in true knowledge, righteousness, and holiness;[30] the "sparks" of revelation that remain after the fall;[31] the mystical union with Christ and the Holy Spirit as the bond of that union; the *testimonium Spiritus Sancti internum*;[32] the distinction between "bare law" and "whole law";[33] the states and offices of Christ; the Kingdom of God; the relation of baptism to the *duplex beneficium* and union with Christ;[34] the parallel physical and spiritual eating

24. Ibid., 14.

25. A letter from Calvin to Olevianus dated October 27, 1562 is reprinted ibid., 481–82.

26. *Epitome institutionum Joh. Calvini* (Herborn, 1586).

27. Knodt, "Briefe von Olevianus," 628–29.

28. See, for example, *Evangelisches Kirchenlexikon,* s.v. "Olevian," by Moltmann; and *Allgemeine Deutsche Biographie,* s.v. "Olevian, Caspar," by Cuno.

29. *Calvin: Theological Treatises,* trans. J. K. S. Reid, vol. 22 of *The Library of Christian Classics* (Philadelphia: Westminster, 1954), 27–28.

30. Calvin, *Institutes,* I.xv.4; Olevianus, Comm. on Col. 3:10, pp. 160–61.

31. Calvin, *Institutes,* I.v.14; Olevianus, *De substantia,* 319.

32. Olevianus, *De substantia,* 225, 249.

33. Calvin, *Institutes,* II.ix.4; II.xi.10; Olevianus, Comm. on Rom. 10:5–8, p. 499; Comm. on Gal. 4:26, pp. 98–99.

34. Calvin, *Institutes,* IV.xv.4,5,6.

and the growth in one's union with Christ in the Lord's Supper; the so-called "extra-Calvinisticum";[35] and the third use of the law.[36] Olevianus takes all of these noncovenantal themes and incorporates them into the creedal structure of his covenant theology. As one scholar has put it, the spirit of Calvin breathes, as it were, in Olevianus's writings.[37]

To assert, however, that Olevianus combines these teachings of Calvin with *Bullinger's* covenant doctrine is not at all warranted. For one thing, while one might detect the outlines of Bullinger's doctrine of the covenant in Olevianus, there is nothing *distinctively* Bullingerian about Olevianus's concept of covenant. To the extent that he was dependent on earlier Reformed sources for his covenant ideas, Olevianus drew upon a common legacy of covenant thought that in its fundamentals differed little from one thinker to the next. Like Bullinger, for example, Olevianus identifies the biblical terms "covenant" and "testament," but so, for that matter, did Calvin and Ursinus before him.[38] Like Bullinger, Olevianus employs the distinction between the *substantia* and *administratio/dispensatio* of the covenant, but so did Calvin and Ursinus.[39] Like Bullinger, Olevianus appeals to the covenant idea in Scripture to explain the development of salvation history from Adam through Christ, the similarities and differences between the Old and New Testaments, and the rationale for infant baptism, but so did Zwingli, Calvin, Musculus, and Ursinus—and all, for the most part, in similar

35. Reu, *Vester Grundt,* 1567 ed., 1360, 1367.

36. Olevianus, *De substantia,* 294–95.

37. "Mit dem Geiste Calvins hatte er sich so vertraut gemacht, dass derselbe, so zu sagen, in seinen Schriften athmet." *Allgemeine Deutsche Biographie,* s.v. "Olevian, Caspar," by Cuno.

38. For Olevianus, see above, p. 64; for Bullinger, see *De testamento seu foedere dei unico & aeterno* (Zurich, 1534), fol. 2–3b; for Calvin, see Andrew J. Bandstra, "Law and Gospel in Calvin and Paul," in *Exploring the Heritage of John Calvin,* ed. David E. Holwerda (Grand Rapids: Baker, 1976), 12; for Ursinus, see *The Commentary of Dr. Zacharias Ursinus on the Heidelberg Catechism,* trans. G. W. Williard (Grand Rapids: Eerdmans, 1954), 97, and *Summa theologiae,* 14 (Q. 32).

39. For Olevianus, see above, pp. 74–75, 81–82; Bullinger, *The Decades* (1557), 5 vols., ed. Thomas Harding (Cambridge: University Press, 1849–52), 3.8, 294; 3.6, 170; Calvin, *Institutes,* II.x.2; Ursinus, *Commentary,* 98–9; *Summa theologiae,* 14 (Q. 33).

fashion.[40] Finally, like Bullinger, Olevianus recognizes both a unilateral and a bilateral dimension to the covenant of grace within the context of a monergistic soteriology; so did Zwingli, Calvin, Musculus, and Ursinus.[41] None of these covenantal emphases in Olevianus can be attributed solely to Bullinger's influence; they are all part of a broader theological tradition.

To identify Bullinger as the source of the covenantal elements in Olevianus's theology also overlooks the fact that prior to Olevianus only Calvin had used the terms *foedus legale, conditio legalis,* and *conditio evangelica* or had applied the terms *dispensatio* and *oeconomia* to the twofold administration of the covenant of grace. It is also possible that the origins of Olevianus's understanding of the *ius creationis* are to be found in Calvin,[42] though Calvin never spoke of this obligation in an explicitly covenantal sense.

Olevianus's colleagues in Heidelberg may also have made distinctive contributions. Ursinus could very likely have been the source of Olevianus's doctrine of the *foedus naturale* or *foedus creationis*, his definition of the covenant of grace as reconciliation with God, the twofold benefit of salvation as the *blessing* of the covenant, his view of Christ as the Mediator of the covenant, his understanding of the Apostles' Creed as a summary of the doctrine of the covenant,[43] and the very personal and practical emphasis in his covenant theology. Diestel and Schrenk also suggested the influence on Olevianus of Peter Boquinus (?–1582), Professor of New Testament at the University of Heidelberg from 1558 to 1576.[44] Olevianus's predilection for

40. See Chapter II.

41. See Chapters II and III above. For an elaboration of this argument see Bierma, "Federal Theology in the Sixteenth Century: Two Traditions?" *Westminster Theological Journal* 45 (Fall 1983):304–21.

42. Calvin, *Institutes,* I.ii.2: "Quomodo enim mentem tuam subire queat Dei cogitatio, quin simul extemplo cogites, te, quum figmentum illius sis, eiusdem imperio esse ipso *creationis iure* addictum et mancipatum?" (Italics added.) See also *Calvini opera* 24:209. Calvin also uses the expression *sponsor foederis* (ibid., 23:587) to refer to Christ.

43. Ursinus, *Summa theologiae,* 14 (Q. 39): "Quae est igitur summa eorum, quae nobis credenda proponit Evangelium, ut foederis divinis simus participes? Comprehensa est in articulis fidei sive symbolo Apostolico."

44. Diestel, *Geschichte des Alten Testaments,* 288; Schrenk, *Gottesreich und Bund,* 56, 59, 62.

the Greek term *koinonia* to express the essence of the covenant relationship between the believer and Christ[45] may well have its roots in Boquinus, who constructed his entire theology on the *koinonia* theme.[46]

Finally, the thesis that Olevianus's covenant theology represents a synthesis of Bullinger and Calvin gives no account of Olevianus's own additions to and deviations from the tradition before him or of the new directions in which he was leading Reformed covenant thought:

(1) In the first place, he introduced into Reformed theology three new covenants: a pretemporal redemptive *pactum* between the Father and the Son,[47] a *foedus* with the Devil contracted at the fall,[48] and a *foedus* that believers have with other creatures.[49] These three covenants are significant not only because with Olevianus they are mentioned in Reformed theology for the first time but also because they indicate how Olevianus is expanding covenant thinking beyond the covenant of grace to include, respectively, the doctrines of the eternal plan of salvation, the fall, and special providence.

(2) Although Ursinus was the first theologian in the Reformed tradition to speak of a creation covenant (*foedus naturale*) in addition to the *foedus gratiae*,[50] Olevianus was actually the first to use the term *foedus creationis* and to treat this doctrine in some detail.[51]

(3) Olevianus helped to redirect the course of covenant theology in the late sixteenth century by altering the definition of the *foedus legale*. Calvin had used this term as a synonym for the old administration of the *foedus gratiae*, more particularly as the laws and ceremonies appended to the promise of grace dur-

45. See, e.g., *Expositio*, 2, 17, 36; *De substantia*, 230, 232, 331, 335, 355, 360, 368.

46. "Boquin fasst hier [*Exegesis divinae atque humanae koinonias* (1561)] die Loci der christlichen Glaubenslehre unter dem Begriff *koinonia hominis cum Deo*, worin er den scopus der gesammten Offenbarung sieht, zusammen, um das Ganze der Heilslehre systematisch zu ordnen und abzuschliessen." Heppe, *Dogmatik des deutschen Protestantismus*, 1:148.

47. See above, pp. 107–12.

48. See above, pp. 120–22.

49. See above, pp. 126–30.

50. See above, p. 58.

51. See above, pp. 112–20.

ing the ministry of Moses.[52] Like Zwingli, Bullinger, and Musculus, he insisted that the Mosaic or Sinaitic covenant was a confirmation of the eternal covenant of grace established with Abraham.[53] Olevianus, however, understands the *foedus legale* as a renewal not of the *foedus gratiae* but of the *foedus creationis*, humanity's innate obligation to God of perfect obedience.[54] For him the *foedus legale* and *foedus gratiae* coexisted throughout the Old Testament age. Circumcision, in fact, served as a sign of initiation into both the *foedus legale* (the "accidental" purpose of circumcision) and the *foedus gratiae* (the "proper" purpose of circumcision).[55] But they were only parallel, not identical, covenants in the Old Testament. Unlike the earlier Reformed tradition, Olevianus separates rather than equates these two covenants.

It has been suggested, of course, that the credit for these innovations in the doctrine of the *foedus legale* actually belongs to Ursinus. According to Paul Althaus, it was Ursinus who moved Reformed covenant thought a major step forward by designating the *foedus naturale* as the content of both natural law and the written law. Melanchthon, Althaus argued, had already equated the *lex Dei* with the *lex naturae*, but Ursinus, his student, was the first to disentangle the *foedus legale* (expressed in the Decalogue) from its uneasy relationship with the old dispensation of the *foedus gratiae* and to identify it instead with the *foedus naturale* (expressed in the law of nature). What Ursinus did, in other words, was place Melanchthon's doctrine of the law within a covenantal framework.[56]

---

52. *Institutes*, II.xi.4.
53. See above, Chapter II, n. 68, under the development of salvation history.
54. See above, p. 122.
55. "Sed hic finis Circumcisionis, ut initiaret quoque in foedus legale, erat accidentalis. Proprius enim erat ut initiaret Abrahamum eiusque semen in fidem de semine promisso: atque iustitiam fidei gratuitam & cordis renovationem eis obsignaret." Comm. on Rom. 2:25–28, pp. 114–15. Cf. also Comm. on Phil. 3:3, pp. 36–37.
56. ". . . konnte, solange das foedus legale noch an das novum foedus nahe herangerückt wurde, solange es noch als halb evangelisch erschien, eine Gleichsetzung mit dem foedus naturae nicht stattfinden. Diese wurde erst möglich, als das calvinische Ineinander zweier Gedankenreihen zu reinlicher Scheidung des Gesetzesbundes von dem nunmehr deutlich als alttestamentlich und neutestamentlich differenzierten Evangeliumsbunde entwickelt war, und

Althaus's analysis, however, needs to be qualified in two ways. First of all, Ursinus never identifies the *foedus naturale* with what Althaus calls the *"foedus legale."* In fact, he does not even employ the term *foedus legale*. He says only that the Decalogue contains the *foedus naturale* entered into at creation[57] and that the law teaches what that creation covenant requires.[58] Ursinus's contribution lay in relating the *foedus naturale* to the *lex natura* and *lex divina*; Olevianus was the first to connect it to the *foedus legale*.

Second, Ursinus's separation of the legal covenant (really the natural covenant in the Decalogue) from the old economy of the covenant of grace is not as "reinlich" as Althaus thinks. Ursinus distinguishes them more sharply than did, say, Calvin, but he does not separate them altogether. In his commentary on the Heidelberg Catechism, for instance, he clearly attaches the law to the Old Covenant:

> The old testament, or covenant, is often used in Scripture by a figure of speech, called synecdoche (in which a part is taken for the whole), for the law. . . . For in the old covenant the law was enforced more strenuously, and there were many parts of it. The gospel was also more obscure. The new testament, or covenant, on the other hand, is for the most part taken for the gospel, because in the new a great part of the law is abrogated, and the gospel is here more clearly revealed.[59]

The law, which contains the natural covenant, is portrayed here as an integral part of the Old Covenant. This may well reflect Ursinus's retreat, for whatever reason, from the double covenant scheme he had outlined in the *Catechesis maior*. It is possible that he detached the law from the *foedus naturale* and brought it again within the embrace of the *foedus gratiae*. But

---

als zweitens auch innerhalb des engeren Kreises der Dogmatik die lex Dei ausdrücklich mit der lex naturae gleichgesetzt wurde. Beide Voraussetzungen sind bei Ursinus erfüllt. Der Schuler Melanchthons wandte die Lehre seines Meisters von der lex naturae auf die Föderaleinteilung . . . an . . ." *Die Prinzipien der deutschen reformierten Dogmatik im Zeitalter der aristotelischen Scholastik* (Darmstadt: Wissenschaftliche Buchgesellschaft, 1967), 155.

57. See above, Chapter II, n. 140.
58. See above, Chapter II, n. 138.
59. *Commentary*, 100.

the fact that in the commentary he retains the connection between the natural and written law[60] raises the question whether the links between *foedus naturale* and *"foedus legale"* and between *"foedus legale"* and *foedus gratiae* are, as Althaus implied, mutually exclusive. In Ursinus's mature theology, at least, quite the opposite appears true.[61] It is not until Olevianus that the separation of *foedus legale* from the *foedus gratiae* is clear and complete.

(4) Not only did Olevianus expand and, to some extent, alter the use of the covenant concept in early Reformed theology, but he did so with the assistance of a wide range of terms and principles borrowed from Roman contract law.[62] It should be recalled that Olevianus spent the first phase of his university education pursuing a doctorate in civil law at Orléans and Bourges at a time when the study of Roman law was at the peak of its humanistic revival in France,[63] and he later brought this legal training to bear upon his theological work. Such terms as *consensus, contractus, fideiussio, ius naturale, iusiurandum, mandatum, mancipare, obligatio, pactum, pignus, spondere, stipulatio, sub conditione, syngrapha*, and *vinculum*, which appear throughout his discussions of the various covenants, are all technical expressions from the Roman law of obligations which Olevianus employs in his theological analysis of covenant.

At the heart of his doctrine of the covenant of creation, for example, is the notion of a *naturalis obligatio* between God the Creator and humanity created in His image.[64] In the Roman law

60. "The Decalogue is, therefore, the renewal and reinforcing of the natural law." Ibid., 492. Cf. also 490–91.

61. Stoever is vulnerable to the same criticism when he concludes: "In contrast to the treatment of Bullinger and Calvin, the distinction [in Ursinus] between old and new (biblical) testaments is no longer simply identifiable with the distinction between old and new covenants." "Covenant of Works," 30.

62. Moltmann (*Evangelisches Kirchenlexikon*, s.v. "Olevian"), McCoy ("Covenant Theology of Cocceius," 74), and Goeters (*Religion in Geschichte*, s.v. "Olevian") all make this same point but provide no evidence to substantiate it.

63. "Thus its [the humanistic treatment of Roman laws] real home became France, where Alciatus had sometimes taught. It was chiefly at the new school at Bourges that humanistic jurisprudence came to its highest flowering. In the sixteenth century a series of men taught here whose work is admired even today." Wolfgang Kunkel, *An Introduction to Roman Legal and Constitutional History*, trans. J. M. Kelley (London: Oxford University Press, 1966), 175.

64. See above, Chapter IV, n. 39.

of obligations this term *obligatio* denoted not merely the *duty* of one party to another, like the English word "obligation," but the whole relationship between the two parties, "the bond which unites creditor and debtor . . . a bond by which one party is bound, and the other entitled to some act of forbearance."[65] This is precisely how Olevianus understands the *naturalis obligatio* that he equates with the *naturale foedus* or *ius creationis* established at creation: a *relationship* of conformity between Creator and creature which involved certain rights and entitlements on the part of the former and certain duties or responsibilities on the part of the latter.[66]

Another example of Olevianus's application of Roman legal terminology to covenant doctrine can be found in his treatment of the pretemporal pact of redemption between the Father and the Son. Here he employs technical language from both verbal and consensual contract law to describe the agreement between the two persons of the Trinity regarding the salvation of the elect. First of all, Olevianus identifies the Son as the *sponsor* of the covenant of grace, His act of promising as *spospondit*, and the promise itself as His *sponsio* and *fideiussio*.[67] The use of this particular vocabulary is striking, for in ancient Roman law verbal contracts were established through a formal exchange of question and answer containing the verb *spondere* ("*Spondesne? . . . Spondeo* ["Do you solemnly promise? . . . I do solemnly promise"]).[68] A *fideiussio*, moreover, was a special kind of verbal contract by which a third party bound himself as surety to a creditor to meet the obligation of a debtor to the creditor in case of the debtor's failure to repay.[69] In applying this language to the covenant of redemption Olevianus sees the Son binding Himself as surety to the Father to meet elect humanity's obligation to the Creator in light of their foreseen fall. The *sponsio* of the Son, therefore, is really a *fideiussio* or contract of suretyship.[70]

65. Barry Nicholas, *An Introduction to Roman Law* (London: Oxford University Press, 1962), 158.

66. See above, p. 113.

67. See above, Chapter IV, ns. 2–5.

68. Nicholas, *Introduction*, 159; William C. Morey, *Outlines of Roman Law* (New York: G. P. Putnam's Sons, 1889), 358.

69. Morey, *Outlines*, 360; Nicholas, *Introduction*, 204–5.

70. See above, p. 108.

Olevianus also employs terminology from consensual contract law when he frequently refers to the *mandatum* that the Father gives the Son in Their pretemporal agreement.[71] Olevianus likely has in mind Jesus's own claim that the giving up of his life was by the "command" (Vulgate: *mandatum*) of the Father (John 10:18), but he interprets this command as a consensual contract known as a *mandatum*. In Roman law a *mandatum* was a

> contract in which one person *(mandator)* commissions another *(mandatarius)* to do something. . . . The service must necessarily be gratuitous. . . . The agent, or *mandatarius*, is under obligations to execute faithfully the terms of the agreement, and to give up to the principal all the property entrusted to his care, or all the proceeds resulting from the execution of his commission. The principal, or *mandator*, on his part, is bound to reimburse the agent for all necessary expenses, and to protect him from any loss incurred in faithfully executing the mandate.[72]

As such, a *mandatum* was "imperfectly bilateral."[73]

All of these features are present also in Olevianus's pact of redemption: the Father commissions the Son to undertake the work of redemption; the Son voluntarily agrees to perform this service; and the Father in turn promises to glorify the Son and to accept His obedience for all eternity. Like the civil *mandatum*, this agreement has, as we saw in Chapter IV, the markings of a bilateral covenant, but one in which the agent (Son) takes a decidedly submissive posture before the principal (Father).[74]

These are but a few of many examples of how Olevianus brought his background in Roman law to bear upon his theological treatment of covenant. In so doing, he was the first in a century-long line of covenant theologians—Olevianus, Sohnius, Martinius, Crocius, Cloppenburg, Cocceius—who in the course of broadening the scope of the covenant theme in Reformed dogmatics increasingly turned to the language of civil law to

71. See above, pp. 111–12.
72. Morey, *Outlines*, 367–70.
73. Nicholas, *Introduction*, 187.
74. See above, pp. 111–12.

elucidate this theme.[75] Melanchthon and Calvin had made modest beginnings in the application of legal language to covenant doctrine, but Olevianus was the first to do so on such a comprehensive scale.[76] Once again, the student had moved considerably beyond his teacher.

(5) Finally, Olevianus's covenant theology has a significantly different focus from that of his predecessors. Heppe, Diestel, and Schrenk all made some attempt to describe Olevianus's special place in the history of Reformed theology by pointing out how he and Ursinus incorporate the doctrine of the mystical union with Christ into the older doctrine of the covenant and thus add a distinctive experiential dimension to the covenant.[77] But that observation by itself does not explain the theological *tour de force* that Olevianus's work on the covenant represents. What Olevianus has in fact done is to move the drama of God's covenant making in history onto the stage of the individual's experience of salvation. *Sub lege* and *sub gratia* are not just two stages in redemptive history for Olevianus but two stages in the life of every believer. The legal covenant is abrogated in history at the advent of Jesus Christ but also, in a personal way, in the life of every Christian at his or her conversion. The covenant of grace is ratified in history in the death of Jesus Christ but also

75. "Begegnete uns schon bei Melanchthon, dann bei Olevianus, ausgesprochener noch bei Sohnius die Neigung, den Föderalgedanken durch die Termini des romischen Verbalkontraktes zur Darstellung zu bringen, so sind darin Martini und Crocius noch weiter gegangen, und Cloppenburg zumal stellt hierin vor Cocceius den Hohepunkt dar." Schrenk, *Gottesreich und Bund,* 74. For more detail on Sohnius's use of Roman law see ibid., 62–63; for Martinius, Crocius, and Cloppenburg, see ibid., 69–81; for Cocceius, see ibid., 82ff.

76. "In dieser Ausdrucksweise [Melanchthon's use of the terms *mutuum foedus, mutua obligatio,* and *stipulatio* in his doctrine of baptism] ist schon der Keim enthalten zu jener späteren Ausbildung des Bundesgedankens nach Analogie des Verbalkontraktes im römischen Recht." Schrenk, *Gottesreich und Bund,* 49. "Wenn bei Calvin ein bescheidener Ansatz zu dieser Methode gemacht wird, so hat er zweifellos, wie eine nähere Untersuchung feststellen kann, auf Olevian, der wie er in Bourges die Rechtswissenschaft studierte, und durch diesen auf die späteren Vertreter der klassischen Föderaltheologie eingewirkt, in der der bis in die Kleinigkeiten gehende Gebrauch der privatrechtlichen Grundbegriffe mitunter die religiosen Werte überwucherte." Bohatec, *Budé und Calvin,* 248.

77. Heppe, *Dogmatik des deutschen Protestantismus,* 1:143–44; Diestel, *Geschichte des Alten Testaments,* 288; Schrenk, *Gottesreich und Bund,* 55, 57, 61–62.

in the life of every Christian in the Holy Spirit's application of the promise of reconciliation to his or her heart.[78] It is, of course, the historical abrogation and ratification of these covenants in Christ that make their personal abrogation and ratification in the believer possible. An Old Testament believer, for example, could possess the whole substance of the covenant of grace only in anticipation of the covenant's ratification by Christ. But unlike previous Reformed theologians, Olevianus is much less concerned in his covenant theology with the historical drama than with the personal drama of salvation.

This change of emphasis is reflected in three ways in Olevianus's treatment of the covenant of grace. In the first place, throughout his writings the foundational text of this doctrine is not Genesis 3:15 (the Protoevangelium) or Genesis 17:1ff. (the covenant with Abraham) but Jeremiah 31:31–34 ("I will make a new covenant. . . . I will put my law in their minds . . . and will remember their sins no more"). Situated near the beginning of both the *Expositio* and *De substantia*, this text provides an early clue that Olevianus intends to concentrate on the believer's possession and enjoyment of the benefits of the covenant, particularly in its new administration, rather than on the origins and development of covenant history.

Second, Olevianus never employs the older distinction between the "substance" and "administration" of the covenant to compare the Old and New Covenants; he applies these terms strictly to the New Covenant promised in Jeremiah 31. Even more significant, however, is the different way in which he defines *substantia* here. Bullinger considered the substance or reality of the covenant as God's promise of faithfulness to His people and His requirement of believing obedience in return.[79] Calvin described it as the hope of eternal life, divine mercy rather than human merit as the basis of the covenant, and knowledge of Christ the Mediator.[80] Ursinus regarded the substance as what he called "the principal conditions of the covenant": the divine promise of forgiveness to those who repent and believe, on the one hand, and the human commitment of

---

78. See above, pp. 138–39.
79. *Decades* 3.8, 294; 3.6, 170.
80. *Institutes*, II.x.2.

faith and repentance, on the other.[81] All emphasized that the covenant of grace throughout history was one in substance, differing only in its old and new administrations. Olevianus, however, defines the *substantia foederis* as exclusively the twofold benefit of the covenant: not merely the promise of forgiveness and renewal but the benefits themselves, the very "gift promised and sworn by God."[82] For him the substance has nothing to do with the mutual conditions of the covenant or its underlying structure in the two testaments. It has to do rather with the fulfillment of the covenant promises in the life of the Christian here and now. What Olevianus has done is to bring even the essence of the covenant into the realm of the personal experience of the believer.

Third, Olevianus appeals to the covenant of grace not primarily to explain the continuity of salvation history in the two testaments or to defend the practice of paedobaptism but to provide the believer with the (objective) certitude of salvation.[83] The well-worn arguments for the unity of the testaments and infant baptism are conspicuously absent from his treatises on the covenant.[84] For a discussion of these issues one must turn to his commentaries, where he is compelled by certain biblical texts to treat them. His focus in his systematic works is rather on what he considers to be the original purpose of the covenant of grace: to provide its members with a personal assurance of salvation. Why is the reconciliation of man with God presented to us in the form of a covenant? he asks in *Vester Grundt*. It is in order that we might be "certain and assured" (*gewiss und versichert*) that a

81. *Commentary*, 98–99.

82. "Foedus itaque gratuitum, si essentiam eius spectes, est promissa et iurata a Deo donatio." *De substantia*, 2.

83. Cf. Moltmann's observation that "im Zentrum [Olevianus's] Theologie steht das Gewissheitsproblem." *Evangelisches Kirchenlexikon*, s.v. "Olevian." Cf. also Heppe, *Dogmatik des deutschen Protestantismus*, 2:220: ". . . will [Olevianus] in der Versöhnungslehre die Sicherheit des Adoptionsverhältnisses und des bleibenden Heilszustandes des Gläubigen nachweisen, weshalb als Basis des Versöhnungswerkes das ewige und unabänderliche *pactum* und *consilium salutis* des Vaters und Sohnes hingestellt wird."

84. Cf. Verhoeven, "Olevianus," 102: "Van een verbondstheoloog als Olevianus verwacht men een uitvoerige verdediging van de kinderdoop. Hij is echter verrassend kort van stof over de Doop en brengt de kinderdoop maar terloops en als een vanselfsprekendheid ter sprake."

permanent, eternal peace between Him and us has been made. Just as two warring parties attain "peace of mind" (*gerüwige gemüter*) only when they have bound themselves together in an oath of peace, so too God chose to bind Himself to us with an oath and promise of reconciliation "auff das wir in unserm gewissen ruhe und fried hetten."[85] That this covenant is, moreover, a covenant of *grace* is all the more comforting to our consciences, because it depends solely on the promises of an eternally reliable God, not on our own powers or capabilities.[86]

This peace of conscience is essentially an assurance of forgiveness based on God's covenant promise that He will remember our sins no more (Jer. 31:34).[87] The "certain, firm, eternal ground" of this assurance is the eternal priesthood of Christ, which was established and confirmed in God's eternal decree with an oath, "You are a priest forever . . ." (Ps. 110:4), thereby securing the eternal efficacy of Christ's sacrificial and intercessory work.[88] The ultimate benefit of Christ's priestly work, the eternal forgiveness of sins, comes to us therefore with a double guarantee: God's covenant promise confirmed by His oath.[89] These are in turn eternally unalterable because God is by nature

85. Reu, *Vester Grundt*, 1567 ed., 1333. Cf. also 1345, 1362, 1379; *Expositio*, 9, 12; *De substantia*, 16, 23, 139, 157, 159.

86. "Atque ita totum hoc foedus mere esse gratuitum & nulla conditione virium nostrarum, sed gratuita Dei misericordia in Christo per fidem, quam ipse donat apprehensa constare, certum est." *De substantia*, 16.

87. "Q. Erkläre mir den gewissen Grund, darauf mein Gewissen ruhen könne, noch etwas besser, dass mir nämlich alle meine Sünden vollkommen verziehen und geschenkt sind, dass diess Gottes unwandelbarer Wille sey gegen mich und alle Gläubigen.

"A. Der Gnadenbund und der Eid Gottes begreift vornehmlich in sich diesen Hauptartikel, dass Gott unserer Sünden nicht mehr gedenken will." Sudhoff, *Fester Grund*, 1590 ed., 163.

88. "Denn dies Königreich musste also aufgerichtet und bestätigt werden, dass zugleich der Gerechtigkeit Gottes ein Genüge geschehe in Ewigkeit, und dass also unser Friede mit Gott, und die von ihm verheissene Gnade einen gewissen, festen, ewigen Grund hätten. Der Grund aber, darauf das Königreich Christi bestehet, ist das Priesteramt Christi, welches im ewigen Rath Gottes mit dem Eid Gottes aufgerichtet und bestätigt ist, da der Sohn aus grosser Weisheit und Barmherzigkeit zu einem solchen Mittler, Versöhner and Fürbitter für uns ist geordnet, dass sein Opfer und seine Fürbitte soll Kraft haben vor dem Angesicht Gottes in Ewigkeit, vermöge des Eids, den Gott geschworen hat, Ps. 110:4." Ibid., 57–58.

89. See ibid., 59–60.

truthful, faithful, and holy and thus cannot lie or ever renege on a promise.[90]

For Olevianus, therefore, what God is doing in this covenanting and oath swearing is employing human conventions that best convey the seriousness of His commitment to the believer and the dependability of His redemptive plan. In yet another way Olevianus is more than a synthesizer of Bullinger and Calvin; he has departed from the earlier preoccupation with covenant history and turned his attention to the significance of the covenant for the individual Christian. He continues to use covenant language but to address a different set of theological questions.

Antischolastic?

A number of scholars over the last century have claimed that Olevianus constructed a biblically oriented theology of covenant that helped to correct the scholastic predestinarian theology on the rise in Reformed circles in the late sixteenth century.[91] No one has argued this thesis more forcefully than Jürgen Moltmann in an article in 1957 entitled "Zur Bedeutung des Petrus Ramus für Philosophie und Theologie in Calvinismus."[92] Moltmann maintained that in the late sixteenth and early seventeenth centuries there emerged in Reformed theology an "antibezaistische renaissance" that encompassed such diverse forms of Calvinism as later Zwinglianism (Bullinger et al.), the Heidelberg-Herborn federal theology (Olevianus, Piscator), Arminianism, Amyrauldism, and English-Dutch "Vorpietismus" (Perkins,

90. "Quia totam illam substantiam indubitato testimonio promisit is qui verax & potens est, qui quod promittit reipsa praestat." *De substantia,* 257. "Ac vicissim se obligat conscientiae Deus, iuramentum a se semel praestitum, totamque foederis illius gratuiti substantiam in articulis fidei comprehensam, iis qui in conscientia sua ita se animatos, ut dictum est, sentiunt firmam ac ratam fore, nec ullum esse mutationis sententiae periculum, cum impossible sit ut mentiatur Deus. . . . Obligatio ex parte Dei erga conscientiam sic affectam per ipsius pratiam, iuratum foedus eiusque totam substantiam ratam ei fore in aeternum, nec esse periculum mutationis sententiae, aut si eius non memor fuerit, se non fore sanctum Deum." Ibid., 330.

91. See above, pp. 23–24. Cf. also Heppe, *Dogmatik des deutschen Protestantismus* 1:139ff., 188ff.; J.A. Dorner, *History of Protestant Theology,* 2 vols. (Edinburgh: T & T Clark, 1871), 2:36ff.; A.C. McGiffert, *Protestant Thought before Kant* (New York: Charles Scribner's Sons, 1926), 153–54; and Christopher Hill, *Puritanism and Revolution* (New York: Secher and Warburg, 1958), 245–46.

92. *Zeitschrift für Kirchengeschichte* 68 (1957):295–318.

Ames). All of these movements shared a common opponent in the orthodox Calvinist school of Theodore Beza. But more importantly, all had at some point been deeply influenced by the philosophical method and dialectic of Peter Ramus (1515–1572), a French Huguenot convert and ardent anti-Aristotelian philosopher.[93] The real war being waged, therefore, was that of a Ramist biblical humanism against a Bezan "Aristotelisierung" of theology; a Ramist "heilsgeschichtlicher Aposteriorismus" against a Bezan "dogmatischer Apriorismus"; a Ramist empirical theology against a Bezan rational theology.[94] Olevianus's role in this conflict was to neutralize Beza's predestinarianism with the pre-Bezan covenant idea of Calvin and Budé.[95] This placed him in the opposite theological camp from his Heidelberg colleague Ursinus, who with Beza in Geneva remained a defender of Artistotelian-Reformed orthodoxy.[96]

This thesis, its popularity notwithstanding, is open to criticism from several angles. Its basic flaw is the sharp distinction it draws between Bezan-Aristotelian dogmatic predestinarianism and Ramist *heilsgeschichtlich* covenantalism, which seriously distorts the picture of Reformed theology in the latter half of the sixteenth century. In the first place, Reformed "scholastic" use of Aristotelian logic did not always betray a commitment to Aristotelian metaphysics or epistemology.[97] Ramus himself, it should be remembered, emphasized Aristotelian causality and rejected only some forms of the syllogism.[98] Second, it is misleading to assert that the doctrine of predestination served as the central structuring principle of the systems of early orthodoxy. As Muller's research has shown, early orthodoxy retained the Christological focus of Reformation theology and placed predes-

---

93. Ibid., 297. Various aspects of Ramus's philosophical and theological reform are treated in Paul Lobstein, *Petrus Ramus als Theologe* (Strassburg: G.F. Schmidts Universitäts-Buchhandlung, 1878); Frank P. Graves, *Peter Ramus and the Educational Reformation of the Sixteenth Century* (New York: MacMillan, 1912); Walter J. Ong, *Ramus: Method, and the Decay of Dialogue* (Cambridge, MA: Harvard University Press, 1958); and Keith L. Sprunger, "Ames, Ramus, and the Method of Puritan Theology." *Harvard Theological Review* 59 (April 1966):133–51.

94. Moltmann, "Bedeutung des Petrus Ramus," 317, 304.

95. Ibid., 317.

96. Ibid., 296.

97. Muller, "Predestination and Christology," 6, 41–42.

98. Carl Bangs, *Arminius: A Study in the Dutch Reformation* (Nashville: Abingdon, 1971), 57, 60–61.

tination within a larger Christological-Trinitarian framework.[99] Finally, theologians like Perkins and Olevianus simply do not fit Moltmann's categories: both might have been Ramist in method but they certainly were not anti-Bezan in their theology.[100]

Olevianus provides an especially convincing refutation of the thesis under examination, for he cannot easily be classified a Ramist or anti-Aristotelian, he does not pit covenant against predestination, and he is much more of a dogmatician than a *heilsgeschichtlich* biblical theologian.

First of all, one must be careful in labelling Olevianus a Ramist or anti-Aristotelian. It is true that others beside Moltmann have characterized him as a disciple of Ramus,[101] a Ramist in philosophy,[102] a follower of Ramus's logic,[103] and one of a number of "begeisterte Verehrer" and "einflussreiche Gönner" of the Frenchman's method.[104] It is difficult, however, to know how exactly Olevianus acquired this designation. It may have to do with the fact that he befriended Ramus during a dispute over the latter's appointment to the faculty at Heidelberg in 1569.[105] It may be because at times in his theological works he appears to resort to the method of dichotomization for which Ramus became so well known.[106] Moltmann himself left

99. Muller, "Predestination and Christology." Cf. also John S. Bray, *Theodore Beza's Doctrine of Predestination* (Nieuwkoop: De Graaf, 1974), 137–143.

100. On Perkins see Bangs, *Arminius*, 63, and Muller, "Perkins' *A Golden Chaine:* Predestinarian System or Schematized *Ordo Salutis?*" *Sixteenth Century Journal* 9, no. 1 (April 1978):70. On Olevianus see below.

101. John T. McNeill, *The History and Character of Calvinism* (London: Oxford University Press, 1954), 391.

102. *Allgemeine Deutsche Biographie*, s.v. "Olevian," by Cuno.

103. *Religion in Geschichte*, 3rd ed., s.v. "Olevian," by Goeters.

104. Karl Bauer, *Aus der grossen Zeit der theologischen Fakultät zu Heidelberg* (Baden: M. Schauenburg, 1938), 21.

105. Sudhoff, *C. Olevianus*, 331.

106. Below is a diagram of one example (*De substantia*, 250, 251, 257):

Cf. Robert Letham's comment that there are "undoubted Ramist influences in [Olevianus's] work" ("The *Foedus Operum:* Some Factors Accounting for Its Develop-the impression that it was Olevianus's connections to an anti-scholastic federal theology in the late sixteenth century that numbered him among Ramus's devotees.

The fact of the matter is, however, that as a logician, at least, Olevianus was still very much an Aristotelian. As we have already mentioned, he began his professional career in 1559 as a teacher of Melanchthon's *Dialectices*, an introduction to Aristotelian logic replete with theological examples and applications.[107] In 1583 he published his own handbook on logic,[108] presumably based on those early lectures in Trier a quarter of a century before. What is noteworthy about this book is its similarity to Melanchthon's 1547 edition of his *Dialectices*. Though not identical in every respect, the two works do frequently overlap. Like Melanchthon, for example, Olevianus opens his discussion of *quaestiones* with the same division into *simplex* and *coniuncta* (Melanchthon uses the term *composita*) questions.[109] His list, short descriptions, and longer definitions of the ten Aristotelian *praedicamenta* (categories)—*substantia, quantitas, qualitas, relatio, actio, passio, quando, ubi, situs,* and *habere*—follow Melanchthon nearly word for word.[110] Even the charts he draws of *substantia* and the *divisio actionum* are exact replicas of those found in the *Dialectices*.[111] Other examples could also be cited, all of which suggest that Olevianus was borrowing heavily from Melanchthon when he composed his own textbook. There is absolutely no question, however, about his commitment to the Aristotelian-Melanchthonian dialectical tradition—a tradition that in many respects Ramus sought to discredit.

---

ment," *Sixteenth Century Journal* 14 [Winter 1983]:466). Letham cites as evidence Olevianus's division of the covenant of grace into "substance" and "administration" and sees in Olevianus one example of how "the *foedus operum* was developed in precisely those centers in which Ramism did take root." Ibid., ns. 58, 52.

107. "Statt der durch die mittelalterlichen Kommentatoren verschütteten aristotelischen Dialektik wollte [Melanchthon] die reine Lehre des Aristoteles geben." Karl Hartfelder, *Philipp Melanchthon als Praeceptor Germaniae* (Nieuwkoop: De Graaf, 1972), 216.

108. *De inventione dialecticae liber, e praelectionibus Gasp. Olevianus excerptus* (Geneva: Eustathius Vignon, 1583).

109. Ibid., 1–2; Melanchthon, *Dialectices,* 4a.

110. Olevianus, *De inventione,* 164–65, 170, 172, 187, 193–95; Melanchthon, *Dialectices,* 12a–12b, 15b, 17a, 33b, 34a, 36a–38a.

111. Olevianus, *De inventione,* 176–80, 188–89; Melanchthon, *Dialectices,* 12b–13a, 35a–35b.

Second, Moltmann argues that Olevianus's more biblically grounded covenant theology (under the influence of Ramus) served as an antidote to Beza's more philosophically grounded decretal theology (under the influence of Aristotle). But Moltmann assumes an incompatibility here that in reality never existed—at either the personal or theological level. Personally, Olevianus and Beza were friends and mutual admirers. Beza, in fact, had such high regard for Olevianus's preaching that he edited and composed the prefaces to three commentaries based on Olevianus's sermons on Galatians (1578), Romans (1579), and Philippians-Colossians (1580). Theologically, the two were no less compatible. Olevianus's understanding of the Lord's Supper, for example, more nearly fits Moltmann's description of Beza's view[112] than of Ramus's.[113] Like Beza, Olevianus insists that the believing communicant partakes of the true body and blood of Christ, not just His benefits, and is thereby brought into closer union with Him.[114] Furthermore, to portray Olevianus's "foedus-Begriff" as a theological mitigator of Beza's "prädestinatianische Dekretenlehre"[115] is to misread him completely. For Olevianus the covenant of grace in no way mollifies the double decree of election and reprobation, either by shifting attention from God's decrees to His acts in history or by shifting ultimate responsibility for one's destiny from the divine to the human partner in the covenant. If anything, Olevianus tends to "dehistoricize" the covenant rather than historicize the decrees.

112. "Seine [i.e. Christi] Wohltaten sind nicht zu trennen von der personalen, und das heisst: von seiner substantiellen Gegenwart. Nicht nur die Frucht seines Sterbens, sondern er selbst in Person ist Gabe des Sakramentes und wird vom Glauben ergriffen. Es entsteht daher nicht nur eine ethische, sondern eine ausgesprochenen 'personale Christusgemeinschaft'. . . , das 'mysterium mysticae *concorporationis.*'" "Bedeutung des Ramus," 310.
113. "Nicht Christus in Person, sondern ein Satisfaktionswerk ist Quelle des Heils. Es entsteht daher im Abendmahl keine substantielle Christusgemeinschaft, weder realiter noch spiritualiter, sondern nur eine Assoziation der Affekte und eine Konsoziation zwischen Christi Willen und Werk und dem Willen und Werk der Gläubigen." Ibid., 308.
114. See above, p. 88. For a detailed discussion of the presence of Christ and union with Christ in the Supper in Beza, see Jill Raitt, *The Eucharistic Theology of Theodore Beza,* A.A.R. Studies in Religion, no. 4 (Chambersburg, PA: American Academy of Religion, 1972), 27–29, 33ff., 44, 48, 58, 65–66.
115. Moltmann, "Bedeutung des Ramus," 317.

His concern, as we have previously pointed out, is much more with the subjective ratification of the covenant in the heart of each believer than with its objective ratification in history. Full membership in the covenant, moreover, is reserved exclusively for those in whom God elected from all eternity to fulfill the conditions of faith and obedience. In Olevianus's theology, therefore, God's covenant making and His decree making are not held in tension but are, to use Althaus's phrase, "friedlich vereinigt."[116]

Finally, if there was anything like the late-century revival of biblical theology that Moltmann describes, Olevianus can be held responsible only in a negative sense, for he was much more of a systematician than a biblical or *heilsgeschichtlich* theologian. As we have seen, the development of redemptive history for Olevianus is neither an ordering principle for his theology nor a major theme in his theology. Even his commentaries are more the work of a dogmatician than of an exegete: he often passes over the finer nuances of meaning in a text to treat the theological locus or loci that the pericope suggests.[117]

Nonetheless, Olevianus cannot be considered a Protestant scholastic in the sense in which this term has traditionally been defined.[118] He is without dispute an Aristotelian logician, but there is also evidence of Ramist influence on the organization of his argument. He shows a penchant for the syllogism but only in single, scattered arguments, not in long series of connected argu-

116. Our own research confirms Althaus's conclusion "dass Föderalgedanke und strenger Prädestinationismus bei vielen theologen friendlich vereinigt gewesen sind. . . . In Wahrheit vertraten Ursinus and Olevianus, der Schuler Calvins, sowohl die Föderaltheologie wie den Prädestinationismus." *Prinzipien der Dogmatik*, 150, 151. Cf. also Lang, *Heidelberger Katechismus*, 21–22.

117. Cf. Sudhoff's remark that Olevianus's commentaries are "vorwiegend dogmatisch." *C. Olevianus*, 460.

118. Brian G. Armstrong (*Calvinism and the Amyraut Heresy* [Madison: University of Wisconsin Press, 1969], 32), e.g., identifies four main tendencies in what is often labelled "Protestant scholasticism": 1) The attempt to produce a logically coherent system of belief through deductive (usually syllogistic) reasoning from given assumptions or principles. This theological approach invariably involves an Aristotelian philosophical commitment. 2) The placing of reason on an equal standing with faith, thus displacing some of the authority of revelation. 3) The reduction of the biblical record to a definitive creedal statement, which can be used to measure orthodoxy. 4) A pronounced interest in abstract, speculative matters, especially with reference to the doctrine of God.

ments sustaining a single proposition. Most of all, he is not a speculative theologian. He is not primarily interested in abstract metaphysical questions but in the experience of personal redemption and in the practical life of the Christian within the community of the redeemed. As Schrenk suggested, it may have been more because of this practical interest than because of his creedal ordering of the data of Scripture that the *heilsgeschichtlich* emphasis of some earlier Reformed theologians recedes in Olevianus. In any case, as a systematic yet nonspeculative theologian, Olevianus is neither the anti-scholastic that Moltmann made him out to be nor the kind of scholastic that Moltmann portrayed him as attacking. He can better be regarded as a transitional figure between the *theologia pietatis* of Calvin and the more developed Protestant orthodox dogmatics of the next century.

Broader Context

Medieval Background

It is widely recognized today that Reformed theologians in the sixteenth and seventeenth centuries were not the first in the history of theology to make use of the covenant motif. Already in the ancient church Irenaeus, Tertullian, Lactantius, and Augustine had all appealed to the covenant idea to support, for various reasons, the basic unity of the Old and New Testaments.[119] Representatives of the Latin mystical tradition, such as Bernard of Clairvaux and the Franciscan spiritualist Ubertino of Casale (d. ca. 1350), employed covenant language to describe the bond of love between the crucified Christ and the soul of the be-

---

119. For a summary of these patristic views of the covenant, see Baker, *Bullinger and the Covenant,* 19–22. Cf. Preus's comment that the late medieval nominalist Gabriel Biel, too, had discovered "the basis of a real continuity between the Old and New Testaments in the *pactum,* the covenant, understood historically." James S. Preus, *From Shadow to Promise: Old Testament Interpretation from Augustine to Luther* (Cambridge, MA: Harvard University Press, 1969), 232. Cf. also Martin Greschat, "Der Bundesgedanke in der Theologie des späten Mittelalters," *Zeitschrift für Kirchengeschichte* 81 (1970):56: "Nach Biel hat sich jenes ewige Dekret der potestas ordinata immer wieder in der Geschichte konkretisiert. Der vor aller Zeit mit dem Menschengeschlect geschlossene Bund begegnet an immer neuen Punkten der Geschichte. Sachlich allerdings zeigen Gottes Bundesschlüsse mit Abraham, mit Mose, und endlich auch der gegenwärtig geltende Bund Gottes mit der Kirche stets genau die gleiche Struktur."

liever.[120] Covenant terminology (*pactum, pactio, pollicitatio, promissio,* etc.) can be found in various formulations of the medieval scholastic doctrine of grace, according to which the order of salvation is grounded not in the essence of God but in the free, self-binding decisions of His divine will.[121] In the late medieval nominalist Gabriel Biel there is a strong emphasis on the bilateral structure or conditionality of this *pactum* of salvation: to those who do their very best God will not deny His grace.[122] And for Scotus, Staupitz, and the late medieval nominalists it is the dependability of the will of God and His faithfulness to His covenant commitments that provide the basis for the (objective) certitude of salvation.[123] Even Luther has been characterized as a covenant theologian of sorts.[124]

120. "Vergeistiger, d.h. die heilsgeschichtliche Dynamik auf ein innerliches Verhältnis reduzierend, redet dann das Werk, dessen Verbreitung und Wirkung in Italien, Spanien, den Niederlanden . . . kaum zu überschätzen ist: der *Arbor vitae crucifixae Jesu* des Ubertin von Casale. Hier wird jener Bund zum Liebesbund des gekreuzigten Christus mit der Seele des demütigen Armen (confoederatio animarum). . . . Die Menschheit Christi, sein exemplum und dementsprechend eine affective-voluntaristische Einigung des Menschen mit ihm sind fur Bernhard und seine Nachfolger kennzeichnend. In diese Konzeption lässt sich die Vorstellung vom Bunde Gottes mit den Armen und Demütigen ohne Schwierigkeiten einzeichnen, wie an Bonaventura oder auch an dem bereits erwähnten Spiritualen Ubertin von Casale erkennbar wird." Greschat, "Bundesgedanke des Mittelalters," 48, 50.

121. Berndt Hamm, *Promissio, Pactum, Ordinatio: Freiheit und Selbstbindung Gottes in der scholastischen Gnadenlehre,* vol. 54 of *Beiträge zur Historischen Theologie* (Tübingen: J. C. B. Mohr, 1977).

122. Heiko A. Oberman, *The Harvest of Medieval Theology: Gabriel Biel and Late Medieval Nominalism* (Cambridge, MA: Harvard University Press, 1963), 173, 218–20, 227–30. Cf. also Baker, *Bullinger and the Covenant,* 24–34, and Greschat, "Bundesgedanke des Mittelalters," 55–56.

123. For Staupitz, see David C. Steinmetz, *Misericordia Dei: The Theology of Johannes von Staupitz in Its Late Medieval Setting,* vol. 4 of *Studies in Medieval and Reformation Thought* (Leiden: E. J. Brill, 1968), 28, 53, 55, 122ff., 182. For Scotus and late medieval nominalism, see Steven E. Ozment, *The Age of Reform, 1250–1550: An Intellectual and Religious History of Late Medieval and Reformation Europe* (New Haven: Yale University Press, 1980), 39–40, 61–62, 244; William J. Courtenay, "Nominalism and Late Medieval Religion," in *The Pursuit of Holiness in Late Medieval and Renaissance Religion,* ed. Charles Trinkhaus with Heiko A. Oberman, vol. 10 of *Studies in Medieval and Reformation Thought* (Leiden: E. J. Brill, 1974), 51.

124. "Wir sind es mit Recht nicht gewöhnt, Luther als einen 'Bundestheologen, anzusehen: seine Theologie ist kein System, in dem der Bundesgedanke ein element darstellt, das alles andere beherrscht und überschatter. . . .

It is clear, therefore, that the covenant notion served a variety of theological functions well before the Reformation. The question is whether early Reformed covenant doctrine was to any extent influenced by these patristic and medieval covenant traditions, as some have suggested. Oberman, for example, concluded in his *Forerunners of the Reformation* that in the centuries to come Covenant theology would continue to provide a structure for the understanding of revelation. Elaborated in many different directions, it became an even more basic and explicit theme in the theology of Ulrich Zwingli, John Calvin, and Johannes Cocceius (d. 1699), and was carried from the Dutch to the English shores. It finally came into full bloom in New England Puritan theology.[125]

In his 1970 article on the covenant in medieval theology, Martin Greschat expressed astonishment that so little scholarly attention had been paid to the connections between late medieval and Reformation covenant thought.[126] Apart from his argument for Erasmus's influence on Zwingli, however, he himself offered no evidence for his conclusion that "von diesem Erbe [of late medieval covenant theology] zehrt . . . auch noch die Reformationszeit."[127] Neither, unfortunately, did Berndt Hamm, who because of a "notwendige Selbstbeschränkung" of his study of covenantal themes in medieval theology, could say only that the "Linien von der mittelalterlichen Selbstbindungstradition in das Zeitalter der Reformation und Gegenreformation führten."[128] The case for direct continuity between the late medieval and early Reformation doctrines of covenant has yet to be made.

Perhaps, however, no such case can be made. Cottrell's and Baker's recent works on the covenant in Zwingli and Bullinger,

---

Dennoch lässt es sich zeigen, dass der Bundesgedanke in einer bestimmten Form auch für den jungen Luther zum Problem und zugleich zur Hilfe geworden ist, und zwar in einer Weise, die unmittelbar mit der Entfaltung seiner Humilitatstheologie zusammenhängt." Heiko A. Oberman, "Wir sein Pettler. Hoc est verum: Bund und Gnade in der Theologie des Mittelalters und der Reformation," *Zeitschrift für Kirchengeschichte* 78 (1967):242.

125. Heiko A. Oberman, *Forerunners of the Reformation: The Shape of Late Medieval Thought* (New York: Holt, Rinehart, and Winston, 1966), 136–37.

126. Greschat, "Bundesgedanke des Mittelalters," 44.

127. Ibid., 63.

128. Hamm, *Promissio, Pactum, Ordinatio,* 390.

respectively, both conclude that no direct lines of influence from the late Middle Ages can be detected. Cottrell concedes that the question requires further study but is still of the opinion that

> even if Zwingli had been familiar with the nominalists' *pactum*, it is unlikely that he would have been impressed by it or influenced by it towards the development of his own covenant doctrine . . . because the nominalists' "covenant" seems to be different in kind from the covenant as Zwingli saw it.[129]

Baker does note Bullinger's acquaintance with some of the patristic materials on the covenant and even allows for an "indirect effect" of the bilateral element in the nominalist *pactum* on the development of Bullinger's covenant thought. But "the nominalist idea of 'pact' seems to have had little if any direct influence on the development of the Reformed covenant idea." Not only was Bullinger not trained in the nominalist tradition, but the two conceptions of covenant are simply too dissimilar to be directly related.[130]

The same must be said of Olevianus. There are no indications in his educational background either that he was familiar with the nominalist tradition (he learned his theology from Calvin), nor is there any *prima facie* evidence in his writings of his dependence on medieval sources. As we have seen, he is primarily indebted to the Reformed covenant tradition of his immediate theological predecessors.

This absence of clear ties to the medieval theological tradition is not especially problematic, however, if we keep in mind the adaptability of the covenant motif to more than one theological framework. The covenant concept has a range of theological uses—it can explain the relationship between Old and New Testaments, the believer's personal union with Christ, the self-imposed obligations of God, the conditionality of salvation, and the believer's assurance of salvation—all of which are employed in pre-Reformation theology and appear again in a new context in Reformed circles. The recurrence of these covenant themes

---

129. Cottrell, "Covenant and Baptism in Zwingli," 382.
130. Baker, *Bullinger and the Covenant*, 24.

in the Reformation does not have to be explained by a direct line of influence from the Middle Ages. Rather, the dearth of evidence for such links might suggest that as the covenant idea in Scripture was again explored, the theological flexibility it had manifested in earlier ages was discovered anew and adapted to a new theological framework. If this be the case, then one of Olevianus's distinctive contributions to Reformed covenant theology was the rediscovery of part of the theological and pastoral potential of the covenant motif—its use as a basis for certitude of salvation.

The absence of clear ties to medieval theology also does not mean that the search for connections between Protestant covenant doctrine and the Middle Ages should be abandoned altogether. A more profitable line of inquiry might be the investigation of the influence of medieval political and juristic conceptions of covenant. A few scholars have already pointed us in this direction. Leonard Trinterud, for example, maintained in his essay on the origins of Puritanism that the covenant theology of the Rhinelanders and English Puritans "utilized most of the ideas found in medieval [state-contract theories]," especially in their formulation of the covenant of works.[131] Gottfried Locher concluded that both Swiss and Scottish understandings of covenant had a longstanding political as well as religious character associated with them.[132] Josef Bohatec saw the influence on Calvin's covenant doctrine of both the Roman law tradition in general and Budé's humanistic reassessment of it in particular.[133] We ourselves have shown how this same tradition of Roman law, revived in the High Middle Ages and mediated through the humanist law faculties in France, also had an impact on Olevianus: not only did he study civil law at the time of its highest humanistic flowering, but he stood in a long line of Reformed lawyer-theologians who employed terms, distinctions, and principles from Roman con-

131. Trinterud, "Origins of Puritanism," 42, 48. Cf. also Francis Lyall, "Of Metaphors and Analogies: Legal Language and Covenant Theology," *Scottish Journal of Theology* 32 (1979):9–10.

132. Gottfried W. Locher, *Zwingli's Thought: New Perspectives*, vol. 25 of *Studies in the History of Christian Thought* (Leiden: E. J. Brill, 1981), 376.

133. Bohatec, *Budé und Calvin*, 247–8.

tract law to give greater clarity to the covenantal patterns they found in Scripture.[134] The research on this question, however, so far has been only suggestive. We still await a definitive study of the links between the theological conception of covenant in the Reformed tradition and the legal and political thought of the Middle Ages.

Late Sixteenth and Seventeenth Centuries

In attempting to measure Olevianus's impact on the generations of Reformed theologians that followed him, one might best begin with Schrenk's conclusion in 1923 that Olevianus was an important link between the first framers of a doctrine of covenant and the federal theologians of the late sixteenth and seventeenth centuries.[135] Schrenk pointed out that many of the later continental federal theologians studied or taught at the renowned Reformed academy at Herborn, founded by Olevianus in 1584 with the financial support of Count John the Elder of Nassau-Dillenberg: Johannes Piscator (1546–1625), a professor at the academy from its founding until his death;[136] Matthias Martinius (1572–1630), student (1589ff.)[137] and later professor and pastor (1595–1607) in Herborn;[138] Ludwig Crocius (1586–1655), educated in Herborn;[139] and Johannes Alsted (1588–1638), also educated at the academy and a teacher there from 1610 until 1629.[140] Schrenk might also have mentioned Hermann Ravensperger (1586–1625), who was trained at Herborn and became an influential federal theologian in Groningen.[141] Olevianus, of course, was long dead (1587) by the time most of these men arrived in Herborn, but it is not at all improbable that Piscator, his son-in-law, colleague on the faculty, and first biographer introduced the students at Herborn to the theological

134. See above, pp. 155–58.
135. "Ursinus und Olevianus sind die wirksamsten Mittelglieder zwischen Bullinger und den späteren Föderaltheologen." Schrenk, *Gottesreich und Bund*, 55.
136. *Schaff-Herzog Encyclopedia*, 1949 ed., s.v. "Piscator, Johannes."
137. Schrenk, *Gottesreich und Bund*, 71, n. 1.
138. McCoy, "Covenant Theology of Cocceius," 78.
139. Schrenk, *Gottesreich und Bund*, 73–74.
140. *Schaff-Herzog Encyclopedia*, 1949 ed., s.v. "Alsted, Johann Heinrich."
141. McCoy, "Covenant Theology of Cocceius," 69.

writings of the academy's distinguished founder,[142] several of which were published and republished in Herborn years after his death.[143]

The most prominent of the "spätere Föderaltheologen" Schrenk had in mind, however, was Johannes Cocceius (1603–1669), Professor of Theology in Bremen and Franeker and perhaps the best-known covenant theologian of the seventeenth century. In his case a direct line of influence can be drawn from Olevianus, for Cocceius not only studied in Bremen under two of the Herborn-trained covenant theologians, Martinius and Crocius, but in his major work on the covenant, *Collationes de foedere et testamento Dei* (1648),[144] he cited Olevianus as the chief source of inspiration for the treatise: "Other learned men have laid the foundation for this disquisition, especially that man of such worthy memory, Caspar Olevianus."[145] And indeed there are elements of Cocceius's covenant theology that appear to bear Olevianus's stamp: God's decree as the foundation of the covenant of grace; a pretemporal covenant in which the Father commands the Son to assume the role as *sponsor* of the covenant of grace; the covenant of works (Olevianus: covenant of creation) as an original *communion* with God by virtue of hu-

142. It is interesting to note that several distinctive features of Olevianus's covenant theology recur in Martinius: *ius creationis* as a designation of the covenant contracted at creation; the forgiveness and renewal promised in Jeremiah 31 as the double benefit of the New Covenant; and the Mosaic covenant as a reiteration of the covenant of creation. See Schrenk, *Gottesreich und Bund,* 71–72. In addition, Althaus notes that "[Alsted's] populäre 'Katechetik' wie das Buch seines Lehrers Martinius die 5 Hauptstücke im Anschlusse an Olevianus unter föderalistische Gesichtspunkte stellt." *Prinzipien der deutschen Dogmatik,* 151.

143. *Notae Gaspar Oleviani in Evangelia* (1587, 1589, 1593); *Notae in Epist. ad Ephesios ex Oleviani concionibus excerptae* (1588); *Notae in Evangelia et Epistolas Pauli ad Galatas, Ephesios, Philippenses et Colossenses* (1589); *Der Gnadenbund Gottes* (1590, 1593); *Expositio Symboli Apostolici* (1593); "Kurzer Bericht [Abendmahlpredigten VII]" (1617).

144. Later, and considerably expanded, editions of this work appeared under the title *Summa doctrinae de foedere et testamento Dei* (1653, 1660). McCoy, "Covenant Theology of Cocceius," 105–6.

145. "Exemplum huius disquisitionis alii quoque Viri Docti praebuerunt; imprimis laudatissimae memoriae Vir Caspar Olevianus," Quoted in Von Korff, *Anfänge der Föderal-theologie,* 9. Bizer ("Historische Einleitung," xxxvi) is certainly mistaken when he asserts, "Cocceius hat sich später auf *Ursin* als seinen Vorgänger in der Föderaltheologie berufen" (italics added).

manity's creation in His image; the continuation of the obligation of this first covenant after the fall; the covenant of grace embracing the *whole* person;[146] tranquility of heart/conscience as a peculiar blessing of the New Covenant;[147] the coupling of covenant and kingdom of God;[148] and, perhaps most significant, the recapitulation of the stages of salvation history in the salvation experience of the individual believer.[149]

Schrenk's thesis, then, is basically sound. Through his influence on the "Herborn School" of federal theologians, especially Cocceius, Olevianus played a significant part in the transmission of Reformed covenant theology to the seventeenth century. Even some not educated at Herborn acknowledged a debt to him.[150] The question, however, is whether Schrenk went far enough in applying his own thesis, for he saw fit to examine Olevianus's role only in the development of covenant theology on the continent. All this while, a theology of covenant was also emerging in Reformed circles in England and Scotland. Did Olevianus also exert some influence there?

A "Scottish connection" can indeed be documented. Robert Howie, a leading figure in the introduction of covenant theology

146. Olevianus, *De substantia*, 95: ". . . cum non solum animae nostrae sed & corpora Deo sint foederata & quidem membra capitis nostri Jesu Christi per vinculum Spiritus fidei."

147. For a fuller discussion of the foregoing themes in Cocceius, see McCoy, "Covenant Theology of Cocceius," 169, 170, 184, 188, 191, 197, 211–13, 255, 260–61, 274.

148. "So hat [Cocceius] denn auch nach Olevianus's Vorgang Bund und Reich miteinander verbunden, und erst diese Verbindung gibt seine ganze Theologie." Schrenk, *Gottesreich und Bund*, 147.

149. "Zo vindt men bij Coccejus de konstruktie, dat de Geest de heilsgeschiedenis in ons leven tot herhaling brengt. In de heilsorde komen dezelfde stadia voor als in de heilshistorie." Verhoeven, "Olevianus," 117. "Unter dem Einfluss von J. Coccejus ist im späteren Pietismus die Heilsgeschichte mit der Heilsordnung verbunden, so dass die Glaubensgeschichte des Christen strukturiert wurde wie eine persönliche Applikation der Heilsgeschichte. Diese Verinnerlichung und Individualisierung der Heilsgeschichte." C. Graafland, "Hat Calvin einen Ordo Salutis gelehrt?" Paper presented at the 3rd International Calvin Congress, Geneva, Switzerland, September 6–9, 1982. Both Verhoeven and Graafland attribute this personalizing of the *Heilsgeschichte* to Cocceius. It actually can be found already in Olevianus. See above, pp. 138–39.

150. For example, Adolph Lampe (1683–1729), *Verborgenheit des Gnadenbundes*, I.1.17, and Johann Grammlichius in his *Tractatus theoretico practico de foederibus divinis*, according to Sudhoff, *C. Olevianus*, 460.

to Scotland, not only studied under Olevianus at the Herborn Academy (1585–1588) but in his work *De reconciliatione hominis cum Deo* (1591) spoke of Olevianus with great respect and, according to Henderson, closely followed his teaching.[151] Howie, in turn, was a close friend of Robert Rollock (1555–1599), one of the most influential covenant theologians in Scotland at the turn of the century. That Rollock might have been indirectly influenced by Olevianus is further suggested by the fact that his friend and colleague in Edinburgh, Charles Lumsden, had owned a copy of Olevianus's *De substantia foederis* since October 1590.[152]

Evidence of Olevianus's influence in England is slimmer and largely circumstantial, but it is intriguing enough to warrant a closer look. The place to begin, perhaps, is with William Perkins (1558–1602), the foremost Puritan theologian at the end of the sixteenth century and a major influence on the next generation of Puritan divines.[153] When one begins to examine Perkins's covenant theology, one cannot help but notice a remarkable similarity to that of Olevianus. Like Olevianus, Perkins writes an exposition of the Apostles' Creed in which he interprets the individual articles of the creed as promises of the covenant.[154] Christ is the "foundation and ground" (cf. Olevianus: "fundament und grundt") of the covenant,[155] and the "substance of the covenant" includes the actual benefits of salvation procured by Christ.[156] At the heart of the covenant of grace is

151. Henderson, "The Idea of the Covenant in Scotland," *Evangelical Quarterly* 27 (1955):8.

152. Ibid., 9.

153. Christopher Hill maintains that Perkins was "the dominant influence in Puritan thought for the forty years after his death." *Puritanism and Revolution* (London: Secher and Warburg, 1958), 216. For a more detailed description of Perkins's shaping influence on seventeenth-century Puritanism, see Priebe, "Covenant Theology of Perkins," 3–10.

154. Ibid., 34.

155. *The Workes of That famous and worthy Minister of Christ in the Universitie of Cambridge, Mr. William Perkins,* 3 vols. (London: John Legatt, 1616–18), 1:165.

156. "Now then that we may proceed at large to open the substance of the Covenant, wee are in the next place to come to that part of the Creede, which concerns the second person in Trinity . . . from which words to the very end of the Creede, such points onely are laide downe as notably unfolde the benefits & the matter of the covenant." Ibid.

the believer's personal union with Christ, that mystical relationship that binds the individual to God.[157] The *foedus gratuitum* and *foedus legale* are separate but concurrent covenants.[158] The "three assaults" of the Devil on the Christian pilgrim are similar, though not identical, to the "drei Anklagen" of the Devil in Olevianus.[159]

What is most striking, however, is Perkins's treatment of the believer's assurance of salvation. For him, as for Olevianus, the covenant idea provides objective certitude by assuring the believer of the absolute reliability and trustworthiness of God: "In the person of Abraham, God . . . hath made covenant with us; and he hath sworne unto us. What can we more require of him? What better ground of true comfort?"[160] Subjective certitude, moreover, is attained through the practical syllogism, by way of inference from the evidences of election in the believer's experience. Using precisely the same approach as Olevianus in *Vester Grundt*,[161] Perkins argues against the possibility of ob-

---

157. Priebe, "Covenant Theology of Perkins," 93, 110, 116ff., 120ff, 261.

158. Ibid., 40ff.

159. Perkins, *Workes*, 1:86–89; Sudhoff, *Fester Grund*, 1590 ed., 562–68.

160. Perkins, *A Commentarie, Or, Exposition upon the first five Chapters of the Epistles to the Galatians . . .* (1617), 186, quoted in John von Rohr, "Covenant and Assurance in Early English Puritanism," *Church History* 34 (June 1965):196.

161. "Und ist dreierlei Wirkung Christi darin zu bedenken, daraus wir schliessen können, dass wir durch den Glauben Glieder Christi sind. Die erste ist das Zeugniss des heiligen Geistes. . . . Die andere . . . ist die Tödtung des alten Menschen. . . . Die dritte Wirkung ist die Lebendigmachung des Geistes. . . . Derhalben wer einen Anfang dieser drei Wirkungen und herzliche Begierde drinnen fortzufahren in sich empfindet, der soll für gewiss bei sich selbst schliessen, dass er den Glauben habe, und derhalben auch Christum besitze mit allen seinen Wohlthaten zur volkommenen Gerechtigkeit und Seligkeit. Wer nun gläubig ist, der ist auch auserwählt. . . . Derhalben auch wider die allerschwerste Anfechtung, ob du auserwählt seyest, musst du nicht in den Rath Gottes mit deinen Gedanken, hinauffahren, sondern musst dich an dem Wort halten, welches zusagt, dass alle Gläubigen aus Gnaden auserwählt seyen zum ewigen Leben, und dass die gläubig sind, die Hunger und Durst haben nach der Gerechtigkeit. Wie man denn durch die drei Wirkungen Christi in uns als Staffeln hinaufschreiten kann, daraus zu schliessen, dass, dieweil wir die Wirkung Christi in uns haben (wie schwach sie uns auch dünkt), dass wir auch die Ursache der Wirkung, nämlich Christum, durch den Glauben besitzen. Haben wir den Glauben, so sind wir auch auserwählt; denn der Glaube keinen, denn den Auserwählten Gottes gegeben wird." Sudhoff, *Fester Grund*, 1590 ed., 191–93.

taining knowledge of one's election directly from God and encourages the believer to look for the effects of election in himself, viz., in the witness of the Holy Spirit in his heart and in the work of sanctification (mortification and vivification) in his life.[162] Sanctification is to election as heat is to fire: "we use to judge by heat that there is fire when we cannot see the flame itself."[163]

In some respects Perkins's covenant theology is more like that of Olevianus than is Cocceius's. Cocceius was first and foremost a biblical theologian, highly trained in Near Eastern languages, exegesis, and rabbinics. While he was also to some degree a systematician, even his dogmatic works reveal his interest in the language of Scripture and in God's redemptive activity in history. As McCoy concluded in a study of Cocceius's covenant theology, "his theology grew out of his understanding of the Bible, not the reverse."[164] Like Olevianus he believed the Scriptures contained a single, harmonious system of truth, yet the framework of this system was provided by the stages of salvation history represented in the progression of biblical covenants.[165] For the Herborn and Puritan federal theologians, on the other hand, this *heilsgeschichtlich* development

> is overshadowed by the theological architectonic. The covenant-motif functions as a paradigm of God's salvific relationship with men, as a device for arranging and/or interpreting dogmatic material; and the historical particularity of successive covenants after the fall is subordinated to the essential unity, before and after Christ, of the covenant of grace and of the Church founded upon it.[166]

162. R. T. Kendall, *Calvin and English Calvinism to 1649* (Oxford: University Press, 1979), 71–72. Cf. also Priebe, "Covenant Theology of Perkins," 24, 258.

163. Perkins, *Workes*, 1:115, quoted in Kendall, *Calvin and English Calvinism*, 72. Kendall surmises (p. 71) that here Perkins is "apparently following Beza."

164. McCoy, "Covenant Theology of Cocceius," 122.

165. Ibid., 127, 142.

166. Stoever, "Covenant of Works," 35, n. 23. Geerhardus Vos suggested already a century ago that "what was new in Cocceius was not his covenant theology as such, but rather the historical conclusions for the economy of redemption which he drew from the covenant concept." "Covenant in Reformed Theology," 235.

Perkins is no exception here. He, too, stresses primarily the dogmatic and practical, not the historical, implications of the covenant. His covenant theology, like Olevianus's, reflects a concern to make the promises of God specific and personal for the individual believer.[167]

The parallels, then, between Perkins's and Olevianus's covenant theologies are almost too uncanny to be coincidental. And there is at least a smattering of historical evidence that supports the possibility of direct influence. First of all, Olevianus's ideas and writings were easily accessible to the English. English merchants, for example, especially those with business contacts in Holland and France, served as regular intermediaries between the continental Reformed churches and the English Puritans.[168] Furthermore, by the 1570s the University of Heidelberg had surpassed the Genevan Academy in its reputation for instruction in the arts and theology and was drawing a large number of foreign students to its halls. Many of these foreigners were English Puritans, the most celebrated being the exiled Cambridge professor Thomas Cartwright (in Heidelberg, 1574–76).[169] These young Puritans were in constant contact with the professors and ministers of Heidelberg, including Olevianus,[170] and it is not at all unlikely that some of Olevianus's sermons and early theological treatises accompanied them across the Channel when they returned to their homeland.

In the second place, we know for certain that at least one of Olevianus's major works had reached the British Isles by 1580, while Perkins was still a student at Cambridge University. On June 9, 1580, the London publisher H. Middleton received a Stationer's license to publish an English translation of Olevianus's *Expositio Symboli Apostolici* (1576)[171] prepared by John

167. Priebe, "Covenant Theology of Perkins," 24.
168. A. F. Scott Pearson, *Thomas Cartwright and Elizabethan Puritanism* (Cambridge: University Press, 1925), 169.
169. Ibid., 131–35.
170. Cf. ibid., 150.
171. A. W. Pollard and G. R. Redgrave, *A Short-Title Catalogue of Books Printed in England, Scotland, and Ireland . . . 1475–1640*, 2nd ed., rev. and enl. W. A. Jackson, F. S. Ferguson, and K. F. Pantzer, 2 vols. (London: The Bibliographical Society, 1976), 2:197.

Field, the most prominent of the second generation Elizabethan Puritans and leader of the Puritan party before Cartwright.[172] The book appeared the following year and went through a second printing in 1582. Within five years of its publication on the continent, therefore, this treatise had not only arrived in England but had become available to a rather wide audience. Whether Perkins ever read it we do not know. The libraries at Cambridge today house copies of the 1576, 1580, and 1584 Latin editions of the *Expositio* printed on the continent,[173] to which Perkins quite probably had access during his student years at Cambridge in the 1580s. We do know for certain, however, that he was familiar with Olevianus's *magnum opus* on the covenant, *De substantia foederis* (1585), because he cites it in his own exposition of the Apostles' Creed published in 1595.[174]

In sum, we have strong evidence that Olevianus was well known by many of the Puritans studying on the continent in the 1570s, that his works had definitely reached England as early as 1580 and were still being read as late as the mid-seventeenth century,[175] and that Perkins himself had read Olevianus's most extensive work on the covenant sometime within the first decade of its publication. It is not at all unlikely, therefore, that Perkins was acquainted with others of Olevianus's works and was to some extent indebted to Olevianus's doctrine of the covenant. Even if no direct dependence can be established, he must at least have been influenced by the more personal, experiential, and certitudinal type of federal theology that Olevianus had fathered and that he (Perkins) in turn passed on to the next generations of English and New England

172. Charles D. Cremeans, *The Reception of Calvinist Thought in England* (Urbana: University of Illinois Press, 1949), 54–55.

173. H. M. Adams, *Catalogue of Books Printed on the Continent of Europe, 1501–1600, in Cambridge Libraries*, 2 vols. (Cambridge: University Press, 1967), 2:21–22.

174. *An Exposition of the Symbole or Creed of the Apostles* (Cambridge: John Legatt, 1595), 305. This reference is found in Moller, "Beginnings of Covenant Theology," 58, n. 4.

175. Olevianus is cited by both William Eyre, *Vindiae Justificationis Gratuitae* (1654), 198, and John Graile, *A Modest Vindication of the Doctrine of Conditions in the Covenant of Grace* (London, 1655), 67ff.

covenant theologians.[176] In the last analysis, Schrenk was perhaps more right than he realized: Olevianus's influence on later federal theology did extend to Bremen and Franeker (Cocceius), but it also crossed the Channel to Aberdeen (Howie) and possibly even Edinburgh (Rollock), Cambridge (Perkins), and beyond.

176. For the importance of the assurance of salvation in Puritan covenant theology, see Perry Miller, "Preparation for Salvation in Seventeenth-Century New England," *Journal of the History of Ideas* 4 (June 1943):253–86; John von Rohr, "Covenant and Assurance in Early English Puritanism," *Church History* 34 (June 1965):195–203; and Richard A. Muller, "Covenant and Conscience in English Reformed Theology," *Westminster Theological Journal* 42 (Spring 1980):308–34.

6

Conclusion

If there is any one thing that the foregoing research has shown, it is that the picture of Olevianus's covenant theology developed over the last century and a half needs to be modified in a number of ways. The most important of these can be summarized as follows:

(1) Olevianus was not the first Reformed theologian to employ the covenant idea as the organizing principle of his theology. He was the first to use it as a sustained theological *leitmotiv*, but the structure of his systematic theological works was provided by the articles of the Apostles' Creed.

(2) Olevianus did not portray the covenant of grace as strictly a divine unilateral promise or testament. Like *all* sixteenth-century Reformed covenant theologians—Zwingli, Bullinger, Calvin, Musculus, Ursinus, Perkins, etc.—he recognized both a unilateral (divine) and a bilateral (divine-human) dimension to the covenant of grace within the context of a monergistic soteriology.

(3) Olevianus's covenant theology does not deal exclusively with a covenant of grace. He introduced into Reformed theology three new covenants (a pretemporal redemptive pact between the Father and the Son, a covenant with Satan, and a covenant with creatures) as well as the term *foedus creationis* (covenant of creation), and enlarged upon the doctrines of the *foedus creationis* and *foedus legale* (legal covenant).

(4) Olevianus was not part of a late sixteenth-century *"heilsgeschichtlich"* reaction against an encroaching predestinarian scholasticism in Reformed circles. Not only are covenant and predestination perfectly compatible in his theology, but the focus of his covenantal theology is the experience of salvation in

183

the individual believer rather than the history of salvation in Scripture.

(5) Finally, Olevianus's role and significance in the history of Reformed covenant theology can best be described as mediatory: chronologically, geographically, and theologically, he stood midway between the first appearances of a Reformed doctrine of covenant in Switzerland in the 1520s and its full flowering in Holland, England, and Scotland a century later. Chronologically, his life spanned the second generation of Swiss covenant theologians, some of whom were his teachers, and the second generation of Herborn and Puritan federalists, some of whom were his students and theological heirs. Geographically, in part because of Olevianus's work there, Heidelberg and Herborn became important way stations for covenant theology as it proceeded down the Rhine from Switzerland to the Lowlands and British Isles. Theologically, his covenant teaching was paradigmatic of, and in part responsible for, the transition taking place in Reformed covenant doctrine from a minor to a dominant dogmatic role, from a single to a double and triple covenant schema, from a modest to a heavy dependence on the Roman law tradition, and from a preoccupation with the history of salvation to a new concern with the personal assurance of salvation. In short, Caspar Olevianus was neither the founder nor the final architect of sixteenth-century Reformed covenant theology but a key intermediary figure in its development. The Heidelberg preacher and church administrator must also be given place among the more important Reformed theologians of the Confessional Age.

Bibliography

I. Primary Sources

A. The Works of Caspar Olevianus
(Listed in the chronological order of their first editions)

Vester Grundt, das ist, die Artikel des alten, waren, ungezweifelten, christlichen Glaubens, den Christen, die in diesen gefärlichen, trübseligen zeiten einen gewissen trost aus Gottes Wort suchen, zu gutem erkleret und zugeschreiben. Heidelberg: Michael Schirat, 1567. Excerpts reprinted in *Quellen zur Geschichte des kirchlichen Unterrichts in der evangelischen Kirche Deutschlands zwischen 1530 und 1600.* Pt. 1: *Quellen zur Geschichte des Katechismusunterrichts.* Vol. 3: *Ost-, Nord-, und West-deutsche Katechismen.* Pt. 2: Texte, pp. 1330–86. Ed. by Johann M. Reu. Gütersloh: C. Bertelsmann, 1924. Expanded edition included in *Der Gnadenbund Gottes* (Herborn: Christopher Rab, 1590) and reprinted in Sudhoff, Karl, *Fester Grund christlicher Lehre. Ein Hilfsbuch zum Heidelberger Katechismus.* Frankfurt: Theodor Volcker, 1854.

Expositio Symboli Apostolici, sive Articulorum Fidei: in qua summa gratuiti foederis aeterni inter Deum & fideles breviter & perspicue tractatur. Frankfurt: Andreae Wechel, 1576. English translation: *An Exposition of the symbole of the Apostles, or rather of the Articles of Faith. In which the chief points of the everlasting and free covenant between God and the faithful is briefly and plainly handled.* Translated by John Field. London: H. Middleton, 1581. Dutch translation included in *Geschriften van Caspar Olevianus.* The Hague: Het Reformatorische Boek, 1963.

In Epistolam D. Pauli Apostoli ad Galatas notae, ex concionibus Gasparis Oleviani excerptae, & a Theodoro Beza editae. Geneva: Eustathius Vignon, 1578.

In Epistolam D. Pauli Apostoli ad Romanos notae, ex Gasparis Oleviani concionibus excerptae, & a Theodoro Beza editae. Geneva: Eustathius Vignon, 1578.

In Epistolam D. Pauli Apostoli ad Philippenses & Colossenses notae, ex Gasparis Oleviani concionibus excerptae & a Theodoro Beza editae. Geneva: Eustathius Vignon, 1580.

Fundamenta dialecticae breviter consignata e praelectionibus. Frankfurt: N.p., 1581.

De inventione dialecticae liber, e praelectionibus Gasp. Oleviani excerptus. Geneva: Eustathius Vignon, 1583.

De substantia foederis gratuiti inter Deum et electos, itemque de mediis, quibus ea ipsa substantia nobis communicatur. Geneva: Eustathius Vignon, 1585. A Dutch translation can be found in *Geschriften van Caspar Olevianus.* The Hague: Het Reformatorische Boek, 1963.

Institutionis Christianae Religionis Epitome: Ex Institutione Johanni Calvini excerpta, authoris methodo et verbis retentis. Cum praefatione Gasparis Oleviani, ad Theodorum Bezam, in qua editionis consilium exponitur. Herborn: Christophorus Corvinus, 1586.

Notae Gasparis Olevianus in Evangelia, quae diebus dominicis ac festis populo christiano in plerique Germaniae ecclesiis proponi solent. Herborn: Christophorus Corvinus, 1587.

Notae in Epistolam ad Ephesios ex Oleviani concionibus excerptae. Herborn: N.p., 1588.

Der Gnadenbund Gottes. Herborn: Christoff Raben, 1590.

"Bawren Catechismus, das ist, Kurtze anleytung für die einfeltigen, Wie ein Haussvatter seine Kinder und Gesind auss den Artickeln des Glaubens und andern Hauptstücken zum verstand ihres heyls in Christo und gottseligen leben durch Gottes gnade ohne besondere Mühe bringen, möge." N.p., n.d. In *Quellen zur Geschichte,* pp. 1307–18. Ed. by Johann M. Reu. Also in *Der Gnadenbund Gottes,* pp. 235–58. Herborn: Christoff Raben, 1593.

"Fürschlag, wie Doctor Luthers Lehr von den heiligen Sacramenten (so in seinem kleinen Catechismo begriffen) auss Gottes Wort mit den reformierten Kirchen zu vereinigen seye." N.p., n.d. In *Quellen zur Geschichte,* pp. 1318– 27. Edited by Johann M. Reu. Also in *Der Gnadenbund Gottes,* pp. 523–44.

"Kurtzer Underricht von der predig des H. Evangelij und reychnung der H. Sacramenten, nemlich des Tauffs unnd H. Abendmals unsers Herren Jesu Christi." N.p., n.d. In *Quellen zur Geschichte,* pp. 1327–30. Edited by Johann M. Reu. Also in *Der Gnadenbund Gottes,* pp. 515–21.

"Predigten von dem heiligen Abendmahl des Herrn." N.p., n.d. Also in *Der Gnadenbund Gottes,* pp. 259–514. Excerpts reprinted in Sudhoff, Karl, *C. Olevianus und Z. Ursinus: Leben und ausgewählte Schriften,* pp. 185–233. Elberfeld: R. L. Friderichs, 1857.

B. The Works of Other Sixteenth-Century Theologians

Bullinger, Heinrich. *Common Places of Christian Religion.* Translated by John Stockwood. London: Tho. East and H. Middleton, 1572.

———. "De testamento seu foedere dei unico et aeterno . . . brevis expositio." In *In omnes apostolicas Epistolas . . . commentarii*. Zurich: Christopher Froscho, 1537.

———. *The Decades*. Edited by Thomas Harding. 5 vols. Cambridge: University Press, 1849–52.

———. *Das Zweite Helvetische Bekenntnis. Confessio Helvetica Posterior*. Translated and edited by W. Hildebrandt and R. Zimmerman. Zurich: Zwingli Verlag, 1966.

Calvin, John. *Calvin: Commentaries*. Edited by Joseph Haroutunian. The Library of Christian Classics, vol. 23. Philadelphia: Westminster, 1963.

———. *Calvin: Theological Treatises*. Edited by J. K. S. Reid. The Library of Christian Classics, vol. 22. Philadelphia: Westminster, 1954.

———. *Calvin's Commentaries*. Edited by D. W. and T. F. Torrance. Vol. 9: *The Second Epistle of Paul the Apostle to the Corinthians and the Epistles to Timothy, Titus and Philemon*. Translated by T. A. Small. Edinburgh: Oliver and Boyd, 1964.

———. *Commentaries on the Book of the Prophet Jeremiah and The Lamentations*. Translated by John Owen. 5 vols. Grand Rapids: Eerdmans, 1950.

———. *Commentaries on the First Book of Moses, Called Genesis*. Translated by John King. 2 vols. Grand Rapids: Eerdmans, 1948.

———. *Commentaries on the First Twenty Chapters of the Book of the Prophet Ezekiel*. Translated by Thomas Myers. 2 vols. Grand Rapids: Eerdmans, 1948.

———. *Commentaries on the Last Four Books of Moses Arranged in the Form of a Harmony*. Translated by Charles Bingham. 4 vols. Grand Rapids: Eerdmans, 1950.

———. *Commentary on the Book of the Prophet Isaiah*. Translated by William Pringle. 4 vols. Grand Rapids: Eerdmans, 1948.

———. *Commentary on the Book of Psalms*. Translated by James Anderson. 5 vols. Grand Rapids: Eerdmans, 1949.

———. *Commentary on the Gospel According to John*. Translated by William Pringle. 2 vols. Grand Rapids: Eerdmans, 1949.

———. *Institutes of the Christian Religion*. Edited by John T. McNeill. Translated by Ford Lewis Battles. The Library of Christian Classics, vols. 20, 21. Philadelphia: Westminster, 1960.

———. *Ioannis Calvini opera quae supersunt omnia*. Edited by G. Baum, E. Cunitz, and E. Reuss. Vol. 26 (*Corpus Reformatorum*, vol. 54): *Sermons sur le Deuteronome*, Pt. 2. Brunswick: C. A. Schwetschke et Filii, 1883.

————. *Ioannis Calvini opera quae supersunt omnia.* Edited by G. Baum, E. Cunitz, and E. Reuss. Vol. 28 (*Corpus Reformatorum*, vol. 56): *Sermons sur le Deuteronome*, Pt. 4. Brunswick: S. A. Schwetschke et Filii, 1885.

————. *Sermons of Master John Calvin upon the Fifthe Book of Moses called Deuteronomie.* Translated by Arthur Golding. London: N.p., 1583.

Melanchthon, Philip. *Erotemata dialectices, continentia fere integram artem, ita scripta, ut inventuti utiliter proponi possint.* Frankfurt: Chr. Ege., c. 1547.

Musculus, Wolfgang. *Common Places of Christian Religion.* Translated by John Man. London: Henry Bynneman, 1578.

Perkins, William. *An Exposition of the Symbole or Creed of the Apostles.* Cambridge: John Legatt, 1595.

————. *The Works of That famous and worthy Minister of Christ in the Universitie of Cambridge, Mr. William Perkins.* 3 vols. London: John Legatt, 1616–18.

Ursinus, Zacharias. *Catechesis minor, perspicua brevitate christianam fidem complectens.* In *D. Zachariae Ursini . . . opera theologica.* Edited by Quirinus Reuter. Heidelberg: Johan Lancellot, 1612.

————. *Catechesis, summa theologiae per questiones et responsiones exposita.* In *D. Zachariae Ursini . . . opera theologica.* Edited by Quirinus Reuter. Heidelberg: Johan Lancellot, 1612.

————. *Commentary of Dr. Zacharias Ursinus on the Heidelberg Catechism.* Translated by G. W. Williard. Cincinnati: Elm Street Printing Co., 1888.

Zwingli, Ulrich. "Antwort über Balthasar Hubmaiers Taufbuchlein." In *Huldreich Zwinglis Sämliche Werke*, vol. 4 (*Corpus Reformatorum*, vol. 91). Edited by Emil Egli, et al. Leipzig: M. Heinsius Nachfolger, 1927.

————. "De providentia dei." In *Huldrici Zwinglii opera*, vol. 4. Edited by M. Schuler and J. Schulthess. Zurich: Ex Officini Schulthessiana, 1841.

————. "Farrago annotationum in Genesim. . . ." In *Zwinglis Werke*, vol. 13 (*Corpus Reformatorum*, vol. 100). Edited by Emil Egli, et al. Zurich: Verlag Berichthaus, 1963.

————. "Gutachten im Ittinger Handel." In *Zwinglis Werke*, vol. 3 (*Corpus Reformatorum*, vol. 90). Edited by Emil Egli, et al. Leipzig: M. Heinsius Nachfolger, 1914.

————. "In catabaptistarum strophas elenchus." In *Zwinglis Werke*, vol. 6/1 (*Corpus Reformatorum*, vol. 93/1). Edited by Emil Egli, et al. Zurich: Verlag Berichthaus, 1961.

————. "Subidium sive coronis de eucharistia." In *Zwinglis Werke*, vol. 4 *(Corpus Reformatorum*, vol. 91).

———. "Von der Taufe, von der Wiedertaufe und von der Kindertaufe." In *Zwinglis Werke*, vol. 4 (*Corpus Reformatorum*, vol. 91).

———. "Zwingli an Urbanus Rhegius." In *Zwinglis Werke*, vol. 8 (*Corpus Reformatorum*, vol. 95). Edited by Emil Egli, et al. Leipzig: M. Heinsius Nachfolger, 1914.

II. Secondary Sources

A. Books

Adam, Melchior. *Vitae germanorum theologorum*. Frankfurt: N.p., 1653.

Adams, H. M. *Catalogue of Books Printed on the Continent of Europe, 1501–1600, in Cambridge Libraries*. 2 vols. Cambridge: University Press, 1967.

Althaus, Paul. *Die Prinzipien der deutschen reformierten Dogmatik im Zeitalter der aristotelischen Scholastik*. Darmstadt: Wissenschaftliche Buchgesellschaft, 1967.

Armstrong, Brian G. *Calvinism and the Amyraut Heresy*. Madison: University of Wisconsin Press, 1969.

Baker, J. Wayne. *Heinrich Bullinger and the Covenant: The Other Reformed Tradition*. Athens, OH: Ohio University Press, 1980.

Bangs, Carl. *Arminius: A Study in the Dutch Reformation*. Nashville: Abingdon, 1971.

Barth, Karl. *Church Dogmatics*. Vol. 4/1: *The Doctrine of Reconciliation*. Translated by G. W. Bromiley. New York: Charles Scribner's Sons, 1956.

Bauer, Karl. *Aus der grossen Zeit der theologischen Facultät zu Heidelberg*. Baden: M. Schauenburg, 1938.

Berkhof, Louis. *Systematic Theology*. Grand Rapids: Eerdmans, 1939.

Bohatec, Josef. *Budé und Calvin: Studien zur Gedankenwelt des französischen Frühhumanismus*. Graz: Hermann Böhlau, 1950.

Boumeester, G. *Caspar Olevianus en Zijn Reformatorische Arbeid*. The Hague: Willem de Zwijgerstichting, 1954.

Bray, John S. *Theodore Beza's Doctrine of Predestination*. Nieuwkoop: De Graaf, 1974.

Cremeans, Charles D. *The Reception of Calvinist Thought in England*. Urbana: University of Illinois Press, 1949.

Cuno, Friedrich W. *Blätter der Erinnerung an Dr. Kaspar Olevianus*. Barmen: Hugo Klein, 1887.

De Jong, Peter Y. *The Covenant Idea in New England Theology*. Grand Rapids: Eerdmans, 1945.

Diestel, Ludwig. *Geschichte des Alten Testaments in der christlichen Kirche*. Jena: Maukes Verlag, 1869.

Dillistone, F. W. *The Structure of Divine Society*. Philadelphia: Westminster, 1949.

Donnelly, John P. *Calvinism and Scholasticism in Vermigli's Doctrine of Man and Grace*. Vol. 18 of *Studies in Medieval and Reformation Thought*. Leiden: E. J. Brill, 1976.

Dorner, J. A. *History of Protestant Theology*. 2 vols. Edinburgh: T & T Clark, 1871.

Fast, Heinold. *Heinrich Bullinger und die Täufer: Ein Beitrag zur Historiographie und Theologie im 16. Jahrhundert*. No. 7 of *Schriftenreihe des Mennonitischen Geschichtsvereins*. Weierhof (Pfalz): Mennonitischen Geschichtsverein e.V., 1959.

Fisher, George P. *Discussions in History and Theology*. New York: Charles Scribner's Sons, 1880.

Gass, Wilhelm. *Geschichte der protestantischen Dogmatik*. 4 vols. Berlin: Georg Reimer, 1857–62.

Gestrich, Christof. *Zwingli als Theologe: Glaube und Geist beim Züricher Reformator*. Vol. 20 of *Studien zur Dogmengeschichte und systematischen Theologie*. Zurich: Zwingli Verlag, 1967.

Good, James I. *The Heidelberg Catechism in Its Newest Light*. Philadelphia: Publication and Sunday School Board of the Reformed Church in the United States, 1914.

———. *The Origin of the Reformed Church in Germany*. Reading, PA: Daniel Miller, 1887.

Gooszen, M. A. *De Heidelbergsche Catechismus. Textus Receptus met Toelichtende Teksten*. Leiden: E. J. Brill, 1890.

Graves, Frank P. *Peter Ramus and the Educational Reformation of the Sixteenth Century*. New York: Macmillan, 1912.

Hamm, Berndt. *Promissio, Pactum, Ordinatio: Freiheit und Selbstbindung Gottes in der scholastischen Gnadenlehre*. Vol. 54 of *Beiträge zur historischen Theologie*. Tübingen: J. C. Mohr (Paul Siebeck), 1977.

Harbaugh, Henry. *The Fathers of the German Reformed Church in Europe and America*. 2 vols. Lancaster, PA: Sprenger and Westhaeffer, 1857.

Hartfelder, Karl. *Philipp Melanchthon als Praeceptor Germaniae*. Berlin: N.p., 1889. 2nd reprint ed. Nieuwkoop: B. de Graf, 1972.

Heppe, Heinrich. *Dogmatik des deutschen Protestantismus im sechzehnten Jahrhundert*. 3 vols. Gotha: Friedrich A. Perthes, 1857.

———. *Geschichte des deutschen Protestantismus*. 4 vols. Marburg: R. G. Elwert, 1853.

———. *Geschichte des Pietismus und der Mystik in der Reformierten Kirche*. Leiden: E. J. Brill, 1879.

Hesselink, I. John. *On Being Reformed: Distinctive Characteristics and Common Misunderstandings*. Ann Arbor: Servant, 1983.

Hill, Christopher. *Puritanism and Revolution*. London: Secher and Warburg, 1958.

Hollweg, Walter. *Neue Untersuchungen zur Geschichte des Heidelberger Katechismus*. Vol. 13 of *Beiträge zur Geschichte und Lehre der Reformierten Kirche*. Neukirchen: Neukirchen Verlag, 1961.

Kendall, R. T. *Calvin and English Calvinism to 1649*. Oxford: University Press, 1979.

Klooster, Fred H. "The Heidelberg Catechism: Origin and History." Syllabus printed at Calvin Theological Seminary, Grand Rapids, MI, 1981.

Kunkel, Wolfgang. *An Introduction to Roman Legal and Constitutional History*. Oxford: University Press, 1966.

Lang, August. *Der Heidelberger Katechismus und vier verwandte Katechismen*. Leipzig: N.p., 1907.

———. *Der Heidelberger Katechismus. Zum 350 jährigen Gedächtnis seiner Entstehung*. No. 113 of *Schriften des Vereins für Reformationsgeschichte*. Leipzig: Rudolf Haupt, 1913.

Lobstein, Paul. *Petrus Ramus als Theologe*. Strassburg: G. F. Schmidts Universitäts-Buchhandlung, 1878.

Locher, Gottfried. *Huldrych Zwingli in Neuer Sicht: Zehn Beiträge zur Theologie der Züricher Reformation*. Zurich: Zwingli Verlag, 1969.

———. *Die Theologie Huldrych Zwinglis im Lichte seiner Christologie*. Pt. 1: *Die Gotteslehre*. Vol. 1 of *Studien zur Dogmengeschichte und systematischen Theologie*. Zurich: Zwingli Verlag, 1952.

———. *Zwingli's Thought: New Perspectives*. Vol. 25 of *Studies in the History of Christian Thought*. Leiden: E. J. Brill, 1981.

McGiffert, A. C. *Protestant Thought Before Kant*. New York: Charles Scribner's Sons, 1926.

McNeill, John T. *The History and Character of Calvinism*. London: Oxford University Press, 1954.

Marx, J. *Caspar Olevian oder der Calvinismus in Trier im Jahre 1559*. Mainz: Kirchheim, Schott, & Thielmann, 1846.

Menk, Gerhard. *Die Hohe Schule Herborn in ihrer Frühzeit (1584–1660): Ein Beitrag zum Hochschulwesen des deutschen Kalvinismus im Zeitalter der Gegenreformation*. Vol. 30 of *Veröffentlichungen der Historischen Kommission für Nassau*. Wiesbaden: Selbstverlag der Historischen Kommission für Nassau, 1981.

Miller, Perry. *The New England Mind: The Seventeenth Century*. New York: Macmillan, 1939.

Morey, William C. *Outlines of Roman Law*. New York: G. P. Putnam's Sons, 1889.

New, John F. H. *Anglican and Puritan: The Basis of Their Opposition, 1558–1640*. Stanford: Stanford University Press, 1964.

Ney, Julius. *Die Reformation in Trier und ihre Unterdrückung.* Nos. 88–9, 94 of *Schriften des Vereins für Reformationsgeschichte.* Halle and Leipzig: Verein für Reformationsgeschichte, 1906–7.

Nicholas, Barry. *An Introduction to Roman Law.* London: Oxford University Press, 1962.

Oberman, Heiko A. *Forerunners of the Reformation: The Shape of Late Medieval Thought.* New York: Holt, Rinehart, and Winston, 1966.

————. *The Harvest of Medieval Theology: Gabriel Biel and Late Medieval Nominalism.* Cambridge, MA: Harvard University Press, 1963.

Ong, Walter J. *Ramus: Method, and the Decay of Dialogue.* Cambridge, MA: Harvard University Press, 1958.

Ozment, Steven E. *The Age of Reform, 1250–1550: An Intellectual and Religious History of Late Medieval and Reformation Europe.* New Haven: Yale University Press, 1980.

Pearson, A. F. Scott. *Thomas Cartwright and Elizabethan Puritanism.* Cambridge: University Press, 1925.

Piscator, Johannes. *Kurtzer Bericht vom Leben und Sterben Herrn D. Gasparis Oleviani.* In *Der Gnadenbund Gottes.* Herborn: C. Rab, 1593.

Pollard, A. W., and Redgrave, G. R. *A Short-title Catalogue of Books Printed in England, Scotland, and Ireland . . . 1475–1640.* 2nd ed., 2 vols. London: Bibliographical Society, 1976.

Preus, James S. *From Shadow to Promise: Old Testament Interpretation from Augustine to Luther.* Cambridge, MA: Harvard University Press, 1969.

Raitt, Jill. *The Eucharistic Theology of Theodore Beza.* No. 4 of *A.A.R. Studies in Religion.* Chambersburg, PA: American Academy of Religion, 1972.

Ritschl, Otto. *Dogmengeschichte des Protestantismus.* 4 vols. Göttingen: Vandenhoeck & Ruprecht, 1926.

Rolston III, Holmes. *John Calvin versus the Westminster Confession.* Richmond: John Knox, 1972.

Schrenk, Gottlob. *Gottesreich und Bund im älteren Protestantismus, vornehmlich bei Johannes Cocceius.* Gütersloh: C. Bertelsmann, 1923.

Schweizer, Alexander. *Die Glaubenslehre der Evangelisch-Reformierten Kirche.* 2 vols. Zurich: Orell, Füssli, und Comp, 1844–47.

Sepp, Christian. *Het Godgeleerd onderwijs in Nederland, gedurende de 16e en 17e eeuw.* 2 vols. Leiden: De Breuk & Smits, 1873–74.

Staedtke, Joachim. *Die Theologie des jungen Bullingers.* Vol. 16 of *Studien zur Dogmengeschichte und systematischen Theologie.* Zurich: Zwingli Verlag, 1962.

Steinmetz, David C. *Misericordia Dei: The Theology of Johannes von Staupitz in its Late Medieval Setting.* Vol. 4 of *Studies in Medieval and Reformation Thought.* Leiden: E. J. Brill, 1968.

———. *Reformers in the Wings*. Philadelphia: Fortress, 1971.

Sturm, Erdmann K. *Der junge Zacharias Ursin: Sein Weg vom Philippismus zum Calvinismus (1534–1562)*. Vol. 13 of *Beiträge zur Geschichte und Lehre der Reformierten Kirche*. Neukirchen-Vluyn: Neukirchener Verlag, 1972.

Sudhoff, Karl. *C. Olevianus und Z. Ursinus: Leben und ausgewählte Schriften*. Vol. 8 of *Leben und ausgewählte Schriften der Väter und Begründer der reformirten Kirche*. Elberfeld: R. L. Friderichs, 1857.

Von Korff, Emmanuel Graf. *Die Anfänge der Föderal-theologie und ihre erste Ausgestaltung in Zürich und Holland*. Bonn: Emil Eisele, 1908.

Walser, Peter. *Die Prädestination bei Heinrich Bullinger im Zusammenhang mit seiner Gotteslehre*. Zurich: Zwingli Verlag, 1957.

Williams, George H. *The Radical Reformation*. Philadelphia: Westminster, 1962.

Wolf, Hans H. *Die Einheit des Bundes: Das Verhältnis von Altem und Neuem Testament bei Calvin*. Vol. 10 of *Beiträge zur Geschichte und Lehre der Reformierten Kirche*. Neukirchen: Verlag der Buchhandlung des Erziehungsvereins, 1958.

Yoder, John Howard. *Täufertum und Reformation im Gespräch: Dogmengeschichtliche Untersuchung der frühen Gespräche zwischen schweizerischen Taufern und Reformatoren*. Vol. 13 of *Basler Studien zur historischen und systematischen Theologie*. Zurich: EVZ Verlag, 1968.

Zinkand, John M. *Covenants: God's Claims*. Sioux Center, IA: Dordt College Press, 1984.

B. Articles

Allgemeine Deutsche Biographie, 1887 ed. S.v. "Olevian, Caspar," by F. W. Cuno.

Allgemeine Encyklopädie d. Wissenschaften u. Künste, 1832 ed. S.v. "Caspar Olevianus," by K. Förstemann.

Allgemeines Kirchen-Lexikon, 1850 ed. S.v. "Olevian."

Bandstra, Andrew J. "Law and Gospel in Calvin and in Paul." In *Exploring the Heritage of John Calvin*. Edited by David Holwerda. Grand Rapids: Baker, 1976.

Bierma, Lyle D. "Federal Theology in the Sixteenth Century: Two Traditions?" *Westminster Theological Journal* 45 (Fall 1983):304–21.

———. "Olevianus and the Authorship of the Heidelberg Catechism: Another Look." *Sixteenth Century Journal* 13, no. 4 (Winter 1982):17–27.

Bizer, Ernst. "Historische Einleitung des Herausgebers." In Heppe, Heinrich. *Die Dogmatik der Evangelisch-Reformierten Kirche*. Neukirchen: Verlag der Buchhandlung des Erziehungsvereins, 1958.

Boussard, Jacques. "L'Université D'Orléans et L'Humanisme au Début de XVIe S." *Humanisme et Renaissance* 5 (1938): 209–30.

Courtenay, William J. "Nominalism and Late Medieval Religion." In *The Pursuit of Holiness in Late Medieval Religion*. Edited by Charles Trinkhaus and Heiko A. Oberman. Vol. 10 of *Studies in Medieval and Reformation Thought*. Leiden: E. J. Brill, 1974.

Cyclopaedia of Biblical, Theological, and Ecclesiastical Literature, 1969 ed. S.v. "Federal Theology," by C. P. Wing.

————. S.v. "Olevianus," by Henry Harbaugh.

Diestel, Ludwig. "Studien zur Föderaltheologie." *Jahrbücher für deutsche Theologie* 10 (1865):209–76.

Eenigenburg, Elton M. "The Place of the Covenant in Calvin's Thinking." *Reformed Review* 10 (June 1957):1–22.

Emerson, Everett H. "Calvin and Covenant Theology." *Church History* 25 (June 1956):136–44.

Encyclopaedia of Religion and Ethics, 1911 ed. S.v. "Covenant Theology," by William Adams Brown.

The Encyclopedia of Christianity, 1972 ed. S.v. "Covenant Theology," by John Murray.

Evangelisches Kirchenlexikon, 1956 ed. S.v. "Bund (Dogmengeschichtlich)," by Jürgen Moltmann.

————. S.v. "Olevian," by Jürgen Moltmann.

Graafland, C. "Hat Calvin einen Ordo Salutis gelehrt?" Paper presented at the 3rd International Calvin Congress, Geneva, Switzerland, September 6–9, 1982.

Greaves, Richard L. "The Origins and Early Development of English Covenant Thought." *The Historian* 31 (November 1968):21–35.

Greschat, Martin. "Der Bundesgedanke in der Theologie des späten Mittelalters." *Zeitschrift für Kirchengeschichte* 81 (1970):44–63.

Hagen, Kenneth. "From Testament to Covenant in the Early Sixteenth Century." *Sixteenth Century Journal* 3 (April 1972):1–24.

Henderson, G. D. "The Idea of the Covenant in Scotland." *The Evangelical Quarterly* 27 (1955):2–14.

Heppe, Heinrich. "Der Charakter der deutsch-reformirten Kirche und das Verhältniss derselben zum Lutherthum und zum Calvinismus." *Theologischen Studien u. Kritiken* 23 (1850):669–706.

————. "Urkundliche Beiträge zur Geschichte der Reformation in Trier im Jahre 1559." *Zeitschrift für die historische Theologie* 19 (1849):416–44.

Hoekema, Anthony A. "The Covenant of Grace in Calvin's Teaching." *Calvin Theological Journal* 3 (November 1967):133–61.

Jöchers Allgemeines Gelehrten-Lexikon. S.v. "Olevianus."

Knodt, D. "Briefe von Caspar Olevianus." *Theologische Studien u. Kritiken* 79 (1906):628–34.

Letham, Robert. "The *Foedus Operum:* Some Factors Accounting for Its Development." *Sixteenth Century Journal* 14 (Winter 1983):457–67.

Lillback, Peter Alan. "Ursinus' Development of the Covenant of Creation: A Debt to Melanchthon or Calvin?" *Westminster Theological Journal* 43 (Spring 1981):247–88.

Locher, Gottfried W. "Grundzüge der Theologie Huldrych Zwinglis im Vergleich mit derjenigen Martin Luthers und Johannes Calvins." *Zwingliana* 12 (1967):470–509, 545–95.

Lyall, Francis. "Of Metaphors and Analogies: Legal Language and Covenant Theology." *Scottish Journal of Theology* 32 (1979):1–17.

McLelland, J. C. "Covenant Theology — A Re-evaluation." *Canadian Journal of Theology* 3 (July 1957):182–88.

Miller, Charles. "The Spread of Calvinism in Switzerland, Germany, and France." In *The Rise and Development of Calvinism.* Edited by John H. Bratt. Grand Rapids: Eerdmans, 1959.

Miller, Perry. "Preparation for Salvation in Seventeenth-Century New England." *Journal of the History of Ideas* 4 (June 1943):253–86.

Moller, Jens. "The Beginnings of Puritan Covenant Theology." *The Journal of Ecclesiastical History* 14 (April 1963):46–67.

Moltmann, Jürgen. "Zur Bedeutung des Petrus Ramus für Philosophie und Theologie im Calvinismus." *Zeitschrift für Kirchengeschichte* 68 (1957):295–318.

Muller, Richard A. "Covenant and Conscience in English Reformed Theology." *Westminster Theological Journal* 42 (Spring 1980):308–34.

————. "Perkins' *A Golden Chaine:* Predestinarian System or Schematized *Ordo Salutis?*" *Sixteenth Century Journal* 9 (April 1978):69–81.

Neuser, Wilhelm. "Die Väter des Heidelberger Katechismus." *Theologische Zeitschrift* 35, no. 3 (May/June 1979):177– 94.

The New Schaff-Herzog Encyclopedia of Religious Knowledge, 1949 ed. S.v. "Alsted, Johann Heinrich," by E. F. K. Müller.

————. S.v. "Olevianus, Kaspar," by Julius Ney.

————. S.v. "Piscator, Johannes," by E. F. K. Müller.

Oberman, Heiko A. "Wir sein pettler. Hoc est verum: Bund und Gnade in der Theologie des Mittelalters und Reformation." *Zeitschrift für Kirchengeschichte* 78 (1967):232–52.

Realencyklopädie für protestantische Theologie und Kirche. S.v. "Coccejus und seine Schule," by Karl Müller.

————. S.v. "Olevianus," by Julius Ney.

Die Religion in Geschichte und Gegenwart. S.v. "Olevian," by Schaller.

————. 2nd ed. S.v. "Bund (Föderaltheologie, dogmengeschichtlich)," by Gottlob Schrenk.

————. 3rd ed. S.v. "Bund (Föderaltheologie, dogmengeschichtlich)," by P. Jacobs.

————. 3rd ed. S.v. "Olevian," by J. F. G. Goeters.

Rudolf, Friedrich. "Die Kirche in Heidelberg nach den letzten Briefen Bullinger-Beza." *Zwingliana* 8 (1944–48):96–107.

Sprunger, Keith L. "Ames, Ramus, and the Method of Puritan Theology." *Harvard Theological Review* 59 (April 1966):133–51.

Steinmetz, David C. "The Baptism of John and the Baptism of Jesus in Huldrych Zwingli, Balthasar Hubmaier, and Late Medieval Theology." In *Continuity and Discontinuity in Church History*. Edited by F. Church and T. George. Leiden: E. J. Brill, 1979.

Steubing, J. H. "Lebensnachrichten von den Herborner Theologen I." *Zeitschrift für die Historische Theologie* 11 (1841):77– 98.

Trinterud, Leonard. "The Origins of Puritanism." *Church History* 20 (March 1951):37–57.

Von Rohr, John. "Covenant and Assurance in Early English Puritanism." *Church History* 34 (June 1965):195–203.

Vos, Geerhardus. "The Doctrine of the Covenant in Reformed Theology" (1891). Translated by S. Voorwinde and W. Van Gemeren. In *Redemptive History and Biblical Interpretation: The Shorter Writings of Geerhardus Vos*. Edited by Richard B. Gaffin. Phillipsburg, NJ: Presbyterian and Reformed Publishing Co., 1980.

Weltkirchen Lexikon, 1960 ed. S.v. "Bundestheologie," by E. Lewis Evans.

Unpublished Theses

Breward, I. "The Life and Theology of William Perkins, 1558–1602." Ph.D. dissertation, University of Manchester, 1963.

Cottrell, Jack W. "Covenant and Baptism in the Theology of Huldreich Zwingli." Th.D. dissertation, Princeton Theological Seminary, 1971.

McCoy, Charles S. "The Covenant Theology of Johannes Cocceius." Ph.D. dissertation, Yale University, 1957.

Muller, Richard A. "Predestination and Christology in Sixteenth-Century Reformed Theology." Ph.D. dissertation, Duke University, 1976.

Oki, Hideo. "Ethics in Seventeenth-Century English Puritanism." Ph.D. dissertation, Union Theological Seminary (NY), 1960.

Priebe, Victor L. "The Covenant Theology of William Perkins." Ph.D. dissertation, Drew University, 1967.

Stoever, William K. B. "The Covenant of Works in Puritan Theology: The Antinomian Crisis in New England." Ph.D. dissertation, Yale University, 1970.

Veninga, James F. "Covenant Theology and Ethics in the Thought of John Calvin and John Preston." Ph.D. dissertation, Rice University, 1974.

Verhoeven, J. A. W. "Caspar Olevianus: Een Onderzoek naar plaats en funktie van het genadeverbond in zijn theologie." Doctoraal scriptie, Rijksuniversiteit Utrecht, 1982.

Weir, David A. *Foedus Naturale:* The Origins of Federal Theology in Sixteenth-Century Reformation Thought." Ph.D. dissertation, University of Saint Andrews, 1984.

Wilcox, William G. "New England Covenant Theology: Its English Precursors and Early American Exponents." Ph.D. dissertation, Duke University, 1959.

Index

Aberdeen, 181
Abraham, 32–34, 36, 40–41, 44, 48,
    50–52, 54, 65, 67–68, 75–76, 90,
    127, 130–131, 137–138, 146,
    153, 159, 177
Adam, 27, 32, 36–37, 39, 45, 52, 62–
    63, 65, 68, 114, 118–120, 130–
    132, 150
Alsted, Johannes, 173
Althaus, Paul, 153–155, 167
Amyrauldianism, 162
Anabaptists, 31–32, 55, 61
Arminianism, 162
Augsburg, 15, 49
Augustine, 168

Baker, J. Wayne, 23–24, 27–28, 40,
    84, 142–143, 170–171
Barth, Karl, 27, 117, 140
Berkhof, Louis, 84, 105
Berleburg, 18
Bern, 49
Bernard of Clairvaux, 168
Beza, Theodore, 14, 24, 163, 166
Biel, Gabriel, 169
Bohatec, Josef, 172
Boquinus, Peter, 151–152
Bourges, 13–14, 155
Bremen, 174, 181
Brown, W. A., 24
Bude, Guillaume, 163, 172
Bullinger, Heinrich, 14, 22–23, 27,
    31, 35–41, 43–45, 48, 51, 55,
    60–61, 142–143, 145, 147–148,
    150–153, 159, 162, 170

Calvin, John, 14, 19, 23–24, 40–49,
    51, 55, 60–61, 96, 144, 148–152,
    154, 158–159, 162–163, 168,
    170–172, 183
Cambridge, 179–181
Cartwright, Thomas, 179–180
Cloppenburg, 157
Cocceius, Johannes, 22, 25–28,
    117–118, 140, 157, 170, 174–
    175, 178, 181
Collegium Sapientiae 16
Cottrell, Jack W., 32, 170–171
Crocius, Ludwig, 173–174
Cuno, F. W., 25

David, 44, 131–132
De Jong, Peter Y., 84, 105
Diestel, Ludwig, 22, 25, 27, 72, 84,
    105, 117, 151, 158
Dort, 18

Edinburgh, 176, 181
England, 175–176, 180, 184
Erasmus, 31, 170

Farel, William, 14
Fast, Heinhold, 142
Field, John, 179–180
Fisher, George P., 27
France, 13, 155, 172, 179
Franeker, 174, 181
Frederick III (Palatinate), 13, 16, 18

Geneva, 14, 149, 163
    Academy, 179
    form of church discipline, 16
Goeters, J. F. G., 23

Greaves, Richard, 40
Greschat, Martin, 170
Groningen, 173

Hamm, Berndt, 170
Heidelberg, 16–18, 24, 151, 163, 184
  Catechism, 12, 17, 55, 154
  Church Order, 16
  -Herborn federal theology 25, 162
  University of, 16, 21, 55, 151, 164,
    179
Henderson, G. D., 176
Heppe, Heinrich, 22–23, 27–28, 70,
  72, 107, 117, 140, 158
Herborn, 19–20, 26, 173–174, 184
  Academy, 19, 149, 173–176
  Heidelberg-Herborn federal the-
    ology 25, 162
  theology, 178
Hoekema, Anthony A., 49
Holland, 179, 184
Howie, Robert, 175–176, 181

Irenaeus, 168
Ishmael, 41
Israel, 32, 52, 65, 82, 122, 133

Jacobs, P., 23
John the Elder (Nassau-Dillenburg), 19, 173

Klooster, Fred H., 25

Lactantius, 168
Lang, August, 24, 144
Lausanne, 14
Locher, Gottfried, 172
Ludwig VI (Palatinate), 18
Ludwig von Wittgenstein 18
Lumsden, Charles, 176
Luther, Martin, 169
Lutheran 18, 26, 96–98, 105
Lutherans 17

McCoy, Charles S., 28, 117, 178
Marburg, 18
Martinius, Matthias, 173–174

Maulbronn Colloquy, 17
Melanchthon, Philip, 14, 55, 153,
  158, 165
Moller, Jens, 40
Moltmann, Jurgen, 24–25, 162, 164,
  166–168
Moses, 36, 44, 46, 52–53, 82, 146,
  153
Muller, Richard A., 23, 163
Murray, John, 28
Musculus, Wolfgang, 49–52, 60–62,
  150–153, 183

Noah, 32, 36, 62

Olevianus, Caspar (view of the covenant), 12, 23–25, 29
  and Apostles' Creed 145, 147,
    151, 176, 183
  and assurance of salvation, 23–
    24, 89, 100–101
  and baptism, 85–87, 89, 91, 93,
    99–104
  conditions in, 26–27, 29, 68–69,
    74, 99
  and covenant of grace 23–27, 29,
    63–64, 66–67, 69, 74, 76, 78, 83,
    86–87, 99, 101, 104–105, 107
    117–118, 120–121, 125–126,
    130–131 135–136, 138–141,
    146, 151–153, 156, 158–160,
    166, 174, 176, 183
  and the Kingdom of Christ, 70,
    72, 121
  influence of Calvin on, 13–14, 18,
    21, 23, 149–150, 152, 162
  and late medieval nominalism,
    171
  and later federal theology, 21–23,
    181
  and Lord's Supper, 26, 86–87, 94,
    96–98, 150
  and mystical union with Christ,
    70, 72–73, 105, 158
  new definition of legal covenant,
    27–28, 124
  and person of Christ, 73, 77

and predestination, 24, 29, 81, 83,
183
and Protestant scholasticism,
162, 167, 183
and Roman law, 155, 157, 172
as unifying theological principle,
147–148
unilateral and bilateral dimensions of, 66–67, 74–75, 88–89,
105, 112, 151, 183
and work of Christ, 64
Olevianus, Gerhard, 13
Olevianus, Philippina, 16
Olewig, 13
Orleans, 13, 155

Palatinate, 12, 16–17, 20
Paris, 13
Perkins, William, 164, 176–181, 183
Piscator, Johannes, 162, 173
Puritan (covenant) theology/theolo-
gian 11, 118, 170, 176
Puritan Federal theology 26, 178
Puritans (ism), 23, 172, 179–180

Ramus, Peter, 163–166
Ravensperger, Hermann, 173
Ritschl, Otto, 26–28, 96, 98, 105,
107, 109, 111, 117
Rollock, Robert, 176, 181

Schrenk, Gottlob, 22, 24–26, 28, 31,
35, 45, 70, 72, 84, 105, 107, 109,

140, 142, 151, 158, 168, 173–
175, 181
Scotland, 175–176, 184
Sohnius, 157
Sorbonne, 13
Stoever, William K. B., 26
Strasbourg, 16
Sudhoff, Karl, 21, 26

Tertullian, 168
Trier, 12–16, 165
Trinterud, Leonard, 23, 28, 34, 40,
42, 172

Ubertino of Casale, 168
Ursinus, Zacharias, 20–23, 28, 55,
57–62, 144–145, 147–148, 150–
155, 158–159, 163, 183

Van't Hooft, 142
Verhoeven, J. A. W., 23–24, 28, 148
Vermigli, Peter Martyr, 14
Viret, Pierre, 14
Von der Leyen, Johann, 15–16
Von Korff, Emmanuel G., 31, 35,
142
Vos, Geerhardus, 119

Walser, Peter, 144

Zurich, 14, 22, 42, 48, 148
Zwingli, Ulrich, 23, 31–38, 40–41,
43–44, 48, 51, 60–61, 150–151,
153, 170–171, 183